U.S. Government, Book 1
We the People

Augustine Caliguire
Howard M. Jacobs
Jeanne M. Kish
Roberta J. Leach
Carol T. Young

The Center for Learning

v1.0

The Center for Learning
www.centerforlearning.org

Authors

Augustine Caliguire, coauthor of Center for Learning curriculum units in government, history, and Advanced Placement social studies, earned his M.A. at John Carroll University, Cleveland, Ohio. He is a social studies teacher and former social studies department chairperson.

Howard M. Jacobs, who earned his M.Ed. at Cleveland State University, Cleveland, Ohio, has been an elementary teacher and has taught English as a second language. He has coauthored government and history curriculum units for The Center for Learning.

Jeanne M. Kish received her M.A. in history from Cleveland State University, Cleveland, Ohio. She is an experienced social studies teacher and department chairperson who has taught Advanced Placement American and European history courses. She is also a Martha Holden Jennings scholar. Kish has served as content editor and project director for revisions of Center for Learning units including *U.S. Government, Book 2*, the *A.P. European History* series, and the *Basic Skills* series.

Roberta J. Leach, a secondary social studies teacher, earned her Doctor of Arts degree from Carnegie Mellon University, Pittsburgh, Pennsylvania. She has coauthored government, history, and Advanced Placement social studies units for The Center for Learning.

Carol T. Young, revision author, is an experienced teacher of U.S. history and government classes. She is currently enrolled in a graduate program in Washington, D.C.

Editorial Team

Lora Murphy, M.A.
Tammy Sanderell, B.A.
Rose Schaffer, M.A.

Cover Design

Susan Chowanetz Thornton, B.S.

List of credits found on Acknowledgments page beginning on 286.

ISBN-13: 978-1-56077-756-4
ISBN-10: 1-56077-756-7

Contents

Introduction

U.S. Government, Book 1: We the People is intended for use with average high school students. Students are required to process information in order to understand the content and use a variety of sources, including graphs, charts, cartoons, illustrations, and readings. These materials help students to understand the relationship between unit themes and concepts. The activities are interesting, developmental, skill-related, and promote critical thinking.

U.S. Government, Book 1 is divided into six parts, each focusing on a major aspect of the theory behind the structure and operation of our government. Part 1, Foundations, examines the principles upon which our democratic form of government is founded. Lessons show how the Founding Fathers used their understanding of political theory and the American experiences with government under the British—and, later, under the Articles of Confederation—to create a new democratic republic. Part 2, Human Rights, provides an overview of the Bill of Rights and deals in greater detail with the meaning of several of our most important freedoms. Part 3, The Legislative Branch, examines the structure and function of Congress. Part 4, The Executive Branch, covers the many roles of the president, and the checks and balances on the powers of the president as exercised by the Congress and the Supreme Court. The range of activities the national government controls today, including the Cabinet and executive departments, are also explored. Part 5, The Judicial Branch, examines the federal court system, beginning with an overview of the structure of the courts and their responsibilities. Part 6, Public Policy, helps students to define and understand the concept of public policy.

Goals

This approach uses concepts to teach American government and reflects these assumptions:

1. American government requires the active participation of its citizens. To understand how to function as responsible citizens, students need to examine how and why changes have occurred.

2. American government illustrates recurring themes. To understand the place these themes hold today, they must be analyzed and conclusions drawn about them.

3. Finally, government as a discipline requires skills of reading, writing, and critical thinking. Practice leading toward mastery in each of these skill areas is an integral part of learning the unit content.

Objectives

1. To understand the practical workings of the American political system

2. To study government and draw conclusions about it

3. To understand personal values and their relationship to governments

4. To practice writing skills in order to communicate ideas clearly to others

5. To explore our heritage as a means of understanding ourselves and our role in government today

Teacher Notes

U.S. Government, Book 1: We the People presents American government conceptually. This unit is comprised of forty lessons. Included is a list of concepts, themes, and study skills used in this book, and a cross-reference chart that lists the lessons in which each occurs. The student handouts are designed for use in class. The procedural steps for each lesson contain specific ways for using the handouts. Answers to the handouts may vary unless otherwise indicated. Students may need additional paper to complete some handouts. In addition, the lessons are flexible enough to permit adjusting according to the availability of equipment and materials, the individual needs of your students, and your educational goals.

You must read each lesson plan in advance. The lessons are thematic in approach and help students to develop an understanding of essential themes, concepts, and changes over time. The lessons are not, however, intended as a substitute for the textbook.

viii

Cross-Reference Section

Concepts*

1. Absolutism
2. Abuse of power
3. Authority
4. Bureaucracy
5. Change
6. Checks and balances
7. Civil authority
8. Colonialism
9. Compromise
10. Confederation
11. Conflict
12. Continuity
13. Democracy
14. Due process of law
15. Equality of opportunity
16. Equality under the law
17. Federalism
18. Government
19. Jurisdiction
20. Leadership
21. Legislative oversight
22. Lobbying
23. Mass media
24. National interest
25. Poverty
26. Power
27. Property
28. Public policy
29. Public welfare
30. Representation
31. Responsibility
32. Rights
33. Security
34. Separation of powers
35. Special interest groups
36. Strict construction
37. Values
38. Wants and needs

Themes*

1. Governments are institutions that provide leadership and authority to meet people's needs.
2. Governments reflect the varied goals of individuals.
3. Governments may need to restrict individuals or groups to protect the general welfare.
4. Governments reflect human values.
5. Governments reflect changes in human values and needs through laws, structures, and policies.
6. Governments' sovereignty and interdependence affect people's efforts to resolve major issues.
7. Governments in complex societies need to become more representative in order to function more effectively.
8. Governments reflect the interaction of individuals and groups through the process of compromise.
9. Governments differ in providing for achievement of individual and group goals.
10. Governments operate at several levels of authority to achieve varied goals.
11. Government's decision-making processes often produce partisan organizations.
12. Democratic governments impose responsibilities as well as guarantee rights.

*See cross-reference chart, page xi.

Skills*

1. Express personal convictions.

2. Interpret what is read by drawing inferences.

3. Detect cause-and-effect relationships.

4. Formulate generalizations.

5. Develop criteria of evaluation.

6. Read for a variety of purposes: critically, analytically, to predict outcomes, to answer a question, to form an opinion, to skim for facts.

7. Read various forms of printed materials: books, magazines, newspapers, directories, Supreme Court decisions, charts, documents.

8. Identify alternative courses of action, and predict likely consequences.

9. Recognize and understand social studies terms.

10. Write a well-constructed paragraph.

11. Prepare summaries and outlines.

12. Interpret charts, graphs, and diagrams.

13. Write a well-organized essay.

14. Interpret political cartoons.

15. Identify relevant factual material.

16. Determine relationships between items of factual information.

17. Group data in appropriate categories according to appropriate criteria.

18. Predict likely outcomes based on factual information.

19. Recognize the value of interpreting factual information.

20. Recognize instances in which more than one interpretation of factual information is valid.

21. Organize key ideas related to a topic.

22. Examine critically the relationship between and among elements of a topic.

23. Detect bias in data presented in various forms: graphic, tabular, visual, print.

24. Combine critical concepts into a state of conclusions based on information.

25. Propose a new system of operation, create a new system, or devise a plan based on available information.

26. Participate in persuading, negotiating, compromising, and debating in the resolution of conflicts and differences.

27. Brainstorm to reach a possible solution to a stated issue or problem.

*See cross-reference chart, page xi.

Cross-Reference Chart

Lesson	Concepts	Themes	Skills
1	1, 18, 26, 32	2, 4	2, 14
2	3, 8, 10, 17	5	2, 6, 16
3	1, 6, 9, 11, 17, 30	1, 2, 8	2, 6, 10, 21
4	17, 19, 26, 34	10	3, 17
5	2, 6, 17, 34	3	2, 12, 16
6	5, 9, 11, 15, 16, 32	5	7, 16, 24, 28
7	5, 9, 11, 15, 16, 32	5	2, 20
8	9, 32	3	3, 6, 7, 9
9	32, 37, 38	3	2, 9, 22
10	3, 11, 32	3	2, 4, 16
11	31, 32	6	19, 26, 28
12	23, 31, 32	3	6, 13, 15, 24, 28
13	27, 32, 35	3	2, 7, 11, 20
14	3, 14, 32	1	9, 21
15	3, 14, 27, 32	3, 6	9, 10, 16, 18, 22
16	5, 11, 15, 16, 32	5, 9	1, 6, 12, 13, 18, 27
17	2, 3, 6, 11, 20, 26	7	2, 16, 22, 28
18	13, 17, 18, 30	1	3, 16
19	13, 17, 18, 30	1	6, 16
20	9, 17, 20	1, 5	13, 16, 21
21	9, 20	1	2, 10, 20, 22
22	24	1	4, 12, 13, 24
23	3, 6, 11, 21	3	10, 11, 17
24	3, 6, 17, 20, 28	1	2, 15
25	3, 6, 11, 17, 26	8	2, 3, 10, 24
26	3, 6, 11, 17, 26	3	2, 16
27	2, 6, 11, 20, 26	3	10, 14
28	4, 12, 18, 28	1	16, 17
29	3, 5, 20	1	2, 16
30	3, 17, 19	10	2, 9, 16
31	3, 19	10	2, 16
32	3, 6, 11, 19, 26	3	10, 14, 16
33	5, 14, 37, 38	5	2, 10, 16
34	4, 17, 22, 29	3, 4, 5	3, 5, 9, 19, 23
35	3, 7, 11, 20, 28	3, 9	6, 7, 10
36	5, 13, 18, 30	5	6, 7, 12, 21
37	9, 12, 13, 17, 31, 38	2, 4, 8	6, 7, 21
38	25, 29, 37, 38	3	2, 4, 7
39	9, 11, 22, 24, 28, 37, 38	3, 9	2, 5, 13
40	5, 11, 20, 24, 28, 33, 37, 38	5	2, 10, 16

Part 1
Foundations

This part, Foundations, examines the principles upon which our democratic form of government is founded and shows how the Founding Fathers used their understanding of political theory and the American experiences with government under the British, and, later, under the Articles of Confederation. Lesson 1 examines the relevant merits of limited and absolute governments. Lesson 2 develops an understanding of how experience of government under the English colonial system and the Articles of Confederation influenced the Founding Fathers in writing the U.S. Constitution. Lesson 3 explores the political and philosophical differences between the Federalists and the Anti-Federalists and examines the importance of the Federalists and Anti-Federalists to the creation of our Constitution. Lesson 4 examines how the Constitution distributes power between the national and state governments. Lesson 5 develops an understanding of how and why the Constitution limits the power of the different branches of government through the use of a system of checks and balances. Lesson 6 explores ways in which the Constitution may be amended. Lesson 7 examines how the elastic clause stretches the powers granted to Congress.

Lesson 1
Government:
Should It Be Limited or Absolute?

Objective
- To understand the relative merits of limited and absolute governments

Notes to the Teacher

English settlers in the New World brought with them an understanding of England's centuries of struggle for limited government and its long tradition of monarchy. A king was sworn to a coronation oath in which he would observe and honor his obligations to protect his subjects and provide them justice, and a tyrant king who broke such a bond had no constraints. A classic illustration of such a tyrannical leader is that of John (1199–1216), who quarreled with the Church, the papal hierarchy, Englishmen, clergy, and his nobles about his exercise of office. He waged reckless, failed military campaigns and lost valuable territory to France, costing England dearly. In reaction, petitioners organized against the king. In 1215, English nobles forced King John, who had imposed on the English nobility increasingly harsh and heavy personal tax burdens to pay for a lavish lifestyle and military failures, to sign the Magna Carta, which limited his authority and protected their feudal rights.

In England, during the first half of the seventeenth century, a government which was characterized by the divine right of kings with its fickle nature and arbitrary leadership developed. Many Englishmen emigrated to America's colonies. Attempts to limit the power of the king with the Petition of Right (1628) were ignored or circumvented by the monarch. England's monarchs acted according to the theory of divine right, in which God empowered the king to rule in all matters, and the king answered only to God for his actions.

In the seventeenth century, a volatile struggle developed in England between king and Parliament, between Anglicans and Puritans, and between upper and lower classes. This conflict led to civil war and resulted in the beheading of Charles I, the abolition of Parliament, and the establishment of a Puritan dictatorship under Oliver Cromwell. Religious and political conflicts continued after Cromwell's death and eventually led to the restoration of the Stuart monarchy under Charles II.

James II, Charles II's successor, antagonized almost everyone by his contempt for Parliament and his announced intention to reestablish the Roman Catholic Church as the official state church. In 1688, the Glorious Revolution put William of Orange, a Protestant, and his wife Mary, daughter of James II, on the English throne. This bloodless revolution determined the character of modern English government by establishing limited powers for the monarchy. The rule of Parliament was supreme, the Anglican Church was the official state religion, and a Bill of Rights protected the rights of the people, although at first these rights applied only to wealthy, titled, or propertied males in the upper class. These ideas were seen first in early colonial America, where only propertied males could vote, and again later at the Constitutional Convention's debates. The Framers expressed deep concerns about representation by a large, uneducated rural populace versus the mercantile and propertied urban minority.

Not only were America's colonists aware of England's historic past, but also they were informed about the ideas of leading English political theorists. The writings of John Locke particularly inspired them. According to Locke, people create a government to protect their natural rights to life, liberty, and property. Thomas Jefferson, the author of the Declaration of Independence, commented that the great treatise was "pure Locke," having substituted the words "pursuit of happiness" for "property." Jefferson asserted that when the government failed to protect these rights, the people have a right and an obligation to alter or abolish it. Both English political tradition and political theory combined to convince the colonists that a government resting on consent of the governed was better suited to their needs than a distant, authoritarian ruler.

In this lesson, students read excerpts from documents dealing with the power of the monarchy and the rights of Englishmen, which became the basis for English common law. Students conclude by assuming the role of James I or John Locke and prepare a two-minute presentation supporting or opposing the theory of divine right.

Procedure

1. Ask students what should be the extent of a king's power. Ask them if they believe a monarchy would work in the United States today. Encourage discussion. Accept all reasonable answers.

2. Distribute **Handout 1**, and have students complete it individually. Review students' responses.

   Suggested Responses:

   Reading 1

   1. God

   2. Government is the monarchy; the king is God's lieutenant, and he is to follow God's commands.

   3. The people have no legal recourse; it was blasphemy and sedition to disagree with the king.

   Reading 2

   4. desperately poor, few rights, no liberty to move

   5. The king prevented concentration of power by distributing estates over a wide area.

   6. It showed the power of every tenant and how much could be extracted in taxes.

   7. They resented this limitation of their power.

   8. They looked for the opportunity to assert their rights.

   Reading 3

   9. No one is to harm the life, liberty, or property of another.

   10. uncertainty of protection of one's rights; preservation of property

11. established law, indifferent judge, power to back up and execute law

12. war; absolved from obedience, refuge against established government

3. Divide the class into groups of three or four, and assign each group either the role of James I or John Locke. Explain that students are to prepare a two-minute role-play illustrating the position of their character regarding the theory of divine right. After small-group discussion, have each group present its conclusion in a large-group session.

   Suggested Response:

   Divine right theory may be efficient in decision making, but it does not necessarily take into account the needs or rights of the people, and the people have no legal right to demand changes. In Locke's social contract theory, while the procedure may be more cumbersome, the source of power resides in the people, and they have the right to alter or abolish a government they find objectionable.

Enrichment/Extension

1. Have students research and report on the interaction of one of the Stuart or Tudor kings or queens with Parliament.

2. Have students research and report on one of the early royal, proprietary, or charter colonial governments and how the colony conducted affairs.

Government: Should It Be Limited or Absolute?

Read the statements on the nature of government, and answer the respective questions. Be prepared for class discussion.

Reading 1

> James I, King of England between 1603 and 1625, claimed in an address to Parliament, that kings were born with the power of divine right. "The state of monarchy is the supremest thing on earth: for kings are not only God's lieutenants upon earth and sit upon God's throne, but even by God himself they are called gods. As to dispute what God may do is blasphemy, so it is sedition in subjects to dispute what a king may do in height of his power. I will not be content that my power be disputed on."[1]

1. What did James I believe was the source of his power?

2. What did he believe was the purpose of government?

3. According to James I, what recourse do the people have if they are dissatisfied with the government?

[1]G. M. Trevelyan, *England under the Stuarts* (1904; reprint, New York: Routledge, 2002), 99.

Reading 2

The Domesday Book surveyed the property and land of medieval England. Its purpose was to maximize the revenues collected by the king's royal commissioners. It caused widespread resentment and protests that were often violent.

> . . . It was a harsh and rigid system, for the villein was desperately poor, had few rights against his superiors, and was unable to leave the manor; yet he was secure in his tenure, and there was no unemployment. . . .
>
> [T]he feudal system depended on the king's ability to control his great vassals, and to strengthen his position (King) William distributed their estates over various parts of the kingdom, so that there should be no great concentration of power. . . . William also separated church courts from secular courts so that the clergy should not come under feudal jurisdiction, a move of immense significance. Finally, he ordered the compilation of the Domesday Book of 1086: a detailed survey of all the manors of England, showing who held them, their size, number of villeins, amount of stock and value. This showed at a glance the power of every tenant and, equally important, how much could be extracted from him in taxes.
>
> It was an order certainly, far better than disorder, but an imposed order, a despotism, with liberty for the king, a limited liberty for his great subjects, and servitude for the great majority. The barons resented this limitation of their power . . . and were ever watchful for the opportunity to assert what they considered to be their rights.[2]

4. Describe the life of the villein.

5. How did the king solidify his own power?

6. What was the ultimate purpose of the Domesday Book?

7. What was the reaction of noblemen at this time?

8. How might this economic system have contributed to a nobleman or commoner's desire for more political rights?

[2]F. E. Halliday, *A Concise History of England* (New York: Thames and Hudson, 1991), 41–45.

Reading 3

. . . The *State of Nature* has a Law of Nature to govern it, which obliges every one; And Reason, which is that Law, teaches all Mankind, who will but consult it, that being all equal and independent, no one ought to harm another in his Life, Health, Liberty, or Possessions. . . .

If Man in the State of Nature be so free, as has been said; If he be absolute Lord of his own Person and Possessions, equal to the greatest, and subject to no Body, why will he part with his Freedom? . . . To which 'tis obvious to Answer, that though in the state of Nature he hath such a right, yet the Enjoyment of it is very uncertain, and constantly exposed to the Invasion of others. . . . This makes him willing to quit a Condition, which however free, is full of fears and continual dangers: And 'tis not without reason, that he seeks out, and is willing to joyn in Society with others who are already united, or have a mind to unite for the mutual *Preservation* of their Lives, Liberties and Estates, which I call by the general Name, *Property.*

The great and *chief end* therefore, of Mens uniting into Commonwealths, and putting themselves under Government, *is the Preservation of their Property.* To which in the state of Nature there are many things wanting.

First, There wants an *establish'd,* settled, known *Law,* received and allowed by common consent to be the Standard of Right and Wrong. . . .

Secondly, In the State of Nature there wants a *known and indifferent Judge,* with Authority to determine all differences according to the established Law. For every one in that state being both Judge and Executioner of the Law of Nature, Men being partial to themselves. . . .

Thirdly, In the state of Nature there often wants a *Power* to back and support the Sentence when right, and to *give* it due *Execution.* . . .

. . . [W]henever the *Legislators endeavour to take away, and destroy the Property of the People,* or to reduce them to Slavery . . . they put themselves into a state of War with the People, who are thereupon absolved from any farther Obedience, and are left to the common Refuge, which God hath provided for all Men, against Force and Violence.[3]

9. What is law in the state of nature?

10. According to Locke, why does one leave the state of nature and seek a government?

11. What are three things the state of nature wants or needs?

12. What recourse do the people have if they are dissatisfied with the government?

[3]John Locke, "The Second Treatise of Government," in *Two Treatises of Government,* ed. Peter Laslett, rev. ed. (New York: Cambridge University Press, 1963), 311, 395–96, 460–61.

Lesson 2
The Lessons of Experience: Writing the Constitution

Objective
- To understand how the English, colonial, and Articles of Confederation governments influenced the Founding Fathers

Notes to the Teacher

The English settlers who colonized the North American continent brought with them the rights of Englishmen, which included established laws within the framework of a constitution, a representative and limited government, and civil liberties. Neglected by Parliament, the colonists were free to apply these concepts to their new surroundings and to develop a system of local governments designed to meet local needs. Virginia's House of Burgesses, their present-day legislature, is the oldest legislative body in the United States and was a model of representative government for the colonies. When the British emerged victorious in the French and Indian War in 1763, the major foreign threat to the colonies was removed. The colonists perceived less need for the protection of the mother country. Parliament imposed new taxes to pay for the cost of the war and defense of the Empire. The stage was set for a clash between local colonial governments and a British imperial government determined to subject the colonists to the will of Parliament.

In 1777, eager to avoid an authoritarian government similar to the one from which they had declared their independence the previous year, the new American states wrote the Articles of Confederation, a plan of government within which most authority rested in the state legislatures. Almost immediately, foreign and domestic crises threatened the new government. Trade squabbles broke out between merchants of Maryland and Virginia because each exorbitantly taxed the other and there was no court of higher appeal to which to take the complaint. The weak Confederation had no power to tax or raise an army and failed to command respect among the established powers of Europe. During the Revolutionary War, members of the Continental Army died of malnutrition and exposure because neither the Continental Congress nor the states would pay for adequate food, uniforms, or supplies for the state militias that formed the army. The lack of an executive to enforce decisions of Congress or a federal court to resolve disputes among states was a major problem, as was the requirement that all states unanimously approve amendments to the Articles of Confederation, which made change difficult.

The Framers, who came to Philadelphia to revise the Articles of Confederation in 1787, quickly decided to form a new plan of government based on the lessons learned from their experience under the colonial British government and under the Articles of Confederation. Later, as a condition for their support and ratification of the Constitution, opponents of the stronger central government demanded a Bill of Rights that guaranteed liberties once violated by the British, and potentially threatened by a strong national government.

In this lesson, students trace how experiences under British colonial rule and the Articles of Confederation influenced the Framers in creating the Constitution.

Procedure
1. Ask how difficult it is to change our government. (*The Constitution can be amended; Supreme Court rulings can change the interpretation of a law.*) Ask students to give examples of how our government has changed over the last two hundred years (*presidential term limits; direct election of senators; women and African Americans have the right to vote; voting age changes; no poll tax*).

2. Distribute **Handout 2**, and briefly discuss the structure of the government under the Articles of Confederation and the resulting problems. Have students complete **Handout 2** in pairs or individually. Review students' responses.

Suggested Responses:

Part A.

1. They resented the Indian-colonial land settlement and trade policy; they felt the economic squeeze of high land costs and taxes.

2. They fought campaigns against Indians and Berkeley's men because they were angry.

3. The outcome was reforms of elections but also deeper hatred of Indians and spread of their incitement to rebellion and violence to other colonies. Perhaps it could have been prevented if there had been a check on the governor's power, which he used to help his friends.

4. organize a government that prevents abusive and centralized power and encourages accountability

Part B.

1. loss of Western lands to settlers; concern that the British were trying to keep the colonists under their control

2. taxation without representation

3. threatened right to privacy

4. threat of all-powerful Parliament

5. threat of unreasonable searches and more taxes levied without representation

6. threatened economy of Massachusetts, self-government in the province, and due process in courts

Part C.

1. Private property throughout the country was in danger.

2. The ability to protect the country's rights as a sovereign nation seemed in danger.

3. The ability to protect one's own people from hostile attacks was in danger.

4. Uncertainty about the value of money endangered foreign and interstate trade.

5. Numerous taxes threatened the volume of trade among states.

6. Financing of costs of running the government was uncertain.

7. The legislative process was not working due to a possible lack of continuity of members and undue pressure of state legislatures' interests.

8. A leadership void was created, and a leader was needed to keep order.

9. The laws were not easily enforced when in hands of the states—a neutral group was needed.

3. Have students complete **Handout 3** in a large-group session, or individually. Review students' responses.

Suggested Responses:

Part A.

1. The Articles of Confederation did not allow Congress to enforce, through a federal court system, what it passed. It had no authoritative muscle to compel citizens or states to comply with laws.

2. Without an ability to enforce what it passed, Congress had very diminished power.

Part B.

1. The Constitution provides for selection of all branches of government either directly by the people or by their elected representatives.

2. Article I, Section 8 provides for a militia.

3. Article I, Section 9 prohibits grants of titles of nobility.

4. The Third Amendment prohibits the quartering of soldiers.

5. Article I, Section 8 provides for establishment of an army.

6. Article I, Section 8 allows Congress to control interstate trade.

7. Article I, Section 8 allows Congress to coin money and regulate its value.

8. The Fourth Amendment prohibits unreasonable searches and seizures.

9. The Fifth Amendment outlines the rights of due process in court trials.

10. *The First Amendment guarantees freedom of religion.*

11. *The First Amendment guarantees freedom of speech.*

12. *The First Amendment guarantees freedom of the press.*

13. *Article II provides for a national presidency.*

14. *Article III provides for a judicial system.*

4. Have students research and report on one of the signers of the Constitution. Have students assume his persona and write an essay discussing his hopes, goals, fears, and concerns about a balanced government, representative of all free men, and how he would handle critical issues such as the abuse of power. Remind students to address essential points, comparing government under the British and the Articles of Confederation. Provide class time for selected students to share their essays.

Enrichment/Extension

Have students prepare a short-answer essay to the following prompt: The Constitution attempted to strike a balance between an authority and individual rights by creating a stronger, more workable government than the Articles of Confederation while providing checks on government power and written guarantees of individual liberties. Have selected students share their essays.

Colonial Unrest

Part A.

Read the following selection, and answer the accompanying questions. As you read, think about what underlying events and economic discontent led to these actions and whether a government structure or policy could have prevented them.

> Led by the twenty-eight-year-old Nathaniel Bacon, the Virginia planter class rebelled against Virginia Royal Governor Sir William Berkeley's Indian policy. Berkeley's policy allowed friendly Indians to settle on tracts of land north of the York River and trade with settlers. Bacon and others resented this close trade relationship and the economic pressure they felt when land costs increased and taxes were raised. Bacon led aggressive, violent campaigns in 1676 against Berkeley's men and the Indians. He captured the capital, Jamestown, razed its major buildings such as the church, and forced Berkley to flee across Chesapeake Bay. Great Britain sent 1,100 troops to help put down the rebellion. In 1677, Bacon died of swamp fever. The Royal Governor's self-aggrandizing tactics were soon exposed: high taxes, jobs for friends, and increasing centralized power. The House of Burgesses passed reform legislation that extended the vote to freemen and called for new assembly elections. The long-term effect of the rebellion was the development of a feeling of deep hatred for Native Americans. This later prevented friendlier relations based on trade or education, and spread to Maryland and North Carolina, which had brief, but similar uprisings.

1. Why did Bacon and his followers rebel against the governor?

2. What method did they use to change government policy?

3. What was the outcome of the rebellion?

4. Could the Virginia legislature have prevented the rebellion?

5. Given this history of colonial rebellion in Virginia, a model colony, how might the Framers of the Constitution have organized a government to prevent this citizen violence?

Source: *The American People*, ed. Gary B. Nash, et al., 5th ed. (New York: Harper and Row, 2001), 76–77.

U.S. Government, Book 1
Lesson 2
Handout 2 (page 2)

Name_____

Date_____

Part B.

The Framers learned much from the colonial experience under the British colonial government. Using an American history textbook or other references, complete the following chart. Identify what fears the British acts described below aroused among the American colonists in the years before the American Revolution.

Act	Description	Fear
1. Proclamation of 1763	Restricted colonists' settlement beyond the Appalachians; necessary to placate the Indians	
2. Stamp Act of 1765	Taxed all printed matter in the colonies	
3. Billeting Act of 1765	Required colonists to house British troops in private homes	
4. Declaratory Act of 1766	Stated that Parliament had the right "to legislate for the colonies in all cases whatsoever"	
5. Townshend Acts of 1767	Taxed imported lead, glass, tea, and paint; collected by customs officials using blank search warrants called writs of assistance	
6. Intolerable Acts of 1774	Punished colonists for Boston Tea Party; suspended colonial legislature and ended town meetings in Massachusetts; allowed British officials charged with crimes in the colonies to be tried in England	

Part C.

The Framers learned many lessons from the difficulties they encountered in governing the states under the Articles of Confederation. Identify the fears each of the following problems raised among Americans during the years of the Articles of Confederation.

Problem	Description	Fear
1. Shays' Rebellion of 1786–87	Armed rebellion in which angry debtors seized several Massachusetts courthouses	
2. British control of forts in Northwest	British refused to evacuate forts in Northwest Territory after the end of the American Revolution.	
3. Indian raids	Native Americans raided settlers' homes along the western frontier.	
4. Lack of uniform currency	Each state printed its own money; stability of currency varied widely among states.	
5. Each state regulated its own commerce	States taxed commerce coming into their territory from other states.	
6. Congress unable to collect taxes or duties	With no power to tax, Congress could raise money only by borrowing from the states.	
7. Severely limited Congressional power	Each state had one vote regardless of size. A unanimous vote was needed to change the Articles of Confederation by the Congress. Members were selected to serve a one-year term.	
8. No chief executive	The Congress yearly chose one of its members as president or presiding officer— not president of the United States.	
9. No national court system	All legal decisions are in the hands of the states. Unresolved disputes only were to be settled, if possible, by legislative action.	

In Support of Change

Part A.

Read the following excerpt from a speech by John Jay, a U.S. foreign secretary under the Articles of Confederation in 1787 and a supporter of the Constitution. Then answer the questions.

> By the Confederation as it now stands, the direction of general and national affairs is committed to a single body of men, viz. The Congress. They make war, but are not empowered to raise men or money to carry it on—they make peace, but without power to see the terms of it observed—they may form alliances, but without ability to comply with the stipulations on their part—they may enter into treaties of commerce, but without power to enforce them at home or abroad—they may borrow money, but without having the means of repayment—they may partly regulate commerce, but without authority to execute their ordinances—they may appoint ministers and other officers of trust, but without power to try or punish them for misdemeanours—they may resolve, but cannot execute either with dispatch or with secrecy.—In short, they may consult, and deliberate, and recommend, and make requisitions, and they who please may regard them.[1]

1. In your own words, summarize the problem regarding Congress' ability to act under the Articles of Confederation.

2. Why were the restrictions under the Articles of Confederation a particular problem for Congress, the primary federal law-making body?

[1]John Jay, "Extract from an Address to the People of the State of New-York, on the Subject of the Federal Constitution," *American Memory: Documents from the Continental Congress and the Constitutional Conventions, 1774–1789,* 2 February 2001, <http://hdl.loc.gov/loc.rbc/bdsdcc.c0501> (6 October 2004).

Part B.

Use a copy of the Constitution and Bill of Rights to determine how the Framers calmed the following fears. List the solution of the problem and where it is found in the Constitution.

Concerns	Solutions/Locations
1. A monarchy	
2. Security against the masses	
3. Control of the government by the nobility	
4. Quartering of troops in private homes	
5. Security against foreign threats	
6. States imposing taxes and tariffs on trade with other states	
7. States coining money with various values	
8. Freedom from unreasonable searches	
9. Due process in courts of law	
10. Freedom of religion	
11. Freedom of speech	
12. Freedom of the press	
13. Need for a national president	
14. Need for a judiciary	

Lesson 3
Federalist v. Anti-Federalist

Objectives

- To understand the political and philosophical differences between the Federalists and Anti-Federalists

- To develop an understanding of the importance of the Federalists and Anti-Federalists to the creation of our Constitution

Notes to the Teacher

Perhaps the most exciting time in U.S. history to read the newspapers, attend community or school gatherings, vote, or attend political rallies, if one were interested in putting political thought into action, would have been the period when our nation was in its infancy. Citizens, such as Thomas Paine, published their ideas here and abroad. This was a time when men fought for their beliefs in freedom and equality.

When the Revolutionary War ended, individual states crafted their own constitutions to reflect their new economic and political status. In most states, male property owners could vote, the legislature had most of the power, governors were limited in their executive powers, and bills of rights were established. From 1776 to 1787, under the Articles of Confederation, tensions were heightened between states, who argued over trade, geographic boundaries, and tariffs.

A group of influential leaders called a convention in 1787, and the states were invited to send delegates to Philadelphia. Half of the delegates were college graduates, and others were lawyers or government officials trained in the law. Propertied gentlemen and planters came from the South, judges from the Middle States, and merchants from New England. The delegates represented a range of political philosophies and ideas.

Those attending knew from past experience that there was a conflict between certain rights, which were designated in the Declaration of Independence as "inalienable," and the fact that "Governments . . . derive their just powers from the consent of the governed." If rights such as liberty, freedom of the press, and freedom of speech could never be denied, altered, or voted upon, what would happen if state governments did try to change them?

The convention sought to strike a balance between assuring that government was by consent and that the rights of the people were protected. The debate over the ratification of the Constitution revolved around an assessment of whether the Framers had sufficiently resolved this conflict.

When the convention concluded its work, citizens could read in newspapers, broadsides, and pamphlets, or attend speeches and debates, about the pros and cons of ratification. Discussion about the meaning and application of government spread into homes, taverns, and public thoroughfares.

There began a heartfelt, impassioned discussion about human nature, and the ability of the people, who were mostly farmers and tradesmen, to select national representatives even if they themselves were not educated. These men would have to counteract the possibility of an abuse of power by an elite elected body. They had to protect on a national level the fundamental rights already protected in most of the states.

On a fundamental level, the Framers and the later Federalists and Anti-Federalists argued about the efficacy of a democracy, how to deal with a population that was emotional and had the potential to be easily manipulated, and a republicanism, which believed in the consent of the governed but despised mob rule.

Upon leaving the convention, the delegates attempted to sway public opinion regarding ratification in their respective states. Nine of the thirteen states were required to vote for ratification in order for the new Constitution to be accepted. George Washington mailed copies of the proposed Constitution to former governors of Virginia and asked for their support, citing his fear that anarchy would overtake the land if the document was not ratified. Heated speeches often punctuated debates over ratification. Delegates debated the rights and nature of humans and their tendency to self-interest and corruption.

In this lesson, students read a fact sheet on the Constitutional Convention, the Federalists, and the Anti-Federalists, and answer questions. Students also read and answer questions about selections from Federalist and Anti-Federalist writings. They conclude by completing an information organizer illustrating the main points of both sides.

Procedure

1. Explain that when the American Revolution ended, many of our nation's leaders felt that the Articles of Confederation, which had governed the colonies during the rebellion, needed to be replaced. Problems involving trade and commerce, disputes between the states, the absence of a chief executive and court system, and the inability of the Congress to tax the states to support the federal government needed to be addressed. When the Constitutional Convention convened in Philadelphia in 1787, many of the delegates had already chosen sides. Compromise would be necessary in order to accomplish ratification.

2. Distribute **Handout 4**, and have students read the fact sheet and answer the questions. Review students' responses.

Suggested Responses:

Part A.

1. *no ability to tax; weak central government; no chief executive; no courts to settle disputes between states*

2. *Anti-Federalists and Federalists*

3. *A large population cannot be well represented in a republican democracy; a strong central government would lead to the failure of state governments; a federal court system would undermine the authority of the state courts; a strong executive would lead to tyranny and corruption; there would be no need for a bill of rights.*

4. *States should work together for the improvement and betterment of the nation; a federal government would act in the national interest; a republican democracy could resolve issues of economics and politics by reaching a consensus within*

the Congress; a government consisting of three branches with a system of checks and balances would prevent any single branch from becoming too powerful.

5. *The essays served as a blueprint for debate over ratification.*

Part B.

Federalists—*Statements 2, 4, 5, 7, 9*

Anti-Federalists—*Statements 1, 3, 6, 8, 10*

3. Be aware that the writings of the Federalists and the Anti-Federalists are difficult to read. Students might be less intimidated by the reading selection if the class is divided into small groups of three or four. Distribute **Handout 5**, and instruct students to read the excerpts and answer the questions. Review students' responses.

Suggested Responses:

Part A.

1. *factionalism*

2. *by removing the causes and by controlling its effects*

3. *by destroying liberty, which is essential to its existence, and by giving every citizen the same opinions, passions, and interests*

4. *Mankind has divided into parties, which cause quarrels. People are disposed to annoy and oppress each other, rather than to cooperate for the common good.*

5. *because his interests would bias his judgment and corrupt his honesty*

6. *the most powerful party*

7. *The causes of factions cannot be removed, and one can only hope to control the effects.*

8. *by enabling the majority to defeat its sinister views by a regular vote and to secure the public good and private rights*

9. *a republic*

10. *the delegation of government to a small number of citizens who represent the rest; the greater number of citizens and greater sphere of the country over which government is extended*

11. *People elect a representative to speak for them.*

12. *could give rise to a cabal*

13. *more likely to center in men who possess merit and have an established character; unfit to comprehend and pursue great national objectives*

14. *unacquainted with their local interests*

Part B.

1. *to reform the federal system and to strengthen the government; to establish peace, order, and justice in the community*

2. *to make one consolidated government*

3. *Powers were limited and inadequate to fulfill the needs of the Union.*

4. *solve problems of trade and commerce*

5. *No one would have attended.*

6. *to consolidate the states into a single national government*

7. *a bill of rights; to protect inalienable and fundamental rights*

8. *Power rested in the hands of the few, who could use the system to block change.*

9. *There are men who have a dislike for a free and equal government, and who will systematically work to change it.*

Part C.

1. *A large territory cannot be governed by the principles of freedom, other than by a confederation of republics; power, given to the national government under the Constitution, would destroy the powers of the state and create one consolidated government; a national government will give way to an iron-handed despotism; the Constitution is not constructed to guarantee the principles of liberty and happiness to the people.*

2. *the writ of habeas corpus; jury trial in criminal and civil cases; trial by an impartial jury; safety for the rights of the accused in criminal prosecutions; liberty of the press*

4. Have students design a poster supporting either the Federalist or the Anti-Federalist position. Explain that the poster should support one or more of the ideals of the faction they choose. Tell students to be prepared to present and explain their poster. Display posters in the classroom.

Enrichment/Extension

Have students research and prepare a short play for presentation to the class. The play should highlight the writings of prominent Federalists and Anti-Federalists such as Patrick Henry, Melancton Smith, Alexander Hamilton, and James Madison.

Ratifying the Constitution

Part A.

Read the fact sheet, and answer the questions.

The Articles of Confederation failed to address several problems confronting the newly formed United States. During the American Revolution, the failure of the Continental Congress to enact legislation to provide monetary support for the Continental army was rooted in its inability to tax the states without their consent. When the war ended, other problems arose. The Articles were concerned with guaranteeing the rights of the individual states. The central government was weak, and there was no chief executive. No court system was established to settle disputes between states or between states and foreign countries. Trade between states and with other countries was unregulated. States imposed tariffs on goods traded from one state to another, and each state produced its own money. Currency value varied from state to state, and often merchants found that they could not use their state's money to pay for goods in another state. Many agreed that the Articles of Confederation needed to be revised. The question was, how should it be changed.

A constitutional convention was called in Philadelphia in 1787. Each of the states was invited to send a delegation to discuss a revision of the Articles. Only Rhode Island failed to send a delegation. Between May and September 1787, a document that proposed not a revision of the Articles of Confederation but the establishment of a new republican democracy was produced. The delegates agreed to three days of debate and that two-thirds of the states would have to approve the document for it to be accepted. The delegates were divided into two main factions—the Anti-Federalists and the Federalists.

The Anti-Federalists, led by James Wilson, Patrick Henry, and George Mason, had the support of the states. There was a general distrust of a strong national government among America's citizens. The Anti-Federalists argued that large populations represented by a few men would lead to a failure on the representatives' part to know the desires of their constituents. Anti-Federalists believed that a strong federal government would lead to the destruction of the state governments and that a federal court system would undermine the work of local courts. They also opposed the establishment of a strong executive branch, fearing it would lead to tyranny. The Anti-Federalists were particularly concerned with the lack of a protection of individual rights within the document.

The Federalists, led by John Jay, James Madison, and Alexander Hamilton, enjoyed the support of America's two truly national political figures, Benjamin Franklin and George Washington. Strong nationalists, who believed that the states should work together for the improvement and betterment of the nation, the Federalists sought to establish a federal government that could act in the national interest. They believed that a republican democracy could resolve issues of economics and politics by reaching consensus within the Congress. The Federalists proposed a government consisting of three branches, within which a system of checks and balances would prevent any single branch from becoming too powerful. Well-organized and well-financed, the Federalists succeeded in gaining passage of the new Constitution, and the document was sent to the states.

It was at this point that the real debate began. In every town and city up and down the Eastern seaboard, debate raged. Newspapers, pamphlets, and broadsides supported one side or the other. The new Constitution was debated in town meetings, and state conventions gathered to decide the fate of the proposal. Eighty-five letters written by the Federalists served as a blueprint for debate at the state conventions. Two-thirds of these letters were written by Jay, Hamilton, and Madison. Later these letters would by compiled in what we know today as *The Federalist Papers*.

After much debate, the new Constitution, which limited and clearly stated the powers of the federal government, was ratified by the required nine states, and the Articles of Confederation became a memory.

1. What were some of the problems that resulted from the weaknesses of the Articles of Confederation?

2. What were the main factions at the Constitutional Convention?

3. What were the main points raised by the Anti-Federalists?

4. What were the main points raised by the Federalists?

5. What was the purpose of *The Federalist Papers*?

Part B.

Read the numbered arguments. Decide which ones were raised by the Federalists and which ones were raised by the Anti-Federalists. Write the number of each statement in an appropriate space on the graphic organizer.

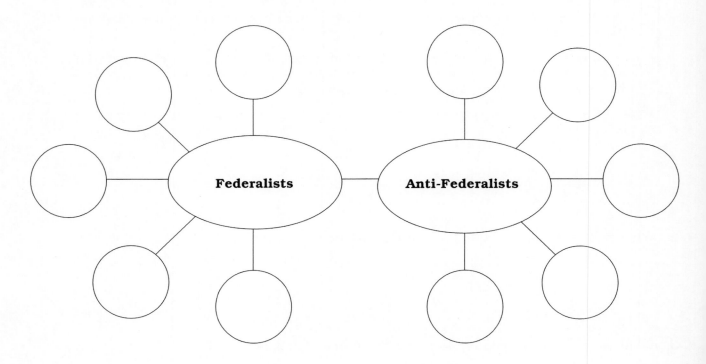

1. The executive branch had too much power.

2. Power needed to be divided between the states and the national government.

3. The "necessary and proper" clause gave too much power to the Congress.

4. The new government needed a strong executive.

5. Since all rights cannot be listed in the body of the Constitution, it is better to add a bill of rights after ratification.

6. No bill of rights had been proposed.

7. Because all branches were equal, no branch could control the others.

8. The national government could maintain an army in peacetime.

9. In a republican form of government, representation is based on the consent of the governed.

10. The proposed constitution gave too much power to the national government at the expense of the states.

Federalist and Anti-Federalist Writings

Part A.

James Madison is believed to have written twenty-nine of the essays that make up *The Federalist Papers*. In the tenth essay, Madison wrote of the problems of factionalism that were confronting the country and the advantages of a republican form of government over a pure democratic government such as the one espoused by the Articles of Confederation. Read the following excerpt from the essay, and answer the questions.

November 23, 1787

Among the numerous advantages promised by a well-constructed Union, none deserves to be more accurately developed than its tendency to break and control the violence of faction. The friend of popular governments never finds himself so much alarmed for their character and fate as when he contemplates their propensity for this dangerous vice. . . .

There are two methods of curing the mischiefs of faction: the one, by removing its causes; the other, by controlling its effects.

There are again two methods of removing the causes of faction: the one, by destroying the liberty which is essential to its existence; the other, by giving to every citizen the same opinions, the same passions, and the same interests. . . .

The second expedient is as impracticable as the first would be unwise. As long as the reason of man continues fallible, and he is at liberty to exercise it, different opinions will be formed. As long as the connection subsists between his reason and his self-love, his opinions and his passions will have a reciprocal influence on each other; and the former will be objects to which the later will attach themselves. . . .

. . . A zeal for different opinions . . . have, in turn, divided mankind into parties, inflamed them with mutual animosity, and rendered them more disposed to vex and oppress each other than to cooperate for their common good. . . . But the most common and durable source of factions has been the various and unequal distribution of property.

Those who hold and those who are without property have ever formed distinct interests in society. . . .

No man is allowed to be a judge in his own cause, because his interests would certainly bias his judgment and, not improbably, corrupt his integrity. . . . [T]he most numerous party or, in other words, the most powerful faction must be expected to prevail.

. . . The apportionment of taxes on the various descriptions of property is an act which seems to require the most exact impartiality; yet there is, perhaps, no legislative act in which greater opportunity and temptation are given to a predominant party to trample on the rules of justice. . . .

. . . The inference to which we are brought is that the *causes* of faction cannot be removed and that relief is only to be sought in the means of controlling its *effects*.

If a faction consists of less than a majority, relief is supplied by the republican principle, which enables the majority to defeat its sinister views by regular vote. It may clog the administration, it may convulse the society; but it will be unable to execute and mask its violence under the forms of the Constitution. When a majority is included in a faction, the form of popular government, on the other hand, enables it to sacrifice to its ruling passion or interest both the public good and the rights of other citizens. To secure the public good and private rights against the danger of such a faction, and at the same time to preserve the spirit and the form of popular government, is then the great object to which our inquiries are directed. . . .

. . . [A] pure democracy, by which I mean a society consisting of a small number of citizens who assemble and administer the government in person, can admit of no cure for the mischiefs of faction. . . . [S]uch democracies have ever been spectacles of turbulence and contention; have ever been found incompatible with personal security or the rights of property; and have in general been as short in their lives as they have been violent in their deaths. . . .

A republic, by which I mean a government in which the scheme of representation takes place, opens a different prospect and promises the cure for which we are seeking. . . .

The two great points of difference between a democracy and a republic are: first, the delegation of the government, in the latter, to a small number of citizens elected by the rest; secondly, the greater number of citizens, and greater sphere of the country, over which the latter may be extended.

The effect of the first difference is . . . to refine and enlarge the public views by passing them through the medium of a chosen body of citizens, whose wisdom may best discern the true interest of their country, and whose patriotism and love of justice will be least likely to sacrifice it to temporary or partial considerations. Under such a regulation, it may well happen that the public voice, pronounced by the representatives of the people, will be more consonant* to the public good than if pronounced by the people themselves, convened for the purpose. On the other hand, the effect may be inverted. Men of factious tempers, of local prejudices, or of sinister designs may, by intrigue, by corruption, or by other means, first obtain the suffrages, and then betray the interests of the people. The question resulting is, whether small or extensive republics are more favorable to the election of proper guardians of the public weal; and it is clearly decided in favor of the latter by two obvious considerations:

. . . [H]owever small the republic may be, the representatives must be raised to a certain number, in order to guard against the cabals** of a few; and that, however large it may be, they must be limited to a certain number, in order to guard against the confusion of a multitude. . . .

. . . [A]s each representative will be chosen by a greater number of citizens in the large than in the small republic, it will be more difficult for unworthy candidates to practice with success the vicious arts by which elections are too often carried; and the suffrages of the people being more free, will be more likely to center in men who possess the most attractive merit and the most diffusive and established character. . . .

. . . By enlarging too much the number of electors, you render the representative too little acquainted with all their local circumstances and lesser interests; as by reducing it too much, you render him unduly attached to these and too little fit to comprehend and pursue great and national objects. The federal Constitution forms a happy combination in this respect: the great and aggregate interests being referred to the national, the local and particular to the state legislatures.

The other point of difference is the greater number of citizens and extent of territory which may be brought within the compass of republican than

*to be in agreement
**small group of people working or plotting in secret

of democratic government; and it is this circumstance principally which renders factious combinations less to be dreaded in the former than in the latter. The smaller the society, the fewer probably will be the distinct parties and interests composing it; the fewer the distinct parties and interests, the more frequently will a majority be found of the same party; and the smaller the number of individuals composing a majority, and the smaller the compass within which they are placed, the more easily will they concert and execute their plans of oppression. . . .

The influence of factious leaders may kindle a flame within their particular States but will be unable to spread a general conflagration through the other States. A religious sect may degenerate into a political faction in a part of the Confederacy; but the variety of sects dispersed over the entire face of it must secure the national councils against any danger from that source. A rage for paper money, for an abolition of debts, for an equal division of property, or for any other improper or wicked project will be less apt to pervade the whole body of the Union than a particular member of it; in the same proportion as such a malady is more likely to taint a particular county or district than an entire State.[1]

1. What does Madison see as the primary problem confronting the new nation?

2. How does Madison believe this problem may be cured?

3. How can this problem be removed?

4. What had happened because of man's zeal for different opinions?

5. Why does Madison say a man should not be permitted to act as a judge in his own cause?

6. Which party does Madison say should prevail?

7. What conclusion does Madison reach about the causes of factionalism?

8. How is relief provided by the principles of republicanism?

9. What does Madison say promises a cure for factionalism?

10. What are the two differences between a democracy and a republic?

11. What does Madison say is the advantage of representative government?

12. Why does Madison caution about having too small a number of representatives?

13. According to Madison, which men are more likely to be elected?

14. What did Madison fear would happen if there were too many representatives?

[1]James Madison, "No. 10," in *The Federalist Papers*, ed. Clinton Rossiter (New York: Penguin Books, 1961), 77–84.

Part B.

Read the following Anti-Federalist responses, which are arguments against the adoption of the Constitution. Then answer the questions.

October 8, 1787

. . . Our object has been all along, to reform our federal system, and to strengthen our governments—to establish peace, order and justice in the community. . . . The plan of government now proposed is evidently calculated totally to change, in time, our condition as a people. Instead of being thirteen republics, under a federal head, it is clearly designed to make us one consolidated government. . . . Whether such a change can ever be effected in any manner; whether it can be effected without convulsions and civil wars; whether such a change will not totally destroy the liberties of this country—time only can determine. . . .

The confederation was formed when great confidence was placed in the voluntary exertions of individuals, and of the respective states; and the framers of it, to guard against usurpation, so limited and checked the powers, that, in many respects, they are inadequate to the exigencies of the union. We find, therefore, members of congress urging alterations in the federal system almost as soon as it was adopted. . . .

The conduct of several legislatures, touching paper money, and tender laws, has prepared many honest men for changes in government. . . . A general convention for mere commercial purposes was moved for—the authors of this measure saw that the people's attention was turned solely to the amendment of the federal system; and that, had the idea of a total change been started, probably no state would have appointed members to the convention. The idea of destroying, ultimately, the state government, and forming one consolidated system, could not have been admitted—a convention, therefore, merely for vesting in congress power to regulate trade was proposed. . . .

The plan proposed appears to be partly federal, but principally, however, calculated ultimately to make the states one consolidated government.

The first interesting question, therefore suggested, is, how far the states can be consolidated into one entire government on free principles. . . . The happiness of the people at large must be the great object with every honest statesman, and he will direct every movement to this point. If we are so situated as a people, as not to be able to enjoy equal happiness and advantages under one government, the consolidation of the states cannot be admitted. . . . [2]

October 9, 1787

. . . There are certain unalienable and fundamental rights, which in forming the social compact ought to be explicitly ascertained and fixed—a free and enlightened people, in forming this compact, will not resign all their rights to those who govern, and they will fix limits to their legislators and rulers, which will soon be plainly seen by those who are governed, as well as by those who govern; and the latter will know they cannot be passed unperceived by the former, and without giving a general alarm—These rights

[2]Melancton Smith, "Letters from the Federal Farmer," in *The Anti-Federalist Papers and the Constitutional Convention Debates*, ed. Ralph Ketcham (New York: Penguin Books, 1986), 257–63.

should be made the basis of every constitution: and if a people be so situated, or have such different opinions that they cannot agree in ascertaining and fixing them, it is a very strong argument against their attempting to form one entire society, to live under one system of laws only.[3]

October 12, 1787

It may also be worthy [of] our examination, how far the provision for amending this plan, when it shall be adopted, is of any importance. No measures can be taken toward amendments, unless two-thirds of the Congress, or two-thirds of the legislatures of the several states shall agree. While power is in the hands of the people, or democratic part of the community, more especially as at present, it is easy, according to the general course of human affairs, for the few influential men in the community, to obtain conventions, alterations in government, and to persuade the common people [that] they may change for the better, and to get from them a part of the power: But when power is once transferred from the many to the few, all changes become extremely difficult; the government, in this case, being beneficial to the few, they will be exceedingly artful and adroit in preventing any measures which may lead to a change; and nothing will produce it, but great exertions and severe struggles on the part of the common people. Every man of reflection must see, that the change now proposed, is a transfer of power from the many to the few, and the probability is, the artful and ever active aristocracy, will prevent all peaceable measures for changes, unless when they shall discover some favorable moment to increase their own influence.[4]

October 13, 1787

. . . It is true there may be danger in delay; but there is danger in adopting the system in its present form; and I see the danger in either case will arise principally from the conduct and views of two very unprincipled parties in the United States—two fires, between which the honest and substantial people have long found themselves situated. One party is composed of little insurgents, men in debt, who want no law, and who want a share of the property of others; these are called levellers, Shayites,* etc. The other party is composed of a few, but more dangerous men, with their servile dependents; these avariciously grasp at all power and property; you may discover in all the actions of these men, an evident dislike to free and equal governments, and they will go systematically to work to change, essentially, the forms of government in this country; these are called aristocrats. . . . The fact is, these aristocrats support and hasten the adoption of the proposed constitution, merely because they think it is a stepping stone to their favourite object. I think I am well founded in this idea; I think the general politics of these men support it, as well as the common observation among them that the proffered plan is the best that can be got at present, it will do for a few years, and lead to something better.[5]

*followers of Daniel Shay

[3]Smith, in *The Anti-Federalists Papers*, ed. Ketcham, 266.
[4]"Letters from the Federal Framer to *The Republican*," in *The Debate on the Constitution: Federalist and Anti-Federalist Speeches, Articles, and Letters during the Struggle over Ratification*, vol. 1, ed. Bernard Bailyn (New York: Library of America, 1993), 281.
[5]Ibid., 284.

1. What did the farmer say was the object of the Anti-Federalists?

2. What is the aim of the new constitution?

3. Why did members of Congress urge changes to the Articles of Confederation?

4. What reason did some members of Congress give when they proposed changing the Articles of Confederation?

5. What does the farmer suggest might have happened if the convention had been proposed to change to a federal system?

6. What was the real purpose of the convention?

7. What did the farmer say needed to be added to the new constitution? Why?

8. What did the farmer say was the danger of representative democracy?

9. What does the farmer say the men he called aristocrats wanted?

Part C.

William Findley, Robert Whitehill, and John Smilie represented the state of Pennsylvania at the Constitutional Convention. They believed that open debate at the convention was discouraged and that secrecy was the order of the day. These actions were supported by the Federalists and prevented dissidents from speaking their minds. Their collective essay was published in *The Pennsylvania Packet and Daily Advertiser* on December 18, 1787. Read the excerpt, and answer the questions.

From "The Address and Reasons of Dissent of the Minority of the Convention of Pennsylvania to Their Constituents"

Our objections are comprised under three general heads of dissent. . . .

We dissent, first, because it is the opinion of the most celebrated writers on government, and confirmed by experience, that a very extensive territory cannot be governed on the principles of freedom, otherwise than by a confederation of republics, possessing all the powers of internal government; but united in the management of their general, and foreign concerns. . . .

We dissent, secondly, because the powers vested in Congress by this constitution, must necessarily annihilate and absorb the legislative, executive, and judicial powers of the several states, and produce from their ruins one consolidated government, which from the nature of things will be *an iron handed depotism*, as nothing short of the supremacy of despotic sway could connect and govern these United States under one government.

As the truth of this position is of such decisive importance, it ought to be fully investigated, and if it is founded to be clearly ascertained; for, should it be demonstrated, that the powers vested by this constitution in Congress, will have such an effect as necessarily to produce one consolidated government, the question then will be reduced to this short issue, viz. whether satiated with the blessings of liberty; whether repenting of the folly of so recently asserting their unalienable rights, against foreign despots at the expence of so much blood and treasure, and such painful and arduous struggles, the people of America are now willing to resign every privilege of freemen, and submit to the dominion of an absolute government, that will embrace all America in one chain of despotism; or whether they will with virtuous indignation, spurn at the shackles prepared for them, and confirm their liberties by a conduct becoming freemen. . . .

We dissent, thirdly, because if it were practicable to govern so extensive a territory as these United States includes, on the plan of a consolidated government, consistent with the principles of liberty and the happiness of the people, yet the construction of this constitution is not calculated to attain the object, for independent of the nature of the case, it would of itself, necessarily, produce a despotism, and that not by the unusual gradations, but with the celerity* that has hitherto only attended revolutions effected by the sword. . . .

The first consideration that this review suggests, is the omission of a Bill of Rights, ascertaining and fundamentally establishing those unalienable and personal rights of men, without the full, free, and secure enjoyment of which there can be no liberty, and over which it is not necessary for a

*swiftness

good government to have the control. The principal of which are the rights of conscience, personal liberty by the clear and unequivocal establishment of the writ of *habeas corpus*, jury trial in criminal and civil cases, by an impartial jury of the vicinage** or county, with the common-law proceedings, for the safety of the accused in criminal prosecutions; and the liberty of the press, that scourge of tyrants, and the grand bulwark of every other liberty and privilege; the stipulations heretofore made in favor of them in the state constitutions, are entirely superceded by this constitution.[6]

1. What were the main objections to the establishment of a representative government?

2. What rights did the Anti-Federalists want to be included in a bill of rights?

**vicinity

[6]"The Address and Reasons of Dissent of the Minority of the Convention of Pennsylvania to Their Constituents," in *The Complete Anti-Federalist*, vol. 3, ed. Herbet J. Storing (Chicago: University of Chicago Press, 1981), 153–57.

Lesson 4
Federalism:
Separated and Overlapping Powers

Objective
- To understand how the Constitution distributes the powers of government between the national and state governments

Notes to the Teacher
Experience with the ill-fated Articles of Confederation in the 1780s convinced the Founding Fathers that a stronger central government was required to solve the pressing domestic and foreign problems of the new American Republic. On the other hand, bitter memories of government under George III cautioned them against too much centralized authority. They tried to create a delicate balance between national and state powers. The powers the national government needs to function effectively are enumerated in the Constitution. All powers not listed in the Constitution, or implied from the powers delegated to the national government, are given to the states. Both levels of government share certain concurrent powers; for example, both must have the power to levy and collect taxes to generate the money they need to operate. This division of power between two levels of government, called federalism, became a major factor in making the Constitution more workable than the Articles of Confederation it replaced.

In this lesson, students define terms associated with federalism, analyze three vignettes about the separation of powers, chart the powers at each level of government, and analyze the application of the powers of government in their daily lives.

Procedure
1. List the following terms on the board, and ask students to define them.

   federalism—*a system of government in which power is shared between central and local governments*

   delegated powers—*specific powers given to one of the branches or levels of government in its Constitution*

   reserved powers—*those powers exclusively for, or reserved to, a certain branch*

   concurrent powers—*the powers shared by more than one level of government, for example, the power to tax*

2. Read the following vignettes aloud. Ask students to identify whether the person would be a supporter of strong national powers, state powers, or concurrent powers.

   - Joel B. Young owns a fleet of ships, which he uses in order to trade with Europe, the West Indies, and ports along the coast of the United States. He wants any new government that might replace the Articles of Confederation to protect his foreign trade as well as his right to carry goods into and out of other American states. Problems with the value of American currency and American prestige abroad also trouble him. (*advocate of strong national government*)

   - Lynn and Elizabeth Jean Wegmann are descendants of Irish landholders who, having lost their holdings to the English crown in a brief rebellion, came to the American colonies and moved into western New York to escape the long arm of the king. Lynn fought in and Elizabeth supported the rebellion against the English king and a tyrannical government. They are suspicious of any central government that would be empowered to raise an army or assess and collect taxes. Lynn feels that he and his family have freed themselves from one tyranny, and they are not willing to accept another. (*advocates of strong state government*)

   - Thomas Ruth, a professor of law at Yale, lectures on the significance of shared powers in a class relating to the new Constitution. Shared powers, as he sees them, allow both the national and state governments the necessary power to tax, apprehend criminals, and enforce laws. On the negative side, he anticipates debates over jurisdiction and a less efficient government. Still, no government could function without these essential powers. (*advocate of concurrent powers*)

3. Ask students to make a t-chart. Have them label one side "State Government" and the other side "National Government." Brainstorm the powers of each government level.

4. Distribute **Handout 6**, and have students complete the activity either individually or in small groups. Review students' responses.

   Suggested Responses:

   Part A.

   National powers—*make treaties, collect import taxes, regulate interstate commerce, declare war, coin money, punish counterfeiters, fix standard weights, naturalize citizens, create post offices, raise an army, grant copyrights*

   State powers—*license professionals, regulate sale of alcoholic beverages, regulate trade within a state, regulate marriage and divorce, regulate gambling, make traffic regulations*

   Concurrent powers—*collect taxes, fund and regulate education, enforce laws*

   Part B.

   National government—*tax exports, suspend writ of habeas corpus, change state boundaries without permission of the states*

   State government—*coin money, enter into treaties, tax federal government agencies, tax imports or exports*

   Both governments—*pass ex post facto laws, pass bills of attainder, deny due process of law, grant titles of nobility, change the Bill of Rights*

5. Ask the following questions:
   - Why did the Framers fail to centralize all powers of government in the national government? (*They remembered the hatred of centralized power under the British and knew that the American people would never approve a centralized government that did not recognize their local needs and their desire for local control.*)
   - Why did the Framers select very specific duties to assign to the national government? (*These were powers necessary for the successful functioning of the nation as a whole, in solving a multitude of domestic and foreign problems.*)
   - Why did the Framers allow both the national and state governments to share powers of taxation? (*Both levels of government need money to operate, and thus both must tax.*)
   - Why did the Framers deny certain powers to the national government, state governments, or both? (*They remembered their experiences under both British rule and the Articles of Confederation, which were characterized by abuse of power, negligence, or both.*)

6. Explain that students have the most contact with their local government and that the Framers would have been surprised at the amount of regulation but pleased that most contact with the government occurs at the state or local level. On the chalkboard or on an overhead transparency, write the following labels: National Powers; Concurrent Powers; State Powers; Local Powers. Have students list their economic and social activities for three days and decide which level of government regulates that activity. Examples of economic and social activities include picking up a paycheck, wearing a helmet while biking, buying shoes, wearing a seat belt while driving a car, and taking a proficiency test.

7. Conduct a class discussion at the end of the three days. Which level of government did students have the most interaction with, and why? Ask students whether the Founding Fathers would be pleased with this balance of power, and why or why not.

Enrichment/Extension

Have students compile a list of examples of how our governments—local, state, and national—affect their daily lives. Have students prepare a photo collage of a selection of these examples for display in the classroom.

Name_____

Date_____

The Separation of Powers

Part A.

Use the Constitution as a reference to place the following powers in the appropriate section of the Venn diagram.

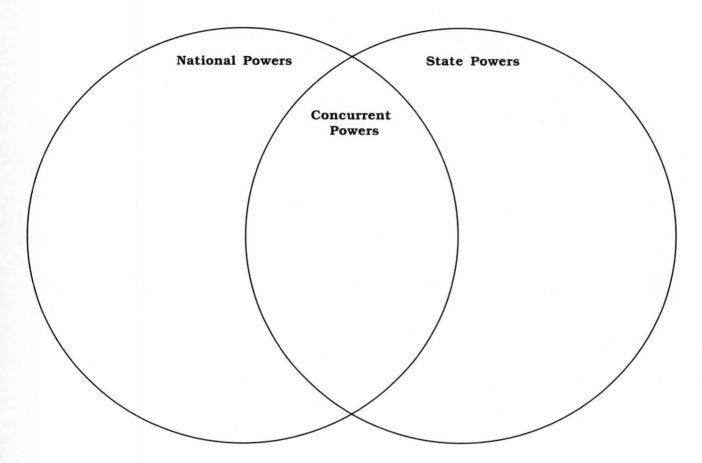

Powers

- license professionals
- collect taxes
- make treaties
- collect import taxes
- regulate interstate commerce
- declare war
- fund and regulate education
- coin money
- punish counterfeiters
- fix standard weights
- regulate sale of alcoholic beverages
- naturalize citizens
- create post offices
- enforce laws
- regulate trade within a state
- raise an army
- grant copyrights
- regulate marriage and divorce
- regulate gambling
- make traffic regulations

Part B.

Use the Constitution as a reference to determine which powers are denied to the various governments. List them in the appropriate sections of the Venn diagram.

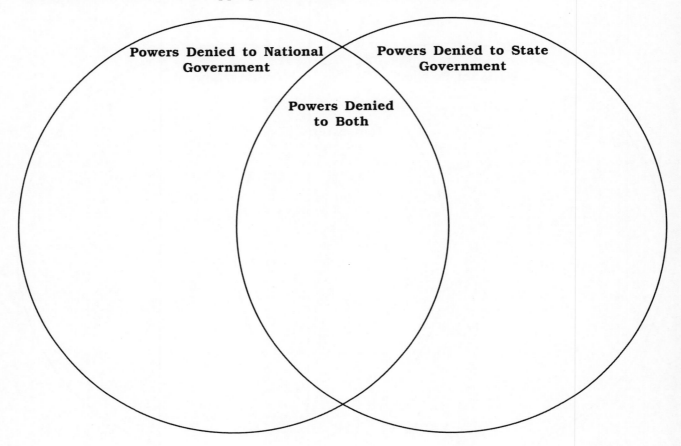

Powers Denied to National Government

Powers Denied to State Government

Powers Denied to Both

Powers

- grant titles of nobility
- coin money
- tax exports
- pass ex post facto laws
- suspend writ of habeas corpus
- enter into treaties
- pass bills of attainder
- tax federal government agencies

- deny due process of law
- tax imports or exports
- change the Bill of Rights
- change state boundaries without permission of the states

Lesson 5
Checking Power with Power

Objectives

- To understand how and why the Constitution limits the power of the people

- To understand how the Constitution separates and checks power within the government

Notes to the Teacher

The combined philosophies of Thomas Hobbes, Jean-Jacques Rousseau, and Baron de Montesquieu, the theology of John Calvin, and the experiences under the colonial and confederation governments all combined to convince early American political leaders of the danger of power concentrated in one person or group. Hobbes viewed man as brutish and selfish, but rational; he believed an authoritarian government would best protect man's natural rights of life and property. Rousseau thought that man in the state of nature is essentially good, could possess property, and could be free. Yet upon entering into a social contract with society, man gives up some of his personal rights but also gains more freedom by submitting to the general will of the group and its laws. French philosopher Montesquieu thought it essential that the powers of government be separated precisely, instead of placing many powers together under one officeholder who could both make and interpret laws and in effect defeat the principle of equality.

Calvin considered man evil and fallen. Although no person merits salvation, Calvin believed that God demonstrates his divine mercy both by providing holy grace to the penitent and by marking "the elect" for salvation. Neither Hobbes nor Calvin saw man as free and responsible persons capable of making rational, intelligent, and responsible decisions. The Constitution's many checks on the power of the people and on the powers of each branch of government reflect the Framers' suspicion of human nature.

The new nation's earlier experiences with government reinforced these fears of unchecked power. Authoritarian British rule, such as the imposition of the Stamp Act and the Intolerable Acts, convinced the colonists of the need to give the people real representation in the government. On the other hand, the horror of unbridled mob action in Daniel Shay's Rebellion (1786–87), when radicals physically attacked the courts, gave them good reason to limit the people's control over their government. In Pennsylvania, the Whiskey Rebellion erupted when Alexander Hamilton, secretary of the treasury, suggested imposing a tax on grain barrels to help pay off the war debt. The rebellion tested the resolve of President George Washington in enforcing federal power against dissenting citizens of a state. Both Washington and Hamilton rode horseback ahead of a vast army to quell the disturbances in rural western Pennsylvania. Washington went only part of the distance, urged by aides who feared for his life.

Although the Constitution laid the foundation for the development of democracy, the Framers had no intention of creating a full-blown democracy at the time of the Constitutional Convention in 1787. They lacked faith in the prudence and character of the common people. Concentrating power in the legislature under the Articles had proven to be equally unwise. The Articles of Confederation lacked a vehicle to enforce decisions and resolve disputes between states. It demonstrated clearly the need for a strong executive office and federal judiciary. The principles of separation of powers and checks and balances carefully distribute power among several branches and use power to check power and ultimately prevent the abuse of power among the branches of government.

In this lesson, students read and discuss selections from Hobbes, Rousseau, Montesquieu, and Calvin. Students examine the basic philosophy of the Founding Fathers and analyze a chart on the question of direct democracy. To conclude, students discuss the merits of our system of checks and balances.

Procedure

1. Discuss why it was necessary to establish a system of checks and balances within the new Constitution. (*The Articles of Confederation had provided little help in solving disputes that arose between and among*

states; each branch of government must be protected from encroachment upon its powers by either of the other two branches.) Ask: What was the purpose of the balance of powers? (*to prevent the abuse of power*)

2. Explain that the political philosophies of the Enlightenment gave birth to America's constitutional government. Stress that no single philosopher served as the model for our government, but that each contributed to the design. Distribute **Handout 7**, and have students complete it in a large-group session. Review students' responses.

Suggested Responses:

Thomas Hobbes

1. *power; desires more, delights to have more*

2. *competition of riches, honor, command; kill, subdue, supplant, repel someone*

3. *laws, judges, marshals, police, someone to execute the law and interpret just consequences for law breakers, when necessary*

Jean-Jacques Rousseau

4. *Man as a baby is free, but he is over-taken when older by laws, regulations, and restrictions.*

5. *The association can be found in democracy, democratic republics, and social democracy because these have the most freedom with the least government.*

6. *popular majority; submitting to its rules even when one, as a citizen, does not like the rules*

Baron de Montesquieu

7. *efficient, yes, but dangerous for liberty, for one branch or person is lawmaker, judge, and executioner*

8. *yes, for it is the clearly stated separation of powers*

John Calvin

9. *to aspire to seek God with our heart*

10. *God determined who is bound for heaven versus damnation.*

11. *organize society and make laws to account for the good and the evil among its citizens*

3. Ask students to select one of the philosophers quoted on the handout and write him a letter explaining how the U.S. Constitution reflects his view of human nature and how such a view is significant today. Allow class time for students to share their work. Letters should reflect a basic understanding of the philosophy and the part(s) of the Constitution that apply to the issue and why it is significant.

4. Distribute **Handout 8**, and have students complete it. Review students' responses.

Suggested Responses:

Part A.

1. *false*

2. *true*

3. *true*

4. *false*

5. *true*

Part B.

Believing humans to be basically evil and motivated by self-interest, the upper-class Framers sought to limit the voice of the people and control the abuse of power through a system of checks and balances.

5. Distribute **Handout 9**, and have students complete it individually. Review students' responses.

Suggested Responses:

Part A.

1. *The Framers had an inherent distrust of the competency of the citizens, mostly uneducated yeomen farmers, trades-people, and artisans.*

2. *House of Representatives*

3. *eliminate the state legislatures to indicate the direct election of senators today*

4. a. *two years*
   b. *six years*
   c. *four years*
   d. *life term*

5. *Supreme Court*

6. *The overlapping or staggered terms of office make it impossible to change all of the leaders of government at once.*

Part B.

1. a. *makes the laws*

    b. *enforces the laws*

    c. *interprets the laws*

2. *Follow the arrows on the diagram for several possibilities in each case.*

3. *The Constitution divides the powers of government among the three branches and creates a system of checks on each branch so that no person or group can act without the consent of the other branches.*

6. Ask students to imagine that they are the current president, a congressional representative, or a federal judge. Ask how they might be frustrated or relieved right now at the checks and balances system that imposes compromises. (Relieved—*The judiciary protects the rights of the minority; Congress can override presidential vetoes; a chief executive officer can immediately take charge of the direction of the government and provide leadership in economic, political, or social crisis;* Frustrated—*Presidents cannot get their federal judges appointed because senators hold up the Senate confirmation hearings; the judiciary interprets popularly voted laws and can declare them unconstitutional; the president threatens to veto or vetoes legislation passed by a majority of the Congress and contributes to legislative gridlock.*)

Enrichment/Extension

Have students review the philosophies represented in this lesson and write a short essay that explains which one they believe is most fully realized in the U.S. Constitution and its present-day application. Have selected students share their essays.

The Balance of Power

The following passages deal with larger, more philosophical questions of government, such as

- What is human nature?
- How is government to be organized, given man's nature?
- Where lies the power within government?
- Can man govern himself?
- Is it in man's interest to be part of a society, of government?

Read the selections, and answer the questions.

From *Leviathan* by Thomas Hobbes

So that in the first place, I put for a general inclination of all mankind, a perpetual and restless desire of power after power, that ceaseth only in death. And the cause of this, is not always that a man hopes for a more intensive delight, than he has already attained to; or that he cannot be content with a moderate power: but because he cannot assure the power and means to live well, which he hath present, without the acquisition of more. . . .

Competition of riches, honour, command, or other power, inclineth to contention, enmity, and war: because the way of one competitor, to the attaining of his desire, is to kill, subdue, supplant, or repel the other. . . .

1. What is the restless desire of man? Why does man seek power?

2. What inclines one to contention? How does one attain such desires from a competitor, according to Hobbes?

3. Given Hobbes' view of nature, how might a government organize itself against such tendencies?

From *The Social Contract* by Jean-Jacques Rousseau

Man is born free, and everywhere he is in chains. There are some who may believe themselves masters of others, and are no less enslaved than they. . . .

. . . Whereas the social order is a sacred right, and provides a foundation for all other rights. Yet it is a right that does not come from nature; therefore it is based on agreed conventions. . . .

Find a form of association which will defend and protect, with the whole of its joint strength, the person and property of each associate, and under which each of them, uniting himself to all, will obey himself alone, and remain as free as before. . . .

If therefore, we set aside everything that is not essential to the social pact, we shall find that it may be reduced to the following terms. *Each of us puts his person and all his power in common under the supreme direction of the general will; and we as a body receive each member as an indivisible part of the whole.*

4. What does Rousseau mean by his first statement? Do you agree?

5. Is it possible for one to find the association he discusses? Is a democratic republic close? Why or why not?

6. Is there a general will in a democracy? What does he mean about subjecting oneself to it?

From *The Spirit of the Laws* by Baron de Montesquieu

When the legislative and executive powers are united in the same person, or in the same body of magistrates, there can be no liberty. . . .

Again, there is no liberty, if the power of judging be not separated from the legislative and executive powers. . . .

7. Is not a government with both legislative and executive power in one body more efficient? Why does Montesquieu argue against it?

8. Would Montesquieu be pleased with the first three articles of the American Constitution?

From *Instruction in Faith* by John Calvin

It is necessary, therefore, that the principal care and solicitude of our life be to seek God, to aspire to Him with all the affection of our heart, and to repose nowhere else but in Him alone.

From *Institutes of the Christian Religion* by John Calvin

Predestination we call the eternal decree of God by which He has determined with Himself what He would have to become of every man. For . . . eternal life is foreordained for some and eternal damnation for others. Every man, therefore, being formed for one or the other of these ends, we say that he is predestinated to life or to death.

9. What is the desire of every man?

10. What is predestination?

11. How might such an outlook affect how one governs?

Name_____

Date_____

The Basic Philosophy of the Framers

Part A.

Read the following selection. Then mark each statement *true* or *false.*

> Long ago Horace White observed that the Constitution of the United States "is based upon the philosophy of Hobbes and the religion of Calvin. It assumes that the natural state of mankind is a state of war, and that the carnal mind is at enmity with God." Of course the Constitution was founded more upon experience than any such abstract theory; but it was also an event in the intellectual history of Western civilization. The men who drew up the Constitution in Philadelphia during the summer of 1787 had a vivid Calvinistic sense of human evil and damnation and believed with Hobbes that men are selfish and contentious. They were men of affairs, merchants, lawyers, planter-businessmen, speculators, investors. Having seen human nature on display in the market place, the courtroom, the legislative chamber, and in every secret path and alleyway where wealth and power are courted, they felt they knew it in all its frailty. To them a human being was an atom of self-interest. They did not believe in man, but they did believe in the power of a good political constitution to control him.[1]

_____ 1. The Framers believed in the basic goodness of human nature.

_____ 2. The Framers represented the interests of the upper, rather than lower, classes.

_____ 3. Man's primary motive is self-interest.

_____ 4. The Framers believed that the legislature is the only branch of government one can trust.

_____ 5. The Framers believed in checking power with power to prevent abuse.

Part B.

Use the information from **Handouts 7** and **8** to construct a statement summarizing the basic philosophy of the Founding Fathers.

[1]Richard Hofstader, *The American Political Tradition and the Men Who Made It* (New York: Alfred A. Knopf, 1948), 3.

A Question of Direct Democracy

Part A.

Examine the following diagram, and use it to answer the questions about the structure of the government.

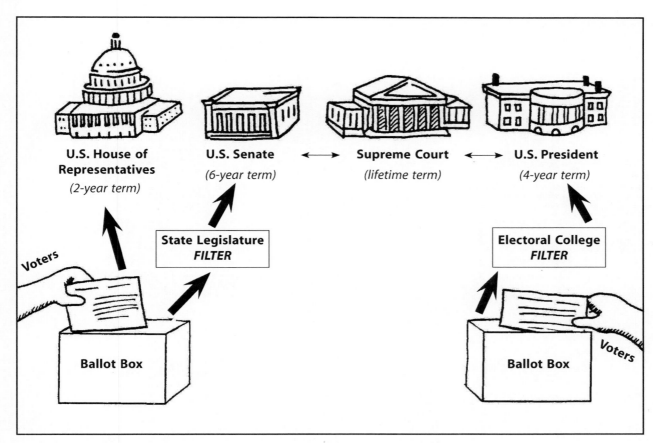

1. Why did the makers of the Constitution place filters between the voters and the U.S. Senate and the presidency?

2. Under the original Constitution, which was the only part of the national government directly elected by the people?

3. What change would be required in the chart to reflect the reality of the electoral process today?

4. What is the term of office of each of the following?

   a. House of Representatives

   b. Senate

   c. President

   d. Supreme Court

5. What part of the government is most removed from control of the people?

6. Explain why this system makes it impossible to change the philosophy of government in one election.

Part B.

Study the diagram below, and use it to answer the questions about checks and balances within the government.

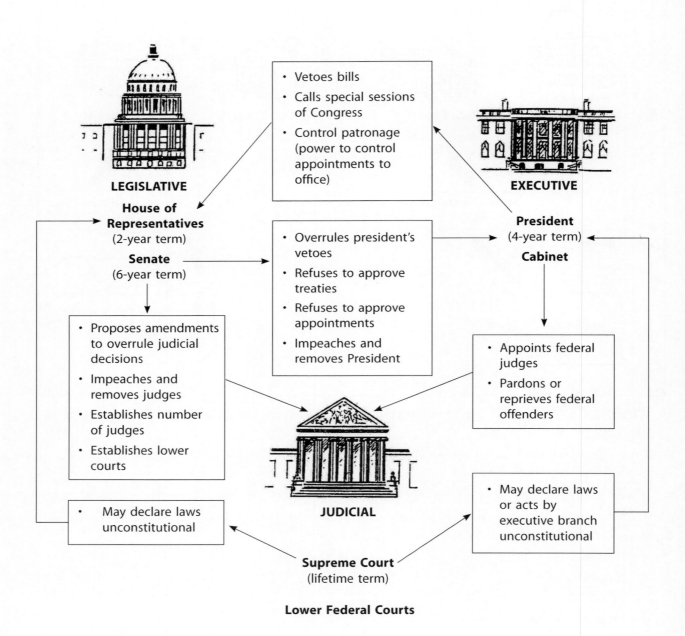

1. What is the function of each branch of government?

    a. Legislative

    b. Executive

    c. Judicial

2. List one check that limits power in each of the following situations.

    a. How does the president check the power of Congress?

    b. How does Congress limit the power of the president?

    c. How does the president check the Supreme Court?

    d. How does the Supreme Court limit the power of the president?

    e. How does the Supreme Court limit the power of Congress?

    f. How does Congress check the power of the Supreme Court?

3. Explain the ways that this diagram illustrates how the Constitution prevents the concentration and abuse of power.

Lesson 6
The Living Constitution

Objective
- To examine the ways amendment, judicial review, and custom and usage have changed the U.S. Constitution

Notes to the Teacher
Since 1787, the U.S. Constitution has demonstrated an amazing resiliency in meeting the needs of both rural/agricultural and urban/industrial societies. Its flexibility has also accommodated the demands of Americans for an increasingly larger role played by the national government in promoting the general welfare. Although the U.S. Constitution has lasted longer than the constitution of any other nation, it is not the same document adopted in 1787.

Changes in the Constitution have come in a variety of ways: formal amendment, congressional legislation, Supreme Court interpretation or judicial review, and custom and usage. The formal amendment process usually works slowly and has been used infrequently.

The twenty-seven amendments adopted between 1791 and 1992 and the six proposed by Congress but not ratified by the states make up about one-third of one percent of the more than ten thousand proposals introduced in Congress since the beginnings of government under the Constitution. Not only do these numbers indicate how difficult the amending process is to use but they also suggest how high the stakes are when we consider using it.

When we amend the Constitution, we alter the matrix of law within which we live our lives and govern ourselves.[1]

Congressional legislation has fleshed out the skeleton outline of government found in the Constitution by establishing executive departments and creating a system of inferior courts. More important, Supreme Court interpretations of the Constitution's broad, general phrases and clauses, as well as years of usage, have altered fundamentally the meaning of the supreme law of the land. For example, today political parties hold conventions at which they elect their nominees for president and vice president, instead of an electoral vote whereby the winner is president and the loser is vice president, as stated in Article I of the Constitution. Another example is the way Congress altered the American economy by creating the Resolution Trust Corporation to help liquidate the assets of failed savings and loans in the 1980s. These are customs, or practices, of American government, but are not written into the Constitution

In this lesson, students read about three major ways of changing the U.S. Constitution. Students then consider which method offers the best way to resolve a constitutional issue of their choice.

Procedure
1. Ask students the following questions about the process of amending the Constitution.

   - How are amendments proposed? (*either by a two-thirds vote of each house of Congress or by a national convention called by Congress at the request of two-thirds of the states*)

   - How are amendments ratified? (*either by three-fourths of the states or by conventions in three-fourths of the states*)

   - How many states must approve an amendment? (*thirty-eight*)

   - How many times has this process been used to date? (*twenty-six times, including the Bill of Rights, which might be considered a part of the original Constitution*)

   - Why is the amendment process easier under the Constitution than it was under the Articles of Confederation? (*The Framers made it nearly impossible to change the Articles of Confederation in order to balance stability with flexibility: Every state legislature had to approve changes, which made passage of amendments—even good ones—very difficult, if not impossible.*)

[1]Richard Bernstein, *Amending America: If We Love the Constitution So Much, Why Do We Keep Trying to Change It?* (New York: Random House, 1993), xii.

2. Pair students, and distribute **Handout 10**. Have students read the selections, answer the questions, and be prepared for class discussion.

Suggested Responses:

1. men would be tyrants if they could; the inspiration of the American and French Revolutions; women's intellectual prowess, when trained and educated; morally proper to give women the vote; women's suffrage was tied to the fight for abolition of slavery

2. campaigned and gave speeches across the country; wrote newspaper articles and books; attempted to take their case to the Supreme Court; formed political organizations to lobby senators, congressmen, and state legislators; held marches, rallies, and parades

3. seventy-two years after the New York Seneca Falls Convention

4. The question was, were separate railway carriages for African Americans and whites constitutional?

5. Separate accommodations for African Americans imply racial inferiority and violate the Fourteenth Amendment guarantee of equality before the law.

6. According to the Supreme Court, legislation cannot overcome social prejudices; the Constitution can enforce civil and political equality but not social equality, which must be the result of natural affinities.

7. The Court decided that "separate, but equal" facilities were constitutional.

8. A dissenting opinion by one or more justices challenges the majority opinion.

9. The Thirteenth Amendment banned slavery and all of its vestiges, such as Jim Crow laws. The Fourteenth and Fifteenth Amendments removed the "race line" by defining citizenship and equal protection. Harlan's dissent reinforced the principle that the Constitution protects all citizens equally under the law, regardless of race.

10. The question was, are segregated public schools constitutional?

11. The plaintiffs argued that denial of admission to integrated schools violated the Fourteenth Amendment right to equal protection under the law.

12. Segregated schools are inherently unequal and are a violation of the Fourteenth Amendment guarantee of equal protection of the law.

13. There were different men on the Court who had different philosophies and different perspectives on the concept of equality.

14. They may be less permanent than amendments. Getting the required majorities to protect the rights of a minority would probably have been impossible at the time because of popular resistance in some places.

15. expansion of government power during wartime, Cabinet, political parties, congressional committee system, senatorial courtesy, executive privilege, seizure of steel mills

16. Amendments passed after the Civil War abolished slavery and involuntary servitude, provided the due process and equal protection of all citizens, and protected a citizen's rights without regard to race, color, or previous condition of servitude. Amendments are not self-executing and depend on the will of the people to enforce them. Eventually the amendment itself was validated by the judicial interpretation of Brown v. Board of Education (1954).

3. Discuss the three major ways—formal amendment, Supreme Court interpretation, and custom and usage—in which changes in the Constitution have occurred.

4. Divide students into groups of four, and assign **Handout 11**. Allow two weeks for research and preparation of a simulation of the process of amending the Constitution. Have each group make its presentation. Have the class evaluate the presentations using the criteria in **Handout 11**.

46

5. Have students consider the following issue: Given the framework of government provided by the Constitution, how can your generation best achieve real and lasting guarantees of equality for all citizens? Ask students to consider which amendment method is best to accomplish a permanent, lasting change to the Constitution and the greatest public acceptance. Ask them to consider the advantages and disadvantages to each method.

Enrichment/Extension

Have students write a short essay on the following topic: The Constitution, written during a time when American society was primarily rural and agricultural, has worked equally well since America became urban and industrialized. How did the Framers create a living document that laid a foundation for meeting the changing needs of people? Have selected students share their essays.

Name_____

Date_____

Ways to Alter the Constitution

Read the selections, answer the questions, and be prepared for class discussion.

The Amendment Process—Women and the Vote

Millions of American women today vote in elections, probably without giving the right too much thought; however, the process of amending the Constitution for women's suffrage took nearly one hundred years. Although the official suffrage campaign began in 1848, long before then American women lobbied for the political and social freedom for the fairer sex.

As early as 1790, in a publication called *A Vindication of the Rights*, English author Mary Wollstonecraft said society could benefit from enfranchising women. Men such as Frederick Douglass and Aaron Burr acknowledged the intellectual equality of women when given proper education. In the early nineteenth century, Frances Wright, a Scottish utopian socialist, spoke on behalf of women's rights in Eastern and Midwestern cities of the United States. Around 1836, Sarah and Angelina Grimké moved north from North Carolina and began to oppose the tyranny of slavery. In Philadelphia, they joined the Quakers and began to seek justice and equal rights for all. Calling slavery a sin, they declared that African Americans and whites were equal, and adamantly supported women's rights.

On July 19–20, 1848, Elizabeth Cady Stanton and Susan B. Anthony hosted the Seneca Falls Convention where the full citizenship of America's women was discussed. The famous "Declaration of Sentiments," which enumerated the rights of women, was based in form and content on Thomas Jefferson's Declaration of Independence. The delegates passed ten of the eleven resolutions. The ninth resolution, which declared that the duty of the women of this country was to secure to themselves their sacred right to elective franchise, was not approved.

For the next fifty years, both women worked tirelessly in the campaign for women's suffrage. Anthony, born and raised in Massachusetts, became a bold, sometimes austere, but always determined advocate for women. She travelled by sleigh, carriage, and horseback to deliver her message about women's property and suffrage rights. Often she endured harsh criticism in newspaper editorials and cartoon caricatures. Stanton, a wealthy New York socialite from a prominent family, and the devoted wife and mother of several children, published magazine and newspaper articles supporting woman suffrage from 1854 to 1859.

In 1872, Anthony voted in the eighth district of New York, along with fifteen other women. Three weeks later a U.S. marshal arrested her. Judge Ward Hunt, a political devotee of New York Senator Roscoe Conkling who opposed suffrage, wrote his opinion before one word of evidence was presented by Anthony or her counsel. She was not permitted to testify. Hunt stated that women were not competent to do so. He disallowed the jury's deliberations and instead instructed them to find her guilty as charged. Anthony was found guilty, but was given no sentence or consequence, which would have been grounds for an appeal.

To the end, both Stanton and Anthony championed the cause of woman suffrage by testifying before the U.S. Senate, publishing historical works such as *The History of Women*, organizing political groups such as the American Women Suffrage Association and the International Council of Women, and planning state suffrage campaigns. Though Stanton was outspoken and Anthony was prolific in her writing, they made little progress from 1848 to 1900. Only four states—New

York, Utah, Colorado, and Idaho—gave women the right to vote, and neither Stanton nor Anthony thought she would live to see all American women going to the polls.

American suffragists continued to organize public marches, rallies, hunger strikes, and parades. They lobbied and picketed at the federal, state, and local levels and participated in large protests in Washington, D.C., and New York. Women arrested in Washington, D.C., were always let out of jail early, out of courtesy and duty, just before dinner in order that they might cook for their families.

In spring 1919, Congress finally passed the Nineteenth Amendment. Thirty-six states had to be convinced to ratify the amendment. By midsummer 1920, seventy-two years after the Seneca Falls Convention in New York, Tennessee became the last state needed to ratify the amendment.

1. Before the official suffrage campaign began, on what grounds did Americans argue for women's equality?

2. What methods were used to secure passage of the Nineteenth Amendment?

3. How many years did it take to pass the Nineteenth Amendment?

Supreme Court Interpretation—*Plessy v. Ferguson*

Homer Adolph Plessy, who was one-eighth black, refused to comply with a Louisiana law that required him to sit in an area on a train for African Americans. He chose to sit in a seat designated for white passengers and refused to vacate it. Plessy was forcibly removed by railroad officials and a police officer and sent to the parish jail. He was denied the option of paying a fine, a possible penalty under the statute. Plessy's counsel argued that segregation violated the Thirteenth and Fourteenth Amendments, which abolished slavery and contained the equal protection clause for all citizens. The Supreme Court's opinion follows:

> This case turns upon the constitutionality of an act of the general assembly of the state of Louisiana, passed in 1890, providing for separate railway carriages for the white and colored races. . . .

> The object of the [Fourteenth] amendment was undoubtedly to enforce the absolute equality of the two races before the law, but in the nature of things it could not have been intended to abolish distinctions based upon color, or to enforce social, as distinguished from political, equality, or a commingling of the two races upon terms unsatisfactory to either. Laws permitting, and even requiring their separation in places where they are liable to be brought into contact do not necessarily imply the inferiority of either race to the other, and have been generally, if not universally, recognized as within the competency of the state legislatures in the exercise of their police power. The most common instance of this is connected with the establishment of separate schools for white and colored children, which have been held to be a valid exercise of the legislative power even by courts of states where the political rights of the colored race have been longest and most earnestly enforced. . . .

> We consider the underlying fallacy of the plaintiff's argument to consist in the assumption that the enforced separation of the two races stamps the colored race with a badge of inferiority. If this be so, it is not by reason of anything found in the act, but solely because the colored race chooses to put that construction upon it. . . . The argument also assumes that social prejudices may be overcome by legislation, and that equal rights cannot be secured to the negro except by an enforced commingling of the two races. We cannot accept this proposition. If the two races are to meet on terms of social equality, it must be the result of natural affinities, a mutual appreciation of each other's merits and a voluntary consent of individuals.

> Legislation is powerless to eradicate racial instincts or to abolish distinctions based upon physical differences, and the attempt to do so can only result in accentuating the difficulties of the present situation. If the civil and political rights of both races be equal, one cannot be inferior to the other civilly or politically. If one race be inferior to the other socially, the Constitution of the United States cannot put them upon the same plane.[1]

Justice John Marshall Harlan, the lone dissenter in the Plessy case, reminded his colleagues that railroads were considered public highways, open to all, and that the Thirteenth Amendment had "struck down the institution of slavery . . . but it prevent[ed] the imposition of any burdens or disabilities that constitute badges of slavery or servitude" and continued with discussion of the Thirteenth, Fourteenth, and Fifteenth Amendments.

[1]Saul K. Padover, *The Living U.S. Constitution*, 3rd ed. (New York: Penguin/Meridian Books, 1995), 283–85.

. . . [I]n view of the Constitution, in the eye of the law, there is in this country no superior, dominant, ruling class of citizens. There is no caste here. Our Constitution is color-blind, and neither knows nor tolerates classes among citizens. In respect of civil rights, all citizens are equal before the law. . . .

In my opinion, the judgment this day rendered will, in time, prove to be quite as pernicious as the decision made by this tribunal in the Dred Scott Case [1857].[2]

Supreme Court Interpretation—*Brown v. Board of Education*

Chief Justice Earl Warren delivered the opinion of the court:

In each of the cases, minors of the Negro race, through their legal representatives, seek the aid of the courts in obtaining admission to the public schools of their community on a nonsegregated basis. In each instance, they had been denied admission to schools attended by white children under laws requiring or permitting segregation according to race. This segregation was alleged to deprive the plaintiffs of the equal protection of the laws under the Fourteenth Amendment. . . .

. . . There are findings below that the Negro and white schools involved have been equalized, or are being equalized, with respect to buildings, curricula, qualifications and salaries of teachers, and other "tangible" factors. Our decision, therefore, cannot turn on merely a comparison of these tangible factors in the Negro and white schools involved in each of the cases. We must look instead to the effect of segregation itself on public education. . . .

We come then to the question presented: Does segregation of children in public schools solely on the basis of race, even though the physical facilities and other "tangible" factors may be equal, deprive the children of the minority group of equal educational opportunities? We believe that it does. . . .

. . . To separate them [school children] from others of similar age and qualifications solely because of their race generates a feeling of inferiority as to their status in the community that may affect their hearts and minds in a way unlikely ever to be undone. . . .

We conclude that in the field of public education the doctrine of "separate but equal" has no place. Separate educational facilities are inherently unequal. Therefore, we hold that the plaintiffs and others similarly situated . . . are, by reason of the segregation complained of, deprived of the equal protection of the laws guaranteed by the Fourteenth Amendment. . . .[3]

4. On what question did the Supreme Court rule in *Plessy v. Ferguson?*

5. What was the primary argument used by Homer Plessy, the plaintiff?

6. On what basis did the Court consider Plessy's reasoning incorrect?

[2]Padover, *The Living U.S. Constitution,* 285–86.
[3]Ibid., 288–91.

7. What was the decision of the Supreme Court, and in what way did the decision have an application broader than merely railway carriages?

8. What is a dissenting opinion?

9. What are the main constitutional underpinnings of Justice Harlan's dissent? Why is the Harlan dissent so important in the history of the Court?

10. What was the question on which the Supreme Court ruled in the Brown case?

11. What was the argument of the plaintiff?

12. What was the court's ruling in the Brown case?

13. How might you account for the reversal of the 1896 decision?

14. What do the Plessy and Brown decisions tell you about the permanence of Supreme Court decisions as a way of altering the constitution? And why do you think change on school segregation came through Supreme Court interpretation rather than an amendment?

Custom and Usage

The Constitution and its Amendments thus depend for their effectiveness on the other two levels of constitutional change—interpretation (whether by Congress, the executive branch, or the courts) and custom and usage. These levels of change work more gradually, more subtly, and more frequently than the amending process does.

Just as we break in a new car or a new pair of shoes through use, so, too, we break in new constitutional provisions. New Amendments are wellsprings of federal legislative and executive power, opening new fields for the exercise of federal authority. . . . For example, a remarkable expansion of government power, especially federal power, took place during the Civil War and again in the twentieth century in response to war, social upheaval, and economic crisis. An equally notable spectrum of agencies and instrumentalities evolved . . . under the aegis of the Constitution's "necessary and proper" clause and the Amendments' "appropriate legislation" clauses. . . .

Sometimes, unwritten customs and usages develop without any formal exercise of authority—for example, institutions (the Cabinet, political parties, and congressional committee system); practices (senatorial courtesy, executive privilege); and principles (separation of powers, the presumption of innocence). . . .

On occasion, customs and usages create more problems than they solve, as in the clashes during the Watergate crisis of 1973–74 between claims of executive privilege and the demands of Congressional investigations of executive misconduct. Or a government statue or policy in support of one important constitutional interest collides head-on with other, apparently equally important principles, as with President Harry S. Truman's order seizing strike-bound steel mills during the Korean Conflict. Executive or legislative attempts to interpret the Constitution to support their positions do not always command general approval or agreement. Such instances . . . often land before the courts for resolution. . . .

Interpretation, custom, and usage often give new life to provisions previously neglected, as with the Fifteenth Amendment or the due process and equal protection clauses of the Fourteenth Amendment. Just as often, however, they can render constitutional provisions or doctrines rooted in them irrelevant to modern legal problems—as the Supreme Court's decisions of the 1870s and 1880s did to the Civil War Amendments. . . .

Again, we must recall that constitutional provisions are not self-executing. They depend for their enforcement on the will, ingenuity, and authority of those who seek to invoke them. We have seen, for example, how the Civil War Amendments languished, all but neglected, for generations while those whom they were supposed to protect lived at the mercy of hostile state and local authorities and the indifference of the federal government. Amendments to the Constitution thus are as much objects or targets of change as sources of change.[4]

15. List several changes in the meaning of the Constitution that have resulted from custom and usage.

16. What were the Civil War Amendments, and why were they not self-executing, or enforced? How did interpretation, custom, and usage breathe new life into these amendments?

[4]Richard Bernstein, *Amending America: If We Love the Constitution So Much, Why Do We Keep Trying to Change It?* (New York: Random House, 1993), 268–69.

Your Amendment to the Constitution

Assume one of the roles and follow the steps to simulate the process of amending the Constitution. The goal is to convince your classmates to ratify your amendment or to consider it worthy as a constitutional reform. The success of the group, and your grade, will depend on two matters: the research as evidenced in the presentation, and the thoughtful questions you raise about other groups' presentations.

Roles

Recorder—takes notes during discussions

Timekeeper—tracks time, keeps group on task, and arranges two group meetings outside of class (These meetings can be held in person, by e-mail, or on the phone.)

Facilitator—assigns roles and work, makes copies of amendment for final ratification vote

Presenter—checks members' work, leads presentation, requests group's presentation date with teacher

Steps

1. Brainstorm topics and choose one as the subject of the proposed amendment. Be creative, but remember that the success of the amendment will hinge on the number of people affected by it. In other words, an amendment that requests lifelong Super Bowl tickets for you and your friends is a losing battle, but requesting a minimum wage, or excellent financial aid, for teens and college-bound students would interest a large segment of the population.

2. Select one of the following methods of gaining passage of the amendment:

   a. Formal Amendment

      Lobby congressional representatives and senators to propose an amendment, or call for a national convention to propose an amendment that state legislatures or conventions will ratify.

   b. Judicial Interpretation

      Ask the courts, by filing a brief or suing a plaintiff, to examine the constitutionality of a law.

   c. Custom and Usage

      Ask a federal agency, cabinet member, political party, or Congress itself to begin to adopt procedures that would include your change.

3. Research the topic. Depending on the method selected in step 2, gather information about at least three of the following elements: lobbying, signs, surveys, canvassing, costs of television and print ads, other successful court cases, examples of changes to procedures.

4. Write the amendment, using the Bill of Rights as an example. Keep it simple and concise. Organize the results of your research and show how it supports the proposed amendment.

5. Present your amendment and supporting information. Depending on the method selected in step 2, the rest of the class will act as either the state legislatures and Congress or the general public, debating ratification; as the Supreme Court, hearing oral arguments and then rendering a majority and dissenting opinions; or as a political party or institution, adopting new customs and creating new traditions.

Lesson 7
The Elastic Clause:
Stretching the Powers of Congress

Objective
- To understand the powers of Congress relative to the "necessary and proper," or elastic clause, of the U.S. Constitution

Notes to the Teacher

The U.S. Constitution's Article I, Section 8 concerns congressional power and concludes with this phrase: "to make all laws which shall be necessary and proper for carrying into execution the foregoing powers, and all other powers vested by this constitution in the government of the United States, or in any department or officer thereof." In other words, Congress' power can be stretched as defined by the elastic clause.

The Constitution's clear delineation of congressional power, by its architect Virginian James Madison, comes directly out of American political philosophy and its proponents' negative experiences under the Articles of Confederation. Alexander Hamilton, a political conservative, was deeply suspicious of the intemperate nature of the common man and remarked,

> One great error is that we suppose mankind more honest than they are. Our prevailing passions are ambition and interest; and it will ever be the duty of a wise government to avail itself of those passions, in order to make them more subservient to the public good. . . . The people are turbulent and changing; they seldom judge or determine right. Give, therefore, to the first class a distinct, permanent share in the government. They will check the unsteadiness of the second, and, as they cannot receive any advantage by a change, they therefore will ever maintain good government. . . . Nothing but a permanent body can check the imprudence of democracy. Their turbulent and uncontrollable disposition requires checks.[1]

Madison agreed that the new federal government would have more energy; would have centralized federal power; could build roads, secure patents, and borrow money; and would be a government of mixed nature that could safeguard stability and freedom, each essential to human happiness. John Jay, a vehement Federalist and an author of *The Federalist Papers*, thought Congress under the Articles of Confederation lacked the power to enforce what it legislated.

One of the most compelling constitutional controversies in the early years was the extent of Congress' authority under the elastic clause. Early interpreters of the Constitution, who were strict constructionists, argued that Congress can perform only those functions directly expressed in the Constitution. This view of federalism sought to limit Congress to being an agent of the sovereign states. Others argued that Congress could legislate on any matter not specifically prohibited to it in the Constitution. Such a view would obviously expand the powers of Congress enormously. Somewhere between these extremes lies the narrower range within which Congress has found it comfortable to operate. The Supreme Court serves as the final authority on the meaning of the Constitution regarding congressional law.

In the early months of the republic, Hamilton and Thomas Jefferson argued over the interpretation of the elastic clause as they grappled with problems of establishing the new government. The issue first surfaced on the constitutionality of Hamilton's proposed National Bank, a case that was tried eventually in the Supreme Court as *McCulloch v. Maryland* (1819). Hamilton saw the bank as a proper outgrowth of the expressed powers to tax and coin money and regulate its value. Jefferson, the strict constructionist, viewed the bank as an unwarranted attempt to enlarge the power granted to Congress under the Constitution and wanted the phrase to give Congress only those powers strictly necessary. Congress voted

[1]Alexander Hamilton, quoted in *The Living U.S. Constitution,* Saul K. Padover (New York: Meridian/Penguin Books, 1995), 4–5.

to charter the bank, and the Supreme Court later ruled that it was constitutional. Daniel Webster argued that "necessary and proper" reflected that a government ought to do what was usual and suitable. Interestingly, Jefferson himself used a loose interpretation of the elastic clause to purchase the Louisiana Territory when he was president.

Chief Justice John Marshall stated in his opinion in *McCulloch v. Maryland* that Congress had the ability to create a national bank. Marshall weighed in on the issue of the elastic clause. He ultimately considered it a catchall clause that served to make the Constitution a living document. Jefferson, who opposed the creation of a national bank, called the justices "thieves," even though most were appointed by Jefferson or Madison.

In the more modern era, the issue of the necessary and proper clause reemerged as a practical discussion about the purpose of government in promoting the well-being of its citizens, especially in economic hard times. When Herbert Hoover and Franklin D. Roosevelt argued over Congress' proper role in ending the Great Depression, Hoover, who was more inclined toward a strict interpretation of the Constitution and the expressed, limited powers of government, insisted that prosperity would return without government intervention in the economy. Roosevelt, on the other hand, proposed a far more active, or more elastic, role for Congress in ending unemployment and promoting the general welfare. His political philosophy would result in an expansion of the implied powers of Congress.

In the late twentieth century, Ronald Reagan and Bill Clinton represented well their parties' political philosophies regarding the role of government, especially as it relates to more versus less government power. While Reagan desired less federal government and aggressively sought to reduce government bureaucracy and federal taxes, Clinton sought to use the Constitution to lessen the economic hardships of working and middle-class Americans by constructing a national health-care system and promoting an economic stimulus package.

In this lesson, students study the case of *McCulloch v. Maryland* and the necessary and proper clause as it applies to state versus federal power. Students interpret the viewpoints of Hoover and Roosevelt, identify and match their opinions and actions about government, and consider the reasons for an increasingly loose interpretation of the powers of Congress.

Procedure

1. Have students complete **Handout 12**. Answers will vary, but students need to be able to support their position. Explain that those students who agreed with statements 1, 3, and 5 would be considered strict constructionists. Those who agree with 2, 4, and 6 would be considered loose constructionists. Stress that the debate over the elastic clause in the Constitution centered on these philosophical differences: those who wanted to follow the spirit of the law and those who wanted to follow the letter of the law.

2. Discuss the case of *McCulloch v. Maryland*. Stress the role of Congress, its expanding powers, and how judges, from state courts to the Supreme Court, can interpret the Constitution. Ask if judges read the letter of the law, or if they interpret the spirit of the law. Explain that the elastic clause, also called the necessary and proper clause, examines how far the power of government, specifically Congress, may be stressed.

3. Distribute **Handout 13,** and have students complete it as directed. Review students' responses.

   Suggested Responses:

   1. The necessary and proper clause encompassed all powers usual and suitable and not specifically prohibited; the bank was not specifically prohibited in the Constitution.

   2. Powers of the federal government are subordinate to the state government because the Constitution was ratified by the states.

   3. The Constitution was created by state delegates and ratified by people of each state in state conventions; thus, it is a measure of the states.

4. *It would be difficult if every action of Congress had to be absolutely necessary under a certain power.*

5. *Marshall's ruling suggested that granting Maryland the ability to tax the bank would allow states to tax other federal institutions.*

6. *Answers may include subsidized federal lunch programs, national parks, Pell Grants for college-bound students, industrial smog restrictions, limits on lead in drinking water, antiterrorist legislation, and subsidized farm goods.*

7. *Federalists might say Marshall's opinion creates a stronger, more clearly defined role of government. Anti-Federalists might say it is an occasion for more abuses of power by the federal government.*

8. *Without this broader interpretation, there would be less congressional bureaucracy and fewer federal laws; however, with it, there is more accountability by individuals and institutions about their actions and economic transactions.*

9. *It is good because the country is large with many special problems. Society needs a bigger government. People must be held accountable for the way they use the power granted to them under our system of government. The federal government is inefficient, bloated, and wastes money.*

4. Distribute **Handout 14**, and have students complete parts A and B individually. Review students' responses.

Suggested Responses:

Part A.

Students should grasp the contrast between Hoover's philosophy of rugged individualism and Roosevelt's preference for government action to solve people's social and economic problems.

Part B.

Federal Emergency Relief Act—Hoover would criticize it as an example of state socialism, while Roosevelt would see it as Christian charity.

Works Progress Administration—Hoover would prefer rugged individualism and the qualities it instilled in people, while Roosevelt saw it as an act of Christian brotherhood.

Social Security Act of 1935—Hoover feared that it would undermine individualism, while Roosevelt saw it as an appropriate, charitable activity for the national government.

5. Divide the class into pairs, and have students complete **Handout 14**, part C. Review students' responses.

Suggested Responses:

1. *R*
2. *H*
3. *H*
4. *H*
5. *R*

6. Read the following quotation aloud to the class.

The things Hoover believed in—efficiency, enterprise, opportunity, individualism, substantial laissez-faire, personal success, material welfare—were all in the dominant American tradition. The ideas he represented—ideas that to so many people made him seem hateful or ridiculous after 1929—were precisely the same ideas that in the remoter past of the nineteenth century and the more immediate past of the New Era had had an almost irresistible lure for the majority of Americans. In the language of Jefferson, Jackson, and Lincoln these ideas had been fresh and invigorating; in the language of Herbert Hoover they seemed stale and oppressive.[2]

---

[2]Richard Hofstader, *The American Political Tradition and the Men Who Made It* (New York: Alfred A. Knopf, 1948), 282.

Ask whether students believe Hoover's ideas would have seemed stale and oppressive during the Great Depression. (*Hoover's ideas offered no new approaches to moving the nation out of a profoundly lingering economic Depression. Rugged individualism appeared to lead only to greater hardship and more unemployment rather than to recovery.*) Ask for suggestions about the possibility of adopting a strict interpretation of the elastic clause in regard to today's economy. (*The complex task of stabilizing the economy seems to require continued vigilance and activity by the national government and requires a strict application of the elastic clause regarding the economy.*)

Enrichment/Extension

Have students research and report on how other modern American presidents have dealt with the elastic clause. Examples might include Harry Truman and the steel strike, Bill Clinton and the assignment of U.S. troops as a peacekeeping force in Bosnia and Somalia, and Ronald Reagan and the use of American troops in Nicaragua and Grenada.

Name_____

Date_____

What Kind of a Player Are You?

All of you have played games, whether they were board games, tag, or intramural sports. In other words, you have been a player. So what describes you as a player? Decide whether you agree or disagree with the statements below. If you agree, write the word *yes* in the space to the left. If you disagree, write the word *no*.

_____1. Rules are rules. Everyone must adhere to them, and there are no exceptions.

_____2. Rules are supposed to be interpreted. That is why we have referees, coaches, and judges in games: to decide what is fair or not.

_____3. If it is not in the rulebook, then it is fair play by the player. Rules need to be in black and white; if not, chaos will rule on the field or during a game.

_____4. There is the spirit of the rule and the letter of the rule. Rules are to be stretched to account for different variables: a rainy day, person with a handicap, a younger player.

_____5. Rules tell you exactly what is fair and what is not. The referee, not everyone, can have an opinion, or else the players will make judgments just to help themselves.

_____6. Situations change. Just because something is not specifically stated in a rulebook does not mean it is not a rule. Sometimes you have to interpret the rule.

The Elastic Clause on Trial: *McCulloch v. Maryland* (1819)

Read the following information, and then answer the questions.

After the Revolutionary War, the former British colonies sought to establish a new government. The Articles of Confederation created a loosely organized government in which the majority of the power rested in the hands of the states. Within a short time, the leaders realized that the Articles were a failure, and the proposal to hold a constitutional convention was made. After meeting in Philadelphia, representatives of the thirteen states voted to send a new constitution to the state governments for ratification. This new constitution was radically different from the Articles of Confederation. It divided power among three branches of government and between the state and federal governments. Checks and balances were created to control the branches, and any powers not specifically granted to the states in the constitution were to be reserved to the federal government.

One of the institutions created by the new federal government was the Bank of the United States. Branches were established within each state. In 1819, the Maryland legislature passed a law taxing bank notes issued by any bank not chartered by the state or printed on paper made in Maryland. When James McCulloch, the cashier of the Baltimore branch, refused to pay the tax, he was sued by the state of Maryland. He lost and filed a writ with the U.S. Supreme Court, asking that the decision be vacated.

Alexander Hamilton argued in support of the bank. Hamilton believed that the bank was necessary to the new nation's growing economy. A national bank provided a structure through which the new American markets could operate and flourish. Thomas Jefferson was among the strict constructionists who were opposed to the bank. They believed that the creation of the bank was unconstitutional and was based on too broad an interpretation of federal powers.

Daniel Webster, arguing for McCulloch, stated that the necessary and proper clause in the Constitution included all powers which were not specifically prohibited and that the Constitution contained no specific prohibition against the bank. Lawyers for the state of Maryland argued that because the Constitution was adopted by what, at the time, were sovereign states, the power of the states superseded that of the federal government.

There were two issues before the Supreme Court. Did the power to create a bank rest with Congress, and could a state tax the bank, which is a federal institution? Chief Justice John Marshall's majority opinion stated that the power of the Constitution rested with the people, not the states. He said that the delegates who created the Constitution represented the people, who then ratified the Constitution at state conventions. Marshall stated that the Constitution speaks of "We, the people," not "We, the states." He also noted that "Congress must possess the choice of means and must be empowered to use any means which are in fact conducive to the exercise of a power granted by the Constitution. . . . Let the end be legitimate, let it be within the scope of the Constitution, and all means which are appropriate, which are plainly adapted to that end, which are not prohibited, but consist with the letter and spirit of the Constitution, are constitutional."

Marshall then addressed the question of whether Maryland or any other state had the right to tax a federal institution. Marshall stated that if Maryland or any other state had the right to tax the bank, then all other federal institutions—such as the mail, the mint, the granting of patents for use within a state, and the courts and customs houses—could be subjected to a tax. This action would lead to destruction of the means necessary for the federal government to function. The bank was deemed constitutional under the necessary and proper clause, so Maryland had no right to tax the bank. Thus, the act of the state legislature was declared to be unconstitutional and void.

1. What argument does the plaintiff, McCulloch, offer?

2. What argument does the defendant, Maryland, offer?

3. On what basis did Chief Justice Marshall state that the Constitution was a voice of the people?

4. Why did he rule that the creation of the Bank of the United States by Congress was constitutional?

5. Why did Marshall rule, based on the Constitution, that Maryland could not tax the bank?

6. If Marshall entered your classroom, what are some of the expanded congressional powers about which you might tell him?

7. What parts of Marshall's majority opinion correspond with or conflict with the Founding Fathers' view of the federal government?

8. How might Congress' powers today be different if Marshall had narrowly interpreted the necessary and proper clause?

9. Given the legislative powers of Congress today, do you think Marshall's majority opinion was a good idea or a bad one? Explain your reasoning.

Rugged Individualism vs. Governmental Regulation

Part A.

The following statements discuss the philosophy of government of Herbert Hoover and Franklin Roosevelt. Summarize beneath each one the president's basic philosophy.

Herbert Hoover—October 22, 1928

During 150 years we have builded up a form of self-government and a social system which is peculiarly our own. . . . It is the American system. . . . It is founded upon the conception that only through ordered liberty, freedom and equal opportunity to the individual will his initiative and enterprise spur on the march of progress. . . .

When the war closed, . . . [w]e were challenged with a peace-time choice between the American system of rugged individualism and a European philosophy of diametrically opposed doctrines—doctrines of paternalism and state socialism. The acceptance of these ideas would have meant the destruction of self-government through centralization of government. It would have meant the undermining of the individual initiative and enterprise through which our people have grown to unparalleled greatness. . . .

Every step of bureaucratizing of the business of our country poisons the very roots of liberalism—that is, political equality, free speech, free assembly, free press, and equality of opportunity. It is the road not to more liberty, but to less liberty. . . .

Franklin D. Roosevelt—October 4, 1933

With every passing year I become more confident that humanity is moving forward to the practical application of the teachings of Christianity as they affect the individual lives of men and women everywhere.

Part B.

Refer to the philosophies of Hoover and Roosevelt, and explain how each would have responded to the following programs and how he would have justified his position.

Program	Hoover	Roosevelt
Federal Emergency Relief Act of 1933 The act provided $500 million for aid to the unemployed. Most of the aid would be in the form of direct relief to the unemployed.		
Works Progress Administration Congress approved an appropriation of $5 billion to provide jobs for the unemployed in the arts and in public works projects such as building roads, schools, hospitals, and bridges.		
Social Security Act of 1935 The act provided for pensions to needy aged, old-age insurance, unemployment insurance, and benefit payments to the blind, dependent mothers and children, and crippled children. The pension system was to be funded by a complicated system of graduated premiums paid by both employers and employees.		

Part C.

Label each item *H* if it fits Hoover's philosophy of government or *R* if it fits Roosevelt's philosophy of government.

_____1. Massive program of federal works projects

_____2. Private contributions for relief

_____3. Idea that direct relief would undermine character and individualism

_____4. Belief in restraint and cautious use of governmental powers

_____5. Belief that Congress has the power to enact all things necessary and proper for promoting the general welfare

Part 2
Human Rights

When the Constitution was presented to the states for ratification, there was no guarantee that the necessary nine states would agree to passage. An Anti-Federalist faction opposed a new federal government, which would have strong national authority. The Anti-Federalists wanted specific written guarantees that their personal freedoms would be protected. As a result, the first ten amendments became a part of the Constitution in 1791.

This section provides an overview of the Bill of Rights and deals in greater detail with the meaning of several of our most important freedoms. Lesson 8 examines the history surrounding the need for a Bill of Rights and helps develop an understanding of the basic freedoms guaranteed by that document. Lesson 9 explores the separation of church and state and how the Constitution protects an individual's freedom of religion. Lesson 10 examines and analyzes Supreme Court decisions regarding freedom of speech. Lesson 11 shows how conflicting values create both personal and national dilemmas in implementing the Bill of Rights, with emphasis on freedom of the press. Lesson 12 analyzes the issue of how much freedom of the press student newspapers should be afforded. Lesson 13 examines the history of the Second Amendment and determines the validity of a law regulating concealed weapons. In Lesson 14, students learn to apply in context a variety of terms related to due process in criminal proceedings. Lesson 15 develops an understanding of how the concept of due process applies to property rights. Lesson 16 evaluates the Civil Rights Act of 1964 and determines whether it has achieved its goal of equal protection under the law.

Lesson 8
The Bill of Rights

Objectives
- To examine the history and debate surrounding the need for the Bill of Rights

- To understand the basic freedoms guaranteed in the Bill of Rights

Notes to the Teacher
Ten of the thirteen colonies, at the close of the year 1781, had drafted and ratified their own state constitutions. Two of them—Connecticut and Rhode Island—simply modified their colonial charters by removing all references to royal authority. The state constitutions reflected a revolutionary generation wary of political power, unless it was husbanded, divided, and limited.

The inadequacies of the Articles of Confederation compelled the political leadership of each state to call for a constitutional convention. The thirteen articles required unanimous agreement in order to approve any reform, frustrated congressional leadership, and denied the central government the powers necessary to operate effectively. The Articles were written as a result of British colonial rule, which had fostered suspicions of central government among colonists who jealously guarded the sovereignty of their states. The Congress directed that a convention be called for the sole and express purpose of revising the Articles of Confederation. The delegates were to report to Congress and the state legislatures the changes on which they agreed, and those changes were to be confirmed by the states. The aim was to create a federal constitution that would preserve the nation.

At first, few of the states even imagined all of the states' citizens as united. Rhode Island was the strongest adversary of amending the articles because it was distrustful and fearful of its neighbors. Its leaders wanted to strengthen the Articles rather than write a new document that would consolidate power in the hands of a central government. Rhode Islanders felt so strongly about this idea that they refused to send a delegation to the convention.

By 1776, most state constitutions contained a Bill of Rights, and most states had a single-house legislature and operated on the principles of self-government. In general, state delegates to the Constitutional Convention were in agreement about the basic principles of governance: rights should be protected, and the people should give consent to be governed. They differed over the method or means of assuring both of these principles. And it was the former, a protection of rights, over which delegates and politicians most fervently disagreed. Yet when the Constitutional Convention was over, there was much dissatisfaction: first, because some attending delegates, as well as those not in attendance (like Patrick Henry), thought the convention had gone beyond its purview; and second, because they suspected that the new framework of government gave too much power to the president, to Congress, and the judiciary and did little to protect its citizens. Thus, the famous constitution ratification debates began, with each side lobbying for its cause. Alexander Hamilton, Benjamin Rush, John Jay, and James Madison passionately supported the new Constitution, while Thomas Jefferson, Patrick Henry, and George Mason opposed it. Five small states, and the larger Pennsylvania, ratified the Constitution in a controversial manner. This led to bitterness, acrimony, and even violence, as Anti-Federalist fervor increased in Virginia and New York. It was during the ratification debate at the Massachusetts ratification convention, on January 9, 1788, that both sides reached a compromise. They agreed to support ratification and commit to changing the Constitution later with crucial amendments. Two revolutionary war heroes—John Hancock and Samuel Adams—supported the framework for this discussion, which later helped to implement amendment reform.

In the lesson, students review reasons for including a Bill of Rights in the new constitution, read and analyze a selection in which Patrick Henry discussed the importance of a Bill of Rights, and conclude by reviewing the rights guaranteed in the first ten amendments to the Constitution.

Procedure

1. Review the reasons many colonists felt that the new constitution should have a bill of rights (*to enumerate the rights guaranteed to the people, which were not specifically mentioned in the body of the Constitution*). Ask students for examples (*freedom of speech, right to bear arms, right to a jury trial*). Explain that many of these rights had their roots in the actions of the British Parliament, which sought to restrict the rights of British colonists, prior to the American Revolution. For example, the right to bear arms has its roots in the British order to confiscate weapons from potentially rebellious colonists. Freedom of religion was rooted in the requirement that a man be a member of the official church, the Church of England, in order to vote or hold a seat in colonial assemblies. Explain that since the Constitution did not specifically list these rights, the Anti-Federalists demanded a bill of rights be attached.

2. Distribute **Handout 15**. Have students complete it first individually and then reach consensus with a partner. Review students' responses.

Suggested Responses:

1. *Her t-shirt is protected symbolic free speech under the First Amendment,* Tinker v. Des Moines School District *(1969).*

2. *While school-mandated school prayer was declared unconstitutional in* Abington School District v. Schempp *(1963), the Supreme Court has ruled that spontaneous, student-led school prayer is allowable and constitutional.*

3. *Although the Fourth Amendment protects the right of people to be secure in their persons, the Court in* Terry v. Ohio *(1968) ruled that where danger threatens, police may stop and frisk a suspect on a standard of reasonable suspicion.*

4. *While some argue that the death penalty violates the Eighth Amendment, the Supreme Court has ruled in* Gregg v. Georgia *(1976) that it is not cruel and unusual punishment. It should be noted that some states have suspended use of the death penalty pending review of possible unfair application to minorities, especially African Americans and the developmentally disabled.*

3. Separate students into groups of four. Distribute **Handout 16**. Explain that they are to read the selection on three levels. They are to read for direct factual information (part A), interpret the reading to acquire more meaning (parts B and C), and use their experience in a similar situation to understand the passage (part D). Review students' responses.

Suggested Responses:

Part B.

All three statements should be checked.

Part C.

1. *It is true that Henry is implying that Virginians love their liberty and the pro-Constitution Federalists are asking them to give it up.*

2. *He loves liberty and freedom for all—Virginians, patriots, and others.*

3. *No, but present-day Republicans, and Democrats, love their American freedoms.*

4. *Henry was trying to have Virginians and, to a degree, the other Americans stand up for liberty, or they would fall prey to unreasonable searches, seizures, invasion of privacy, and limits to their individual freedom.*

4. Ask students to define the following terms.

civil case—*a case that does not involve criminal charges*

double jeopardy—*being tried twice for the same crime*

due process of law—*a process that guarantees an individual all rights under the law*

eminent domain—*right of the government to buy property for a public purpose*

grand jury—*group that decides whether there is sufficient evidence against an individual to hold a trial*

self-incrimination—*being a witness against oneself*

5. Distribute **Handout 17**, part A, and have students complete it as directed. Review students' responses.

Suggested Responses:

1. religion, speech, press, petition, and assembly

2. the right to bear arms

3. quartering soldiers in one's home

4. unreasonable searches and seizures

5. right to be charged by a grand jury; freedom from double jeopardy; freedom from self-incrimination; right to due process in court; and the government's right of eminent domain

6. speedy and public trial by jury; information on the nature and cause of the charge; right to confront witnesses at trial; defendant must be provided with counsel

7. jury trial in civil cases

8. freedom from excessive bail and cruel and unusual punishments

9. other rights not specifically mentioned in the Bill of Rights

10. those powers not delegated to the United States, to the states, or to the people

6. Have students complete **Handout 17**, part B. Review students' responses.

Suggested Responses:

1. quartering soldiers; Third Amendment

2. right to bear arms; Second Amendment

3. right of eminent domain; Fifth Amendment

4. freedom of assembly; First Amendment

5. procedure in civil cases; Seventh Amendment

6. freedom from illegal searches and seizures; Fourth Amendment

7. freedom from unreasonable bail; Eighth Amendment

8. powers reserved to the states; Tenth Amendment

9. enumerated powers; Ninth Amendment

10. right to confront witnesses; Sixth Amendment

7. Ask students to write a short paragraph on the amendment in the Bill of Rights they feel is the most important. Instruct students to include reasons for their choice. Have selected students share their paragraphs.

Enrichment/Extension

Have students research and report on recent court cases that have resulted in rulings applicable to the Bill of Rights.

Name_____

Date_____

Our Rights under the Constitution

Read each of the following statements, and decide whether the action is constitutional. Write *A* if you agree or *D* if you disagree on the first line before each of the following actions. Afterwards, share your responses with a partner. Try to reach consensus between the two of you, and write *A* or *D* on the second line. Be prepared to report to the class about your opinion.

_____ _____ 1. Kendra wants to protest against the American-government-sponsored School of the Americas. She plans to wear to school a t-shirt that shows bloody, violent images of people tortured by generals and soldiers who were trained at the School.

_____ _____ 2. Philip, the high school quarterback, wants to lead the crowd and his team in a prayer before the big game Friday night.

_____ _____ 3. St. Louis FBI agent Victoria Lee sees two suspicious-looking, trench-coat-wearing teen boys. She thinks they are possibly casing a store to rob it, so she stops them, pats them down, and finds guns.

_____ _____ 4. Texas Governor Caroline Stark denies clemency in the death penalty case of a murderer, who is a born-again Christian who helps both prisoners and guards. The murders were particularly gruesome and cruel.

Patrick Henry Discusses the Importance of a Bill of Rights

Part A.

Virginia patriot Patrick Henry was a stirring public speaker. He was probably the most prominent Anti-Federalist. Read the following excerpts from Henry's speeches.

16 June 1788

Mr. Chairman.—The necessity of a Bill of Rights appear to me to be greater in this Government, than ever it was in any Government before. . . .

All nations have adopted this construction—That all rights not expressly and unequivocally reserved to the people, are impliedly and incidentally relinquished to rulers; as necessarily inseparable from the delegated powers. It is so in Great-Britain: For every possible right which is not reserved to the people by some express provision or compact, is within the King's prerogative. It is so in that country which is said to be in such full possession of freedom. It is so in Spain, Germany, and other parts of the world.

Let us consider the sentiments which have been entertained by the people of America on this subject. At the revolution, it must be admitted, that it was their sense to put down those great rights which ought in all countries to be held inviolable and sacred. Virginia did so we all remember. She made a compact to reserve, expressly, certain rights. When fortified with full, adequate, and abundant representation, was she satisfied with that representation? No.—She most cautiously and guardedly reserved and secured those invaluable, inestimable rights and privileges, which no people, inspired with the least glow of the patriotic love of liberty, ever did, or ever can, abandon. She is called upon now to abandon them, and dissolve that compact which secured them to her. She is called upon to accede to another compact which most infallibly supercedes and annihilates her present one. Will she do it?—This is the question. If you intend to reserve your unalienable rights, you must have the most express stipulation. . . .

In this business of legislation, your Members of Congress will lose the restriction of not imposing excessive fines, demanding excessive bail, and inflicting cruel and unusual punishments.—These are prohibited by your Declaration of Rights. What has distinguished our ancestors? That they would not admit of tortures, or cruel and barbarous punishments. But Congress may introduce the practice of the civil law, in preference to that of the common law.—They may introduce the practice of France, Spain, and Germany—Of torturing to extort a confession of the crime. . . . The officers of Congress may come upon you, fortified with all the terrors of paramount federal authority.—Excisemen may come in multitudes:—For the limitation of their numbers no man knows.—They may, unless the General Government be restrained by a Bill of Rights, or some similar restriction, go into your cellars and rooms, and search, ransack and measure, every thing you eat, drink and wear. They ought to be restrained within proper bounds. With respect to the freedom of the press, I need say nothing; for it is hoped that the Gentlemen who shall compose Congress, will take care as little as possible, to infringe the rights of human nature.—This will result from their integrity. They should from prudence, abstain from violating the rights of their constituents. . . .

17 June 1788

. . . I trust that Gentlemen, on this occasion, will see the great objects of religion, liberty of the press, trial by jury, interdiction of cruel punishments, and every other sacred right secured, before they agree to that paper. These most important human rights are not protected by that section, which is the only safeguard in the Constitution.—My mind will not be quieted till I see something substantial come forth in the shape of a Bill of Rights.[1]

Part B.

Place a check mark next to the statements that contain the same information as the excerpts in part A. The statement may use exactly the same words or it may paraphrase a portion of Henry's speech. Be prepared to support your opinion with evidence from part A.

_____1. Henry believed the Confederation will become just like Germany, Spain, and France if it does not ratify the Constitution.

_____2. The speech reflects Henry's belief that unless the rights of people are put onto paper and ratified, the federal government will necessarily abuse its authority.

_____3. Henry's mind will not be quieted until the Constitution contains a bill of rights.

Part C.

Consider how the following statements relate to the passages in part A. Place a check mark next to the statements that say what Henry meant to say. Then explain why you did or did not check each statement.

_____1. The Federalists were not vigilant about citizens' liberty and freedoms, as were Virginians.

_____2. Henry loved Virginia and what it stood for more than he loved the Confederation and what the new Constitution promised.

_____3. Henry was the forerunner of the present Republican Party.

_____4. Virginians were warned by Henry not to ratify the federal Constitution, because though it has no bill of rights, its power would overrule the constitution of Virginia, which did have a bill of rights.

Part D.

Read the following statements, and think about experiences you have had that relate to the reading. Check the statement with which you and your group members agree because of its similarity both to an experience one of you has had and to the reading selection. Be ready to support your decisions with evidence.

_____1. Power corrupts, and absolute power corrupts absolutely.

_____2. Sticks and stones may break my bones, but words will never hurt me.

_____3. Stand for something, or you will fall for anything.

[1]Patrick Henry, in *The Creation of the Constitution*, ed. William Dudley (San Diego: Greenhaven Press, 1995), 236, 238–241.

Name_____

Date_____

Rights Guaranteed in the Bill of Rights

Part A.

Use your textbook and other sources to answer the following questions about the Bill of Rights.

1. Name the five basic rights protected in the Bill of Rights.

2. What right does the Second Amendment protect?

3. From what does the Third Amendment free citizens?

4. From what does the Fourth Amendment offer protection?

5. What are the five basic provisions of the Fifth Amendment?

6. What four basic rights are protected by the Sixth Amendment?

7. What right does the Seventh Amendment guarantee?

8. What two freedoms does the Eighth Amendment guarantee?

9. What does the Ninth Amendment guarantee?

10. What powers does the Tenth Amendment reserve?

Part B.

Each of these descriptions relates to a guarantee in the Bill of Rights. Note the specific right or freedom involved and the number of the amendment that protects that right or freedom.

Situation	Right or Freedom	Amendment
1. During a weeklong national military convention and ceremony, the Urban family refused to house two members of the Missouri National Guard, even when told to do so by the governor.		
2. Senator Wegmann lists statistics showing the sale of handguns is not linked to an increase in city crime.		
3. The Youngs' house is being purchased by the county for a new highway. Mr. Young is suing the county for more money.		
4. Benjamin and Joel, students at Central High School, plan to meet in the city square to protest curfew laws.		
5. Mr. Martin and Mr. Stark go to court to settle an argument over a tree that is on Mr. Martin's yard but hangs over Mr. Stark's new cement driveway.		
6. Eleanor argued that the police had no right to take belongings from her house even though the police had found illegal drugs there.		
7. Until she was able to post a $500 bond, Megan had to remain in jail after protesting against a federal military nuclear silo.		
8. Governor Thomas wanted his state to consider new liquor laws that are not under the federal government's domain.		
9. Senator Jones argued that the federal government has no right to control marijuana sales since this right is not mentioned in the Constitution.		
10. The defendant, through his attorney James Wilson, demanded to confront, in court, the eyewitness who claimed to have seen him commit a burglary.		

Lesson 9
Freedom of Religion: Separation of Church and State

Objective
- To understand how separation of church and state protects the individual's freedom of religion

Notes to the Teacher
In colonial times, Pilgrims, Puritans, Roman Catholics, and Quakers came to America seeking religious freedom. However, these groups did not always extend tolerance to other religious minorities. The Puritans, for instance, threatened to banish Roger Williams from Massachusetts Bay for preaching complete separation of church and state, equal rights for women, and fair treatment of the Indians. Williams escaped to Rhode Island and there created the model of religious liberty in America in colonial times.

However, the multiplicity of religions in America precluded the creation of an established church in this country. Religious issues had contributed to the support for revolution against England. After the American Revolution, most states included freedom of religion in the Bills of Rights attached to their constitutions. Later, the Anti-Federalists demanded a national Bill of Rights in which freedom of religion was mentioned as an important right of the people.

Although Thomas Jefferson talked of a separation between the church and state, links join the church and state in many instances. The Supreme Court, the final authority on the meaning of constitutional phrases, has dealt with such controversial religious issues as public aid to parochial schools, the right of conscientious objectors to avoid the draft, the obligation of Jehovah's Witnesses to salute the flag, and the right of Christian Scientists to deny medical aid to their children. In *Lemon v. Kurtzman* (1971), the Supreme Court established three rules for judging the constitutionality of laws relating to separation of church and state: the law must have a secular legislative purpose; its primary effect must neither advance nor inhibit religion; and it must avoid excessive government entanglement in religion.

In this lesson, students analyze the evolving concept of separation of church and state by applying the three tests for constitutionality to real issues that have come before the Supreme Court. Students then use this information to write their own definition for the legitimate connection between church and state in this country.

Procedure
1. Ask students to brainstorm answers to the following questions:
   - What examples can you give of references to God in American government and history? (*The motto "In God We Trust" appears on coins and currency; the Pledge of Allegiance; the appointment of a chaplain to Congress, as well as chaplains in the military; the oaths of office for government officials are sworn on a Bible, as are oaths sworn for testimony in court.*)
   - Give examples of evidence against the establishment of a state religion. (*The government does not force one to attend church, pray, or belong to a specific church, temple, or mosque and does not fund a specific religion. A citizen is not required to belong to a specific religious group in order to vote.*)
   - Give evidence of the freedom to practice or not practice religion. (*Students may mention the existence and diversity of small religious sects, as well as court cases that have guaranteed their right to exist.*)

2. Distribute **Handout 18**, and have students complete it as a large-group activity. Review students' responses. Then inform students of the decision made by the court in each case.

Suggested Responses:
1. *In* Everson v. Board of Education of Ewing Township *(1947), the Supreme Court ruled in favor of the school board and said that both the intent and effect of the law was to help individual*

75

children attend school, even parochial schools, and government involvement was minimal.

2. In Gillette v. United States *(1971)*, the Supreme Court ruled in favor of Gillette's receiving conscientious objector status, because his intent was to remain true to his religious and moral upbringing, and he did not deny the right of the country to wage war for self-defense.

3. In King's Garden v. Federal Communications Commission *(1974)*, the Supreme Court ruled against the employers and said that a religious sect had no constitutional right to convert a licensed communications franchise into a church.

4. In Torcaso v. Watkins *(1961)*, the Court struck down the Maryland provision as an unconstitutional invasion of freedom of belief and religion.

5. In West Virginia Board of Education v. Barnette *(1943)*, the Supreme Court reversed an earlier opinion on the same subject. In this case, the Court ruled that compelling students to salute the flag and recite the Pledge of Allegiance transcended the constitutional limits of the First Amendment protecting the sphere of intellect and spirit.

6. In Sherbert v. Werner *(1963)*, the Supreme Court ruled that a denial of employment benefits constituted a restriction on the free exercise of religion.

7. In Walz v. Tax Commissioner of the City of New York *(1970)*, the Court ruled in favor of the tax commission and determined that tax exemptions for religious institutions were not intended to aid religion but instead provide governmental assistance to all institutions offering social welfare services of good works.

8. In McGowan v. Maryland *(1961)*, the Court upheld Sunday Blue Laws, which were designed to provide for a secular state end (a uniform day of rest), not to provide time for religious observances.

9. In Engle v. Vitale *(1962)*, the Supreme Court struck down the prayer rule as a violation of the separation of church and state, since both its intent and effect were religious.

10. In Marsh v. Chambers *(1981)*, the Supreme Court upheld the use of tax funds to support a chaplain for the state legislature on the grounds that this was a practice of long standing and did not establish a religion but was an acknowledgement of beliefs widely held among people of this country.

11. In Wallace v. Jaffree *(1985)*, the Court declared Alabama's moment of silence law was unconstitutional because it contained a special reference to voluntary prayer and was not consistent with the established principle that government must pursue a course of complete neutrality toward religion.

12. In Edwards v. Aguillard *(1987)*, the Supreme Court voided a Louisiana law that provided for the teaching of evolution and creationism because its primary purpose was to endorse a particular religious doctrine and it violated the establishment clause.

13. In Goldman v. Weinberger *(1986)*, the Court ruled the Air Force could forbid the wearing of a yarmulke while an orthodox Jew was on active duty.

14. In Lynch v. Donnelly *(1984)*, the Supreme Court ruled that a city may include nativity scenes as part of its seasonal display but left open the question of the constitutionality of a display that contained only religious symbols.

15. In Board of Education v. Allen *(1968)*, the Court upheld the New York law on the basis of the child benefit theory, which stated the aid was directed at the child, not the school, and reinforced the idea that the state may aid only secular education.

3. Ask students to select cases that they believe extend the separation between church and state. *(Students might cite the decisions*

on school prayer, *Jehovah's Witnesses and the flag salute, the radio station and fair employment, and the decision ending the obligation to profess a belief in God as a condition of office holding. The explanation of how they build the wall of separation will depend upon the cases cited.*) List responses on the chalkboard or on an overhead transparency. Have students describe how the decisions divide church and state.

4. Have students select cases that they believe break down the separation between church and state. (*Students might cite the use of tax funds to pay for transportation to parochial schools and to support a chaplain for the state legislature and the decision upholding tax exemptions for church property. Their explanation will, again, depend upon their choice of cases.*) List responses on the chalkboard or on an overhead transparency. Have students describe how the decisions link church and state.

5. Mention that in the case of *Zorach v. Clauson* (1952), Supreme Court Justice William O. Douglas commented:

> The First Amendment . . . does not say that in every and all respects there shall be a separation of Church and State. Rather, it studiously defines the manner, the specific ways, in which there shall be no concert or union or dependency one on the other. . . . Otherwise the state and religion would be aliens to each other—hostile, suspicious, and even unfriendly.

Conclude the lesson by asking students what, according to Douglas, is the purpose of the First Amendment guarantee of freedom of religion. (*The amendment recognizes an attempt to create a government built upon a religious foundation that guarantees absolute equality in matters of thought and belief for America's many and diverse religious groups.*)

Enrichment/Extension

Divide students into groups of three or four, and have each group select a case being considered by the Supreme Court during its current term. Have students research and report on the case and then attempt to reach consensus on what decision the Court will reach. Have each group track its case until a decision is handed down. Then compare the group's decision with that of the Court.

Freedom of Religion: Separation of Church and State

Part A.

Read the following information. Then use the listed criteria to determine how the Supreme Court would rule in the numbered situations. Using separate paper, write both the decision you believe the Court would make and the grounds in the criteria for that ruling.

The Supreme Court has the task of interpreting the meaning of the phrases "freedom of religion" and "separation of church and state" as they apply to specific cases. In the 1971 decision of *Lemon v. Kurtzman*, the Supreme Court laid down three basic criteria for determining whether or not a specific practice violates the principle of separation of church and state:

a. The law must have a secular legislative purpose. A rule or law that intends to promote or establish a particular religion would thus be unconstitutional.

b. It must have a primary effect that neither advances nor inhibits religion. For instance, financial support that promotes one religion over another is unconstitutional.

c. The law or rule must not cause excessive government entanglement. What is "excessive" is, of course, open to interpretation, but the point is to avoid active involvement of the government in religious matters.

1. In 1941, a New Jersey school system gave bus fare to families of children riding public transportation to parochial schools. A taxpayer challenged this practice as breaking the wall of separation between church and state.

2. Gillette, a Roman Catholic and a conscientious objector, resisted the draft during the Vietnam War. He argued that he had no objection to fighting in a just war, but he considered the Vietnam War unjust.

3. The owners of a church radio station rejected applications of individuals who did not practice the religion of the station owners. Job applicants argued that the radio station, acting as part of the church's mission, should practice fair employment practices.

4. Maryland's constitution has a provision requiring a person to declare his or her belief in the existence of God as a prerequisite for holding public office. A potential officeholder complained in court that this requirement violated his freedom of religion.

5. During World War II, the West Virginia Board of Education passed a resolution that all teachers and students were to salute and pledge allegiance to the flag of the United States every day. Students who refused were expelled until they agreed to participate, and their parents were subject to criminal prosecution. A group of Jehovah's Witnesses took their case to court because contrary to their religious beliefs, the resolution placed loyalty to the nation above loyalty to God.

6. A Seventh-Day Adventist, who had been discharged from his job for refusing to work on Saturday, sued when he was denied unemployment benefits.

7. Frederick Walz, who owned real estate in New York City, went to court to stop the New York Tax Commission from granting tax exemptions to religious organizations for religious properties used solely for religious worship. He argued that a tax exemption to church property indirectly required him to make a contribution to religious bodies and thereby violated his First and Fourteenth Amendment guarantees of freedom of religion.

8. A citizen challenged Maryland's Sunday Closing or Blue Laws in court. He argued that closing businesses on Sunday, the Sabbath of predominantly Christian sects, facilitated and encouraged church attendance and tried to induce people with no religion or marginal religious beliefs to join the predominant sects.

9. The New York Regents wrote a nondenominational school prayer for use in classrooms. Prayers were not required in New York classrooms, but this was the only one allowed. Parents of several students sued the New York state school system for violating their freedom of religion.

10. A citizen challenged the use of tax funds to pay a chaplain to open sessions of the state legislature. He argued in court that this practice clearly violated the separation of church and state.

11. A citizen challenged an Alabama law that allowed one minute of silence for meditation or voluntary prayer on the grounds that the practice violated separation of church and state.

12. A Louisiana law mandated that a balanced treatment in the teaching of evolution must be followed. If evolution was taught, then creationism must also be taught. A suit argued that the law was a violation of the establishment clause.

13. An Orthodox Jew asked the Supreme Court to void an Air Force ruling that said he could not wear his yarmulke, a skull cap, when on active duty.

14. The Supreme Court was asked to rule whether the city of Pawtucket, Rhode Island, was permitted to display a nativity scene, which featured only religious symbols.

15. In the name of a New York state resident, the Supreme Court was asked to rule whether parochial students legally could be provided with secular, or nonreligious, textbooks paid for with funds raised by taxes.

Lesson 10
Freedom of Speech: Criteria and Examples

Objectives

• To analyze the criteria for decisions regarding freedom of speech

• To apply those criteria to specific examples

Notes to the Teacher

The First Amendment to the Constitution states that Congress shall make no law abridging the freedom of speech. The Supreme Court has extended the meaning of freedom of speech to include "symbolic speech," or the use of symbols, emblems, and signs to communicate ideas, as well as parading, demonstrating, writing, and leafleting. However, freedom of speech is not absolute. The Supreme Court applies five major tests in determining the limits of free speech in this country: clear and present danger; fighting words; obscenity; sedition; and slander.

In this lesson, students analyze the dimensions of freedom of speech as defined by the Constitution, courts, and public practice. They then apply these definitions to specific cases and derive their own definition of the limits of freedom of speech in America.

Procedure

1. Write the following terms on the chalkboard or on an overhead transparency, and have students define them:

   clear and present danger—In *Schenck v. United States* (1919), the Supreme Court stated that free speech would not protect a man falsely shouting fire in a theatre and causing panic. If these words are used in such a manner as to create a clear and present danger, they bring about the evils that Congress has the right to protect.

   fighting words—In 1942, the Supreme Court first specified that an utterance that provokes another to anger but has little if any social value may be considered fighting words and violates the concept of freedom of speech.

   obscenity—This is a violation of the public sense of decency. The Supreme Court has not, however, been able to define the term with any precision.

   sedition—This is advocating the violent overthrow of the government.

   slander—Exposing a person or group to contempt, ridicule, or hatred and adversely affecting the person's or group's reputation is a violation of freedom of speech. The Court has further refined its definition of slander to exclude all of the following: the truth; something said with the consent of the individual; an accidental speech where no negligence or malice was intended because an individual was quoted accidentally; and something said by a privileged speaker protected by immunity, such as member of Congress speaking to colleagues or a parent speaking to a child.

2. Distribute **Handout 19**, and have students complete it either individually or in small groups. Review students' responses.

   Suggested Responses:

   Part A.

   1. *True. These are examples of symbolic speech.*

   2. *False. Symbolic speech is permitted as long as the free speech does not present a clear and present danger.*

   3. *False. Obscenity laws are allowable in communities, which may determine what is and what is not obscene.*

   4. *True. It adversely affects a person's reputation.*

   5. *False. The act is considered constitutional and is protected under the First Amendment.*

   Part B.

   1. *It might depend upon whether or not the individual or group presented a "clear and present danger."*

2. *Symbolic speech involves using symbols or emblems to communicate a message.*

3. *False*

4. *Such words will provoke an angry response.*

3. Divide the class into groups of three or four, and distribute **Handout 20**. Have students complete the handout as directed. Review students' responses.

Suggested Responses:

Part A.

1. *in favor of Marilyn; accidental speech*

2. *in favor of students; no clear and present danger*

3. *in favor of Joyleen; statements were untrue*

4. *in favor of Cynthia; no clear and present danger*

5. *in favor of Ajax; not a privileged speaker protected by immunity*

Part B.

1. *The Court upheld congressional limits, ruling that "money is speech."*

2. *These limits did not violate the First Amendment.*

3. *The Court overturned the conviction as action guaranteed by the First Amendment.*

4. *The ban was upheld because the group did not violate the First Amendment.*

5. *The act was declared unconstitutional because it placed an infringement on First Amendment rights.*

6. *The Court ruled in favor of the Klan because the action of the television station violated the 1934 Communications Act and the First Amendment.*

7. *Judgment was vacated by the Supreme Court and remanded to the lower court. The Federal Election Commission Acts were unconstitutional. Contributions used to finance campaign ads could be used for ads that were produced*

independent of a specific candidate and were entitled to the protection of the First Amendment.

8. *The government cannot prohibit communications considered indecent but may investigate and prosecute obscenity or child pornography as prohibited by the act. The use of the terms* indecent transmissions *and* patently offensive materials *abridge the freedom of speech as stated in the First Amendment.*

4. Review the Supreme Court's interpretation of the freedom of speech. Also review the Court's definition of obscenity. Ask students to select a song, listen to the lyrics, and decide whether the song would be considered obscene under the First Amendment. Have students consider the following:

• Does the artist have the right to sing any lyric as an expression of artistic freedom?

• Do radio stations have the right to limit the playing of certain music or conversation based on the community's standards of what is obscene?

• How would you define *decency* and *obscenity*?

Enrichment/Extension

Have students research and report on cases that deal with free speech and are being considered by the Supreme Court during the current term.

Limits to Freedom of Speech

Part A.

Read each statement, and decide whether it is true or false. Give a reason for your choice.

_____1. Black armbands, ribbons of remembrance for breast cancer survivors or AIDS victims, antiwar banners and brochures, and flag-burning are forms of speech.

_____2. The Supreme Court permits symbolic speech.

_____3. Free speech allows me to use curse words if I feel like it.

_____4. You may purposely tell fake stories in which your principal is guilty of illegal drug activity. If there is a police investigation and no charges are filed, your principal may sue you for slander.

_____5. A man burns an American flag during a political party's presidential convention. His desecration of the flag is unconstitutional.

Part B.

Study each case, and then answer the questions.

De Jonge v. Oregon (1937)

Dirk De Jonge was distributing literature about Communism and was arrested, tried, convicted, and sentenced for violating Oregon's Criminal Syndication Act. The Supreme Court reversed the decision of the lower court and stated that De Jonge was entitled to free speech because he presented no clear danger to the government.

Dennis v. United States (1951) and Brandenberg v. Ohio (1969)

In 1949, a group of Communists were tried under the Smith Act (1940), which made it a crime to advocate the overthrow of the government. Found guilty, they appealed to the Supreme Court on the grounds that the Smith Act violated their First Amendment rights. Their appeal was rejected on the grounds that they presented a "clear and present danger." Later the Court said the government can only restrict speech when it advocates the use of violence directed towards inciting imminent and likely lawless action, but does not protect conspiracy to advocate the overthrow of the government.

U.S. v. O'Brien (1968)

Vietnam War protestors were arrested for burning their Selective Service (draft) cards. The Supreme Court defined this as "symbolic speech," or speaking through actions or symbols. The convictions were upheld when the Court found the draft card to be part of the operation of the Selective Service.

Tinker v. Des Moines School District **(1969)**

High school students wore black armbands to protest the war in Vietnam. Their principal ordered them to remove the armbands. They refused to comply and were suspended. The Supreme Court ruled that wearing armbands in school was protected under the principle of "symbolic speech," which did not disrupt the educational process in the school.

Village of Skokie v. National Socialist Party of America **(1978)**

Members of the Nazi party (National Socialist Party of America) wanted to speak and parade while wearing Nazi emblems and carrying flags bearing the swastika in Skokie, a predominantly Jewish suburb of Chicago. The Supreme Court defined this as an example of "fighting words" because many of the citizens of Skokie were victims of the Holocaust. The Court limited the Nazis' use of emblems and signs.

R.A.V. v. St. Paul **(1992)**

On June 21, 1990, several teenagers burned a cross inside the fenced yard of a black family in St. Paul, Minnesota. The teenagers were charged under a provision that prohibited placement of symbols that produced anger based on race, color, creed, religion, or gender. In a majority opinion, the Supreme Court stated that the provision was unconstitutional because it was underinclusive; in other words, the statute was not specific enough.

1. What suggestion does the Supreme Court make in the De Jonge case which indicates that some individuals might be treated differently for the same offense?

2. Judging from these Supreme Court decisions, define *symbolic speech.*

3. True or false: The Supreme Court always permits symbolic speech.

4. In your own words, explain what the Supreme Court means by *fighting words.*

Specific Cases Pertaining to Free Speech

Part A.

Read each selection. Assume the role of the Supreme Court, and, on a separate piece of paper, write an opinion ruling on each case. Include an explanation of your reasoning. Use the criteria on **Handout 19** to help you.

1. Marilyn has been sued for slandering her neighbor, Donald, an automobile service manager. She is accused of harming Donald's business reputation by publicly criticizing some repair work done at Donald's place of employment. Marilyn claimed she was misquoted and that she never intended to harm Donald's reputation.

2. A school rule forbids wearing badges that express anti-American ideas. A group of students chooses to display badges that promote a stand against an unpopular military action. The principal orders them to remove the badges.

3. Joyleen is angry because a fellow employee told coworkers that she was an alcoholic and that was the reason she was frequently late for work. Joyleen, who does not drink and whose tardiness was caused by caring for her terminally ill mother, sued her coworker for slander, saying he had ruined her reputation.

4. Cynthia had been making speeches against a law that she believes is against the basic privacy principles of the Constitution. A federal statute prohibits seditious acts and the promotion of un-American causes. Cynthia is prosecuted and found guilty. She appeals her case to the Supreme Court.

5. Mr. Brown, a school board member, announced that the school district would no longer do business with the Ajax Company, because the business engaged in dishonest practices. The president of the company sued Mr. Brown and the school district for slander.

Part B.

Read the following statements, and use your textbook and other sources to determine the decision of the Supreme Court concerning the principle of freedom of speech. On a separate piece of paper, write a short summary of the decision reached by the Court and the reason behind the decision.

1. The Court was asked to overturn limits Congress had placed in individual donations to candidates for public office.—*Buckley v. Valeo* (1976)

2. The Federal Election Commission placed limits on gifts given by political action committees to candidates for public office.—*California Medical Association v. Federal Election Commission* (1981)

3. A man is sentenced to six months' imprisonment for wearing a flag patch on the seat of his pants.—*Smith v. Goguen* (1974)

4. Members of the Community for Creative Non-Violence were prevented from sleeping in Lafayette Park across from the White House as a protest against the administration's policies regarding the poor and homeless.—*Clark v. Community for Creative Non-violence* (1984)

5. The Court was asked to determine whether the Federal Protection Act outlawing the desecration of the U.S. flag was constitutional.—*U.S. v. Eichman* (1990)

6. The Ku Klux Klan wanted to broadcast a program on the Kansas City cable television network. City Council and community members protested that the broadcast would incite racial tension. The American Civil Liberties Union took up the Klan's case.—*Missouri Knights of the Ku Klux Klan v. Kansas City* (1989)

7. The Colorado Republican Party launched a series of expensive radio ads against Democratic candidates. The Federal Election Commission ruled that the party was in violation of the Federal Campaign Act of 1971, which limited the amount a party could spend on television and radio ads. The Court of Appeals ruled in favor of the Commission and against the Republican Party, which appealed.—*Colorado Republican Federal Campaign Committee and Douglas Jones, Treasurer, Petitioners, v. Federal Election Commission* (1996)

8. The Communications Decency Act of 1996 protected minors from those who would use the Internet to knowingly send or sell "indecent" or "patently offensive" communications to children under the age of eighteen. The Federal District Court declared the law to be unconstitutional because it abridged the right to free speech, under the First Amendment.—*Reno, et al. v. American Civil Liberties Union* (1997)

Lesson 11
Freedom of the Press: Earl Caldwell's Dilemma

Objective

- To understand how conflicting values create both personal and national dilemmas in implementing the Bill of Rights with emphasis on the right of freedom of the press

Notes to the Teacher

During the eighteenth century, critics of kings and governments suffered harsh punishment and were subjected to censorship, licensing acts, the destruction of printing presses and unapproved books, and even imprisonment. In 1735, John Peter Zenger, publisher of the *New York Weekly Journal*, was charged with printing seditious material that criticized the royal governor of New York. Zenger's defense was that what he wrote was true and therefore not seditious. A jury acquitted Zenger. A member of Great Britain's House of Commons, John Wilkes, was charged with seditious libel for publishing tracts critical of the king and his ministers. He was re-elected to Parliament and continued to defend the freedom of the press. In 1798, Congress passed the Sedition Act, which made it a crime to utter, write, or publish anything that would defame or bring into contempt or disrepute the president or other members of the government. This act was allowed to expire in 1801.

The Supreme Court has attempted to clarify a number of controversial issues relating to freedom of the press. Rulings banning reporters from interviewing prisoners, attending presidential press conferences, and releasing information that affects national security have all been considered. Frequently, the courts ask reporters—like Earl Caldwell—to testify about information they have received in confidence. Such situations create a dilemma for reporters: Should they give precedence to their responsibility as citizens to serve as witnesses in court, or should they protect the identity of their confidential informant at the expense of going to jail? The courts face an equally perplexing dilemma: Is it more important to protect freedom of the press or to guarantee due process in court? The Supreme Court has

ruled on this issue on a case-by-case basis and has not established clear guidelines. This lesson illustrates the value conflict that policymakers must resolve in protecting conflicting rights of citizens.

In this lesson, examining Earl Caldwell's dilemma allows students to debate these issues and helps them to see how government policies affect the lives of individuals. First, students read and discuss an excerpt from a letter written by Thomas Jefferson in which he expresses his opinion about the need for a free press in America. Then, they read about Caldwell's dilemma and demonstrate how personal decision making requires ranking one's value priorities. Students write a paragraph explaining their position on the case; they use one of six topic sentences. Students then discuss the reasoning behind their stated advice to Caldwell.

Procedure

1. Have students complete the prereading activity in **Handout 21**. Review students' responses.

   Suggested Responses:

   1. the people and their good sense

   2. The people get information from newspapers and use their good sense and opinion to act.

   3. Answers should include the following: newspapers and television news programs appeal to the people but do not always reflect the people's values and good sense; commercialism and corporate sponsorship can determine the length, subject, and political view of a news show; newspapers and television networks are ultimately accountable to the people and stories involving scandals, problems, and successes need to be reported.

   4. If we had newspapers without a government, then we would not have legislators, courts, mayors, governors, or a president. There would perhaps be a certain amount of chaos, but there would still be an open communication of information and opinions about the state of affairs.

5. Disagree—*People today do not exhibit the good sense he speaks of. There is low voter turnout, an increase in crime, poor public education, and an increase in court litigation, where individuals sue large corporations for their poor personal choices. We need government and its leaders to run the country.*

   Agree—*The purpose of this government is to represent the interests of the people, and by being better informed through the media and newspapers, citizens need to become more active, educated, and involved.*

2. Distribute **Handout 22**. Have students read the dilemma and write the assigned paragraph for homework.

3. Ask a student to explain Earl Caldwell's dilemma in his or her own words. Have other students fill in missing details.

4. Ask students what each of the following groups thinks Caldwell should do:

   - Caldwell's colleagues in journalism
   - the government
   - the Black Panthers
   - the American public
   - Caldwell's family

5. Ask students for examples of the rights involved in this dilemma. Compile a list on the chalkboard or on an overhead transparency as students suggest them.

Suggested Responses:

- *the right of newsmen to protect their sources of tips on important stories*
- *the right of the grand jury to compel witnesses*
- *the right of the government to investigate and apprehend dangerous criminals*
- *the right of the public to know the whole truth*

- *the public's right to protection from dangerous individuals and groups*
- *the right of minorities to espouse unpopular viewpoints*
- *the right of newsmen to pursue their profession without going to jail*

6. Have several students read their paragraphs. Try to use as many paragraphs with different topic sentences as possible. In each case, ask someone to state the writer's strongest point and another to take a different position, framing the question the student would most like to ask the writer of the paragraph. This is a good opportunity for students to learn the persuasive power of a good question. Additional discussion questions for each topic sentence include the following:

   1. Suppose there is good chance that a court of appeals will side with Caldwell. Should the possibility that he might not go to jail make a difference in his action?

   2. Should Caldwell base his decision on the prospect of maintaining the news sources on which his career depends?

   3. Is it important to consider what other people think of one's behavior? Why? Is it more important to consider the reactions of other people or one's conscience? Why?

   4. Should it make any difference if Caldwell had promised the Black Panthers confidentiality? if he agreed with their position?

   5. What would happen to society if an individual defied government authority whenever he or she found it convenient or desirable?

   6. Do reporters always have an obligation to do everything possible to preserve freedom of the press and the public's right to know the truth? Why?

7. Before students turn in their paragraphs, have them write at the bottom of the page one new point they learned in the discussion that they wish they had considered in writing the paragraph.

8. To conclude the lesson, redirect students' attention to **Handout 21** and Jefferson's comment about preferring newspapers without a government. Ask students to explain in their own words what Jefferson meant and why he believed it was so important to maintain a free press. Then ask how Jefferson would have advised Caldwell to act. (*Jefferson would have advised Caldwell to resist the order to testify in court to preserve the essential freedom of the press.*)

Enrichment/Extension

Have students prepare and present a play dramatizing Earl Caldwell's dilemma.

Name_____

Date_____

A Letter from Thomas Jefferson

In 1787, Thomas Jefferson, then minister to France, wrote a letter to his friend Edward Carrington about the violent tax revolt, called Shay's Rebellion, which was taking place in Massachusetts. Read the following excerpt, and answer the questions.

> The tumults in America I expected would have produced in Europe an unfavorable opinion of our political state. But it has not. On the contrary, . . . [t]he interposition of the people themselves on the side of government has had a great effect on the opinion here. I am persuaded myself that the good sense of the people will always be found to be the best army. They may be led astray for a moment, but will soon correct themselves.
>
> The people are the only censors of their governors; and even their errors will tend to keep these to the true principles of their institution. To punish these errors too severely would be to suppress the only safeguard of the public liberty. The way to prevent these irregular interpositions of the people is to give them full information of their affairs through the channel of the public papers, and to contrive that those papers should penetrate the whole mass of the people. The basis of our governments being the opinion of the people, the very first object should be to keep that right; and were it left to me to decide whether we should have a government without newspapers, or newspapers with a government, I should not hesitate for a moment to prefer the latter. But I should mean that every man should receive those papers, and be capable of reading them.[1]

1. What is the "best army" to censor governors and safeguard the public liberty, according to Jefferson?

2. How does one protect against the "irregular interpositions of the people"? Why do you think Jefferson supports this idea?

3. Given his opinion about the role of newspapers, what might Jefferson say about today's print and television journalism?

4. What would happen today if the circumstances were, as Jefferson suggested, newspapers without government?

5. Do you agree with Jefferson's views of the American people? Why or why not? Is he being pragmatic or idealistic? Explain your choice.

[1]Thomas Jefferson to Edward Carrington, January 16, 1787, in *The Creation of the Constitution*, ed. William Dudley (San Diego: Greenhaven Press, 1995), 51.

Earl Caldwell's Dilemma

Part A.

Sometimes we forget how directly government decisions affect people's lives. We forget, too, how difficult it is for government officials to make the *right* choices that all Americans can accept as just and fair. Earl Caldwell's dilemma illustrates both points. A dilemma is a situation where one must decide between a right or a wrong choice. In this case, both Caldwell's view and that of the U.S. government have merit. Read the following information about Earl Caldwell's dilemma.

In the late 1960s, the *New York Times* assigned Earl Caldwell to cover stories related to the Black Panthers and other black militant groups. To gain interviews with Black Panther leaders and spokespersons, Caldwell promised confidentiality to individuals who talked freely with him about the organization's aims, purposes, and activities. Some time later, a New York grand jury summoned Caldwell to give secret testimony about the group. Caldwell remembered his unspoken, but nonetheless sacred, pledge as a journalist: "I will go to jail before revealing the identity of anyone who tells me something confidentially." Consequently, he refused to testify in court, saying his appearance before the grand jury would "suppress vital First Amendment freedoms . . . by driving a wedge of distrust and silence between the news media and the militants." He argued that "so drastic an incursion upon First Amendment freedoms" was unwarranted in his case.

The government viewed the situation quite differently. The grand jury was investigating possible criminal violations against the president, rioting, interstate travel to incite a riot, and mail frauds and swindles. On November 15, 1969, a Black Panther representative had declared in a publicly televised speech that "We will kill Richard Nixon." Caldwell's articles in the *New York Times* had stated that "in their role as the vanguard in a revolutionary struggle the Panthers have picked up guns." He had also quoted an unidentified Panther leader as saying "We advocate the very direct overthrow of the government by way of force and violence" and "we recognize it [the government] as being oppressive and . . . we know that the only solution to it is armed struggle."

As a result, the government considered "every person within the jurisdiction of the government" bound to testify upon being properly summoned. Caldwell received notification from the court that his refusal to cooperate with the grand jury would result in a contempt citation and imprisonment until he agreed to testify or until the expiration of the term of the grand jury.[1]

[1]Adapted from *Communication under Law, Vol. II: Journalistic Freedom*, Joseph J. Hemmer Jr. (Metuchen, N.J.: The Scarecrow Press, 1980), 217–18.

Part B.

Should Earl Caldwell testify? Write a paragraph explaining what you think he should do and why. Build your paragraph around one of the following topic sentences. Support your decision with good reasons, and be prepared to discuss your paragraph in class.

1. Earl Caldwell should testify before the grand jury because he will go to jail if he refuses.

2. Earl Caldwell should refuse to testify before the grand jury because that is the only way to insure that he will be trusted with news tips in the future.

3. Earl Caldwell should testify before the grand jury because the public admires those who uncover and print "the whole truth."

4. Earl Caldwell should not testify because he will lose the respect of those to whom he has promised confidentiality.

5. Earl Caldwell should testify before the grand jury because respect for the law will be destroyed if people believe they can refuse compliance with any orders they find objectionable.

6. Earl Caldwell should refuse to testify because reporters have an obligation to maintain a free press and resist censorship of any information that might upset those in power.

Lesson 12
Freedom of the Press: Student Newspapers

Objective
- To analyze the issue of how much freedom of the press student newspapers should be afforded

Notes to the Teacher
Upon taking his seat in Congress, James Madison proposed adding a Bill of Rights to the new Constitution. His aim was to prevent more radical changes to the document by the Anti-Federalists and to forestall a second convention. His proposed bill of rights differed from those added to state constitutions and contained a short list of specific restraints.

In 1735, Alexander Hamilton argued in the case of John Peter Zenger against the royal governor of New York that a jury was a bastion of liberty and should read and hear Zenger's articles and determine their truthfulness. The judge instructed the jury to determine only whether Zenger had published the articles. The jury ignored the judge's instructions and found Zenger not guilty.

Thomas Jefferson and George Clinton, who were Anti-Federalists, lobbied for a bill of rights, which would protect the freedom of the press. Mercy Otis Warren wrote, "There is no security in the proffered system, either for the rights of conscience, or the liberty of the Press . . . the most unjust restrictions may take place in the first instance, and an *imprimator* [approval] on the Press in the next, may silence the complaints, and forbid the most decent remonstrances of an injured and oppressed people."

Federalists, including Alexander Hamilton, responded to the Constitution's lack of a bill of rights by arguing that several state constitutions lacked bills of rights and that the federal Constitution offered protection for these rights. He stated that protection of a bill of rights depended on the spirit and opinion of the people, as well as public opinion.

In January 1988, the U.S. Supreme Court's decision in the case of *Hazelwood v. Kuhlmeier* gave power to school officials to use editorial control over the content of school-sponsored student publications. The limit placed by the Court was that school officials had the power "so long as their actions are related to legitimate pedagogical concerns." The response was mixed, with many seeking ways to continue to protect these publications as guaranteed by the First Amendment.

In the first two years following the *Hazelwood* decision, the record of success for change was mixed, as the following examples illustrate.

- As of July 1, 1989, students in Iowa are protected from the impact of the *Hazelwood* decision. Iowa became the first state to draft and pass new legislation protecting student free expression rights in the wake of *Hazelwood*.

- California already had a student free expression statute, and Massachusetts made its optional statute mandatory in July 1989. Legislation to protect student expression was defeated in Nevada and Rhode Island.

- A Tennessee high school student was barred from a school election for insulting the assistant principal in a speech. The U.S. Court of Appeals for the Sixth Circuit cited *Hazelwood* and claimed that "civility is a legitimate pedagogical concern" in upholding by 2–1 the action by the school officials.

In this lesson, students examine and analyze opinions regarding the issue of free speech in school newspapers and develop an essay.

Procedure
1. Ask for examples of responsible reporting, sincere editorials, and commentary. Ask for examples of what might be considered to be scandalous and defamatory press. Ask who decides what is responsible reporting.

2. Distribute **Handout 23**, and have students complete it as a large-group activity. Review students' responses.

   Suggested Responses:

   1. A journalist is free from censure as long as what he or she is writing is not criminal.

   2 In a free state, one must be able to criticize the government and its leaders.

   3. The evil shoot is the tendency of the press to degenerate into licentiousness. It is possible to prevent people from publishing immoral, slanderous, and scandalous material. In doing so, perhaps the government helps society become a moral place; however, in rooting out these writings, it could damage a free press to the degree that even good and responsible writing could be curtailed.

   4. Perhaps the courts could determine what is dangerous or threatening speech. Perhaps the legislature could ban the publication of child pornography. Perhaps the president could sign an executive order requesting that all news agencies police themselves.

3. Distribute **Handout 24**, and have students read the comments concerning the impact of the *Hazelwood* decision. Ask students which of these educational leaders support the Court's decision and which ones oppose it. (*Heath and Nebgen support the decision while Goodman and LaPier oppose it.*) On what constitutional grounds or principles do they make their arguments? (*Heath and Negben make the point that the process of editing and writing an article reflects real life, that there is some give and take between publisher and writer and that the contents of the article, as well as the consequences of its printing, must be considered. Finally, the school does have authority over its students. Goodman and LaPier assert that the decision supports censorship of students and disregards the fundamental American principle of free expression and free press. Finally, students are not participating in true journalism, but writing what administrators want to hear.*)

4. Have students write an essay on the following topic: Should principals have the authority to prevent the publication of articles in school-sponsored student newspapers? Instruct students to follow this formula:

   • In paragraph 1, introduce the topic and state the thesis, topic, or position to be discussed.

   • In paragraphs 2–4, discuss the position by citing specific data from the material presented.

   • In paragraph 5, conclude the essay by evaluating the immediate effects of the topic. State what is likely a longer lasting effect and the reason for the prediction.

5. Divide students into small groups of three or four. Have them share their essays and select a representative essay to share with the class. Conduct a class discussion in which students attempt to reach consensus on the topic.

Enrichment/Extension

1. Have students search current newspapers and magazines for stories that deal with free speech and school newspapers. Instruct students to share their findings with the class.

2. Have students research and report on how their state legislature is dealing with this issue.

Should Newspapers Be Censored?

Read the quotations about freedom of the press, and answer the questions that follow.

The liberty of the press is indeed essential to the nature of a free state: but this consists in laying no previous restraints upon publications, and not in freedom from censure for criminal matter when published. Every freeman has an undoubted right to lay what sentiments he pleases before the public: to forbid this, is to destroy the freedom of the press.

—Sir William Blackstone,
Commentaries on the Laws of England, 1765

Among those principles deemed sacred in America . . . there is no one of which the importance is more deeply impressed on the public mind than the liberty of the press. That this *liberty* is often carried to excess; that it has sometimes degenerated into *licentiousness*, is seen and lamented; *but the remedy has not yet been discovered. Perhaps it is an evil inseparable from the good with which it is allied; perhaps it is a shoot which cannot be stripped from the stalk without wounding vitally the plant from which it is torn. However desirable those measures might be which might correct without enslaving the press, they have never yet been devised in America.*

—Charles Cotesworth Pinckney, John Marshall, and Elbridge Gerry,
in a letter to French Foreign Minister Talleyrand, 1798

1. According to Blackstone, is a journalist free from censure?

2. Why could one argue that liberty of the press is essential to a free state?

3. What is the inseparable evil "shoot" on the "stalk" that is free press? Do you think it can be torn away? What does Marshall say?

4. In the twenty-first century, what measure could be used to control the excesses of a free press?

Should School Newspapers Be Censored?

Read the following quotations by various educators on the *Hazelwood* decision.

In January 1988, the U.S. Supreme Court delivered a decision in the case of *Hazelwood v. Kuhlmeier*. This decision gave school officials widespread editorial control over the content of school-sponsored publications (newspapers, magazines, and yearbooks).

I recommend five simple questions to check the appropriateness of material printed for a school newspaper: (1) Does the article deal with a substantive issue that will inform and educate readers? (2) What is the intent of the reporter who wrote or proposed the article? (3) What makes the article questionable? (4) Who will be informed if the article is printed? and (5) Who will be hurt if the article is not printed?

. . . There has to be a give-and-take among the newspaper staff, advisor, and principal to allow publication of thought-provoking and controversial content that is appropriate for a school as determined by local standards.

—Brent Heath is a social studies teacher and department chairperson at De Anza Junior High in Ontario, California.

Principals can help students learn the responsibilities of journalism by assuming a supportive role in the paper's operation. When student journalists cover pertinent, though uncomfortable, issues, principals have the same options as managers of professional publications. They can require modification of the article. They can publish a disclaimer stating that opinions of the journalism staff are not necessarily shared by the administrators of the school. They can write their own responses opposing opinions expressed by student writers. Or they can try to collaborate with students to set an editorial policy that outlines both the rights and responsibilities of the student press.

In no case, however, should principals prevent the publication of an article for reasons other than libel.

—Moody ElLaissi is an associate professor at Georgia Southern University in Statesboro, Georgia.

The 623 telephone calls that the Student Press Law Center received in 1987 from student journalists seeking advice paint a disturbing picture. Routinely censored stories include those critical of school officials or policies and those concerning AIDS, teen pregnancy, drug abuse, race relations, abortion, and similar topics of vital importance to young people that some squeamish adults would prefer to be ignored. Students subject to such censorship receive a troubling message: their school officials have little respect for free expression and a free press, encourage blind acceptance of the government's view of the world, and discourage critical thinking. The real educators involved in this controversy—the nation's classroom journalism teachers and publications advisors—joined with students before the Supreme Court to argue that a school cannot teach good journalism without allowing students press freedoms.

—Mark Goodman is executive director of the Student Press Law Center in Washington, D.C.

Following the *Hazelwood* decision, I met with our school's newspaper sponsor and staff to thoroughly discuss its implications. *Hazelwood* highlighted only what students already knew but had not realized for some time because they liked to "hide" behind the First Amendment. They had always been responsible for the content of the articles in the paper, but the

Court now emphasized that I could have a greater impact on the paper. Once students saw that no major changes were planned, they began to understand their true responsibility and to see the enormous power of the press.

—Bill Harrington is principal of
Newton Senior High School in Newton, Kansas.

Giving complete power to one person, the principal, is against all the tenets of our government. The wording of the *Hazelwood* decision is so nebulous that a principal can be completely arbitrary in censoring student articles. Anything that looks as though it may cause a ripple could be eliminated from the school publication.

. . . Students will not be learning responsible journalism—they will be learning to write what those in control want to hear.

—Cynthia LaPier
is director of school libraries for the Schuyler-Chemung-Tioga
Board of Cooperative Educational Services in Elmira, New York.

My concern is not that a school administration has the authority to stop a publication, but that there needs to be more discussion of what criteria should be used to intervene. Who specifically will make a decision to prevent publication? Will the teacher or advisor be responsible? Will students have a say in the decision? These questions should be answered before a principal steps in.

Helping students to explore the rights and responsibilities of journalism is part of the educational process leading to greater freedoms. Confrontations can be useful as an educational experience. Actually, the resurgence of the free speech issue is a good sign that could foreshadow greater involvement in the political process and a better generation of leaders.

—Suzanne Chapin is Chapter 1 department head for the Rio Blanco
Board of Cooperative Educational Services in Rangely, Colorado.

If we wish to teach students about the "real world," then it is certainly appropriate for them to learn that in any arena of adult American society, the exercise of free speech is not a totally uncontrolled right. The Supreme Court did not grant to school officials unilateral power to unreasonably censor student publications, but it did re-emphasize the authority—and responsibility—of school officials to require of their students a standard of journalism which demands that they exercise their First Amendment rights responsibly.

—Mary Nebgen is deputy superintendent of the
Tacoma, Washington, Public Schools.

Editing is a fact of life in all forms of journalism. Students must learn that censorship, in the form of editing, is one of the realities in the publications profession. Therefore, student newspapers should be operated within the frameworks established by the various newspapers around the country. . . .

Because students in school are legally a captive audience, administrators must ensure that publications balance the constitutional rights of pupils with the maintenance of a learning environment for which schools are held accountable. The *Hazelwood* decision should strengthen efforts for responsible school journalism.

—Kip Sullivan is assistant professor of educational leadership
at Lamar University in Beaumont, Texas.[1]

[1]"Issue," *ASCD Update*, September 1988, 4–5.

Lesson 13
The Right to Bear Arms

Objectives

- To examine the history of the Second Amendment

- To determine the validity of a law regulating concealed weapons

Notes to the Teacher

Issues regarding the ownership and use of guns by private citizens have been controversial for decades. The Second Amendment to the Constitution protects the right to bear arms, stating that a well-regulated militia is necessary to the security of a free state, and that the right of the people to keep and bear arms shall not be infringed upon. Connections between guns and violent crimes have prompted attempts to require that guns be registered. In 1911, New York City set the precedent for gun control when it enacted the Sullivan Law. Later upheld by the Supreme Court, the Sullivan Law requires gun licensing and permits to own a gun or to carry a concealed weapon. By 1934, the National Firearms Act was enacted to regulate the sale and use of firearms.

Some of the Founding Fathers believed that the Constitution gave too much military power to the federal government. They supported the Second Amendment as a way to check the danger of military tyranny.

After the Revolutionary War, state constitutions affirmed the rights of citizens to bear arms and of those same states to raise militias. States have adequately protected the right to bear arms. Federal, state, and local governments have regulated the sale and use of weapons, including those that are concealed. Automatic weapons and those that have been criminally altered, such as sawed-off shotguns, are banned in most states.

The debate over guns and gun control involves the interpretation of the amendment itself. The pro-gun lobby points out that the Second Amendment guarantees the right of the people to a well-regulated militia. Members of this group cite English common law, the English Bill of Rights, and debates over the ratification of the Bill of Rights in support of their position. Gun control advocates respond

that the right to bear arms was essentially the right to defend the state and that owning a personal weapon was never an absolute right but rather one to be controlled.

Both sides in the debate support highly sophisticated lobbies that support their position. The call for gun control, particularly handguns, stems from many groups, and the rise of violent crime has strengthened their cause. The Gun Control Act of 1968, which was dependent upon the commerce clause of the Constitution, tightened federal firearms licensing, limited foreign gun imports, reduced mail-order sales, outlawed federal dealers' licenses to minors, outlawed the sales of rifles, shotguns, or ammunition to minors, and forbade certain types of criminals from carrying firearms over state lines. However, the law did not regulate a type of cheap handgun commonly called a "Saturday night special."

Since 1968, three major federal gun control statutes have been enacted by Congress. In 1978, President Jimmy Carter pushed for serial number registration by the Bureau of Alcohol, Tobacco, and Firearms, but the House of Representatives did not allocate money for its enforcement. The Brady Act (1993) requires background checks of gun purchasers by federally licensed firearms dealers. The Violent Crime Control and Law Enforcement Act (1994) banned the sale of semiautomatic assault weapons, and the Domestic Violence Offender Gun Act (1996) prohibited gun ownership by anyone who commits a misdemeanor domestic violence offense.

In this lesson, students complete a chart outlining the pros and cons regarding gun control. They read selections regarding the history of the government's attempts to regulate the right to bear arms, and they conclude by writing a paragraph in which they express an opinion either for or against gun control legislation.

Procedure

1. Distribute **Handout 25**, and have students complete it either in small groups or as a large-group session. Explain that the purpose of this activity is to help students develop their own position on gun control

and to discuss that position in class. Answers will vary, but students should be able to explain their current opinion. Review students' responses.

Suggested Responses:

Reasons for Gun Control

1. *Handguns are not always handy, can cause accidents, and are often stolen.*

2. *Handgun control would make it more difficult for an individual prone to violence to get a handgun. Fifty percent of all homicides are committed with handguns.*

3. *Great Britain has gun control laws and has a much lower homicide rate than the United States.*

4. *This clause applies to the collective right to form a militia, not the personal right of individuals to own handguns.*

Reasons against Gun Control

1. *Handguns can be a good way to defend one's home and personal safety.*

2. *Violent individuals are the ones who are least likely to obey handgun laws.*

3. *Crime rates have not been lowered with the enactment of gun control laws. Criminals still find ways to obtain guns.*

4. *This clause grants each individual the right to bear arms. Waiting periods and background checks before getting a gun force the law-abiding citizen to justify his or her need for a gun, while the criminal easily obtains his gun illegally.*

2. Explain that interpretations of the Second Amendment have been controversial. Explain that the Founding Fathers sought to prevent the government from taking weapons from its citizens, as the British had done before and during the early days of the Revolutionary War. Stress that the idea of a militia was important in our nation's early history, especially along the frontier. Mention that the use of the term *militia* has become controversial, especially by groups such as the Posse Comitatus and numerous other white supremacy groups. Divide students into pairs. Then have them

read the selections in **Handout 26** and answer the questions. Review students' responses.

Suggested Responses:

1. *to provide for protection against enemies in a country that had no standing army*

2. *They were administrators of the country's laws and probably would not fight.*

3. *The militia shall consist of all able-bodied men between the ages of eighteen and forty-five who were citizens or had declared the intent to become a citizen and all females who are in the National Guard.*

4. *Organized—the National Guard and Naval militia; Unorganized—all other males between the ages of eighteen and forty-five who are not members of the National Guard*

5. *The purpose of the amendment is to prevent rulers from disarming the people. Members of the militia need to learn to handle weapons for efficient use.*

6. *A standing army is considered dangerous to the liberties of the people.*

7. *Arms may be kept for general defense against invasion or oppression; the use of weapons for individual deadly encounters was prohibited.*

8. *to execute the laws, suppress insurrections, and repel invasions*

9. *The law compelled state law enforcement officers to administer and enforce a federal regulatory program.*

10. *to wear, bear, or carry upon the person or in clothing, or a pocket*

11. *The federal government may not disarm its citizens without strong justification; firearms may be used in defense of homes; the right to hunt game and the right to employ firearms to commit aggressive acts against others are not permitted.*

3. Have students write a short paragraph for or against gun control. Allow time for students to share their paragraphs.

Suggested Responses:

- *A gun advocate might say that such legislation is unnecessary but that a more stringent application of the criminal code would solve many of these problems while not restricting the rights of the law-abiding citizen.*

- *A gun control advocate might argue that these laws clarify the meaning of the Second Amendment and guarantee a lawful, regulated gun ownership.*

Enrichment/Extension

Have students research and report on concealed weapon laws that have been passed in several states, including Texas and Ohio.

Name_____

Date_____

Reasons for and against Gun Control

Complete the following chart based on your opinion regarding the main reasons for and against gun control. Be prepared to explain your answers.

Issues	Reasons for Gun Control	Reasons against Gun Control
1. Handguns can be used for defense.		
2. Handguns are often used in crimes of passion.		
3. Handgun control reduces the homicide rate.		
4. The Constitution protects the right to bear arms.		

Interpreting and Regulating the Right to Bear Arms

Read the following excerpts, and answer the questions.

Militia Act of 1792

Sec 1. *Be it enacted* . . . That each and every free able-bodied white male citizen of the respective states, resident herein, who is or shall be of the age of eighteen years, and under the age of forty-five years (except as is herein after excepted) shall severally and respectively be enrolled in the militia. . . . That every citizen so enrolled and notified, shall, with six months thereafter, provide himself with a good musket or firelock, a sufficient bayonet and belt, two spare flints, and a knapsack, a pouch with a box therein to contain not less than twenty-four cartridges, suited to the bore of his musket or firelock, each cartridge to contain a proper quantity of powder and ball: or with a good rifle, knapsack, shot-pouch and powder-horn, twenty balls suited to the bore of his rifle, and a quarter of a pound of powder. . . .

Sec. 2. [Exempting the Vice President, federal judicial and executive officers, congressmen and congressional officers, custom-house officers and clerks, post-officers and postal stage drivers, ferrymen on post roads, export inspectors, {river} pilots, merchant mariners, and people exempted under the laws of their states.]

Current Militia Act (Enacted 1956, Amended 1958)

(a) The militia of the United States consists of all able-bodied males at least 17 years of age and . . . under 45 years of age who are, or who have made a declaration of intention to become, citizens of the United States and of female citizens of the United States who are members of the National Guard.

(b) The classes of militia are—

  (1) the organized militia, which consists of the National Guard and the Naval Militia; and

  (2) the unorganized militia, which consists of the members of the militia who are not members of the National Guard or the Naval Militia.

From *General Principles of Constitutional Law*, Thomas Cooley, 1880

The Constitution—By the Second Amendment to the Constitution it is declared that, "a well-regulated militia being necessary to the security of a free State, the right of the poeple to keep and bear arms shall not be infringed."

The amendment, like most other provisions in the Constitution, has a history. It was adopted with some modification and enlargement from the English Bill of Rights of 1688, where it stood as a protest against arbitrary action of the overturned dynasty [the Stuarts] in disarming the people, and as a pledge of the new rulers [William and Mary] that this tyrannical action should cease. The right declared was meant to be a strong moral check against the usurpation and arbitrary power of rulers, and as a necessary and efficient means of regaining rights when temporarily overturned by usurpation.

The Right is General.— . . . The meaning of the provision undoubtedly is, that the people, from whom the militia must be taken, shall have the right to keep and bear arms, and they need no permission or regulation of law for the purpose. But this enables the government to have a well regulated militia; for to bear arms implies something more than the mere keeping; it implies the learning to handle and use them in a way that makes those who keep them ready for their efficient use; in other words, it implies the right to meet for voluntary discipline in arms, observing in doing so the laws of public order.

*Standing Army.—*A further purpose of this amendment is, to preclude any necessity or reasonable excuse for keeping a standing army. A standing army is condemned by the traditions and sentiments of the people, as being dangerous to the liberties of the people as the general preparation of the people for the defence of their institutions with arms is preservative of them.

*What Arms may be kept.—*The arms intended by the Constitution are such as are suitable for the general defence of the community against invasion or oppression, and the secret carrying of those suited merely to deadly individual encounters may be prohibited.

Opinion in *United States v. Schwimmer,* 1929

The common defense was one of the purposes for which the people ordained and established the Constitution. It empowers Congress to provide for such defense, to declare war, to raise and support armies, to maintain a navy, to make rules for the government and regulation of the land and naval forces, to provide for organizing, arming, and disciplining the militia, and for calling it forth to execute the laws of the Union, suppress insurrections and repel invasions; it makes the President commander in chief of the army and navy and of the militia of the several states when called into the service of the United States. . . .

Concurrence in *Printz v. United States,* 1997

The Court today properly holds that the Brady Act violates the Tenth Amendment in that it compels state law enforcement officers to "administer or enforce a federal regulatory program." . . .

Dissent in *Muscarello v. United States,* 1998

[The question in the case involved a definition of the phrase "carry a firearm" and whether that definition applied only to the carrying of a firearm on a person or also included the "carrying" of a firearm in a car. The majority opinion agreed that the term, *carrying,* applied only to the carrying on a person.]

At issue here is not "carries" but "carries a firearm." . . . Surely a most familiar meaning is, as the Constitution's Second Amendment ("Keep and bear Arms") and Black's Law Dictionary, at 214, indicate: "wear, bear, or carry . . . upon the person or in the clothing or in a pocket, for the purpose . . . of being armed and ready for offensive or defensive action in a case of conflict with another person."

From *American Constitutional Law*, Laurence Tribe, 2000

Perhaps the most accurate conclusion one can reach with any confidence is that the core meaning of the Second Amendment is a populist/republican/federalism one: Its central object is to arm "We the People" so that ordinary citizens can participate in the collective defense of their community and their state. But it does so not through directly protecting a right on the part of the states or other collectivities, assertable by them against the federal government, to arm the populace as they see fit. Rather the amendment achieves its central purpose by assuring that the federal government may not disarm individual citizens without some unusually strong justification consistent with the authority of the states to organize their own militias. That assurance in turn is provided through recognizing a right (admittedly of uncertain scope) on the part of individuals to possess and use firearms in defense of themselves and their homes—not a right to hunt for game, quite clearly, and certainly not a right to employ firearms to commit aggressive acts against other persons—a right that directly limits action by Congress or by the Executive Branch and may well, in addition, be among the privileges or immunities of United States citizens protected by Sec. 1 of the Fourteenth Amendment against state or local government action.

1. What do you think was the purpose of the Militia Act of 1792?

2. Why do you think public officials were exempt from the requirements of the Militia Act of 1792?

3. What is currently considered to be part of the militia?

4. What are the types of militia, and of what does each consist?

5. What does Cooley say is the purpose of the Second Amendment?

6. What does Cooley say about a standing army?

7. For what reason may arms be kept?

8. In *Schwimmer*, what does the Supreme Court say is the purpose of the Second Amendment?

9. In *Printz*, why did the Court hold that the Brady Act violated the Tenth Amendment?

10. In *Muscarello*, how did the Court define the "carrying of firearms"?

11. What does Tribe say is the central purpose of the Second Amendment?

Lesson 14
Due Process: Criminal Law

Objective
- To learn and apply in context a variety of terms related to due process in criminal proceedings

Notes to the Teacher
James Madison wrote, "In Europe, charters of liberty have been granted by power. America has set the example . . . of charters of power granted by liberty." Thomas Jefferson remarked that "a bill of rights is what the people are entitled to against every government on earth, general or particular, and what no just government should refuse, or rest on inference" and later stated to Madison that the purpose of a bill of rights was "the legal check which it puts into the hands of the judiciary." As such, a judiciary protects the people against abuses by other branches of the government. In *The Federalist* (Number 78), Alexander Hamilton concurred with his two colleagues: "The complete independence of the courts is peculiarly essential in a limited Constitution. . . . Without this, all the reservations of particular rights or privileges would amount to nothing."

Twelve of the twenty-seven amendments to the Constitution deal with rights—the first ten as contained in the Bill of Rights as well as the Reconstruction amendments, numbers thirteen and fourteen. The amendments define both the procedure and substance of rights and influence a culture that is diverse in its religion, political philosophies, and means of self-expression. The amendments have shaped for Americans the underlying assumptions upon which they think and act. The judiciary interprets and protects an individual's rights, even when those individuals are accused of criminal acts.

Since 1947, the Supreme Court has ruled several times on the rights of the accused. States are bound to abide by the key components of the Bill of Rights. And phrases such as "read him his rights" or "you have the right to remain silent" have become commonplace.

The Fourteenth Amendment protects a citizen's right to due process and from the arbitrary acts of government. Unlike the Bill of Rights, which focuses on the scope and substance of protection, in the Fourteenth Amendment, the aim is to protect the procedure itself. Due process is important in both criminal and civil law. To assure due process with regard to liberty, it refers to both civil endeavors, such as pursuing a career, marriage, family, or a contract, and criminal safeguards, such as a fair trial. The Supreme Court reviews laws that restrict these fundamental nonprocedural rights as substantive due process.

The source of due process can be traced from English history to early American colonial history. The Magna Carta guaranteed that no freeman could be imprisoned without being tried by a jury of his peers. Colonial law also defined the fact of due process as the law of the land. The Fifth Amendment states that a person may not be deprived of basic essential rights without due process. The Fourteenth Amendment carries this further and extends the requirement to state and local governments. The Supreme Court has strengthened these amendments by ruling that the government must act fairly and not arbitrarily, capriciously, or unreasonably.

In this lesson, students define and apply terms associated with criminal due process and examine the procedure guaranteed a person accused of criminal activity. Students conclude by role-playing the due process procedure.

Procedure
1. Distribute **Handout 27**, and have students complete it for homework. Review students' responses.

   Suggested Responses:

   Part A.

   bail—*money posted by the accused to insure that he or she will appear in court at the appointed time*

   capital punishment—*death penalty*

   contempt of court—*violation of court order or disruption of courtroom proceedings*

   cruel and unusual punishment—*harsh or barbaric punishment*

double jeopardy—*subjecting a suspect to more than one trial for the same offense*

due process of law—*a variety of constitutional guarantees that individuals cannot be deprived of their inalienable rights without fair and reasonable court procedures*

exclusionary rule—*requirement that evidence must be obtained properly to be admissible in court*

ex post facto law—*criminal law applied retroactively to the disadvantage of the accused*

grand jury—*body of jurors who determine whether or not there is sufficient evidence to charge a person and bring him or her to trial*

writ of habeas corpus—*court order requiring law enforcement officials to explain to the court why an individual should not be released from custody*

indictment—*a formal charge brought by the grand jury*

petit jury—*a group of citizens who hear evidence in a case and arrive at a verdict*

Miranda rule—*requirement that a person accused of a crime be informed of his or her rights when arrested*

probable cause—*reliable evidence that a crime has been committed*

right of confrontation—*right of the accused to face and question witnesses testifying against him or her*

right to compel witnesses—*right of the court to force witnesses to testify in court*

right to counsel—*the right of the accused to expert legal representation*

self-incrimination—*testimony against oneself*

speedy and public trial—*open trial conducted without undue delays*

search warrant—*document giving police permission to search and seize property*

Part B.

1. *exclusionary rule*
2. *cruel and unusual punishment*
3. *right to confrontation*
4. *bail*
5. *probable cause*
6. *self-incrimination*
7. *grand jury*
8. *search warrant*
9. *speedy and public trial*
10. *ex post facto law*
11. *double jeopardy*
12. *indictment*
13. *right to counsel*
14. *writ of habeas corpus*
15. *contempt of court*
16. *due process of law*
17. *right to compel testimony*
18. *capital punishment*
19. *petit jury*
20. *Miranda rule*

2. Distribute **Handout 28**, and have students complete it as directed. Review students' responses.

Suggested Responses

Part A.

a. 7
b. 3
c. 1
d. 5
e. 2
f. 6
g. 4

Part B.

1. *probable cause*
2. *search warrant*
3. *Miranda rule*
4. *right to counsel*
5. *writ of habeas corpus*
6. *bail*
7. *grand jury*

8. *indictment*

9. *speedy and public trial*

10. *exclusionary rule*

11. *ex post facto law*

12. *contempt of court*

13. *capital punishment*

14. *self-incrimination*

15. *cruel and unusual punishment*

3. Have students role-play the due process procedure.

Enrichment/Extension

Have students search current newspapers and magazines for articles about cases that deal with procedural due process. The articles can be the basis of a classroom bulletin board display on due process.

Due Process in Criminal Proceedings

Part A.

Using a separate sheet of paper, define each of the following terms.

bail	indictment
capital punishment	petit jury
contempt of court	Miranda rule
cruel and unusual punishment	probable cause
double jeopardy	right of confrontation
due process of law	right to compel witnesses to testify
exclusionary rule	right to counsel
ex post facto law	search warrant
grand jury	self-incrimination
writ of habeas corpus	speedy and public trial

Part B.

Each of the following statements describes the importance of one of the terms from the list in part A. Write the appropriate term in the blank.

_____ 1. Evidence must be properly obtained in order to be used in court.

_____ 2. Our society no longer condones the barbaric punishments of earlier eras.

_____ 3. Unknown persons cannot present secret accusations against a citizen.

_____ 4. The accused is entitled to be released upon the posting of a cash or property bond to guarantee he or she will appear in court.

_____ 5. In order to prevent the development of a police state, the police must have a reason for detaining a person.

_____ 6. A person cannot be forced to give testimony that might lead to his or her own conviction.

_____ 7. The state needs to determine whether or not there is sufficient evidence against the accused to justify the cost and inconvenience of a trial.

_____ 8. Police cannot search a person or a person's property without probable cause or without permission of the court.

_____ 9. The accused is guaranteed the right to an open trial conducted without undue delay.

_____ 10. The state cannot punish an individual by enacting a law after a crime has been committed.

_____ 11. People judged innocent should no longer be harassed by the state for the same charge.

_____ 12. Only after the grand jury has determined that there is sufficient evidence can the state charge an individual with a crime.

_____ 13. The accused is guaranteed the right to a competent defense.

_____ 14. Unless the state is restricted, it could incarcerate an individual without trial forever.

_____ 15. Failure to follow court guidelines may result in a defendant, his counsel, the prosecutor, or witnesses being jailed. At trial, the state must adhere to specific guidelines from arrest to sentencing.

_____ 16. An individual is entitled to fair and reasonable court procedures from arrest to trial.

_____ 17. The court has the right to force uncooperative witnesses to testify.

_____ 18. Some states use the death penalty to deter others from performing violent crimes.

_____ 19. Judgment by one's peers is perceived to offer the fairest form of justice.

_____ 20. The individual should understand that one need not incriminate himself or herself and may have the counsel of a lawyer.

The Basic Steps of Criminal Due Process

Part A.

Listed below are the basic steps in criminal due process. Write *1* next to the first logical step, *2* next to the second step, and so on through the steps in the criminal process.

_____   a. The accused appeals the sentence.

_____   b. The accused is indicted.

_____   c. The accused is arrested.

_____   d. The accused receives the verdict.

_____   e. The accused is informed of the right to counsel and of the right to remain silent.

_____   f. The accused receives the sentence.

_____   g. The accused is tried by a jury.

Part B.

Complete the following story of an individual accused of a crime by filling in each blank with an appropriate term from the following list.

bail	indictment
capital punishment	petit jury
contempt of court	Miranda rule
cruel and unusual punishment	probable cause
double jeopardy	right of confrontation
due process of law	right to compel witnesses to testify
exclusionary rule	right to counsel
ex post facto law	search warrant
grand jury	self-incrimination
writ of habeas corpus	speedy and public trial

On June 3, Mr. Wonnell arrived at home, only to find two policemen at his door. Because of his previous criminal record, the police assumed that a recent rash of burglaries, one resulting in a death, was his doing. They believed they had 1. _____ to question him. They had a/an 2. _____ to search his house and, in the search, found some of the stolen items. They also found some drugs and took them along as evidence. Mr. Wonnell was read his 3. _____ . The police took

Mr. Wonnell to the station where he was locked up but given 4. _____

_____ and was permitted to call his lawyer.

Miss Young, the defense attorney, presented a/an 5._____ ,

and Mr. Wonnell was released, but not until he had paid 6. _____.

The next week, Miss Young represented Mr. Wonnell at his arraignment, and a hearing was set

up with a/an 7. _____ . The result of the hearing was that a/an

8. _____ was issued and Mr. Wonnell had to stand trial. Miss

Young insisted that justice would be done only through a/an 9. _____ ,

but a new and stronger state law, just passed that week, made possession of the amount of

drugs found in Mr. Wonnell's home a felony, so his troubles mounted.

In court, Miss Young argued that using the drugs as evidence in court violated the

10. _____ and the new law did not apply to Mr. Wonnell because

it was an example of a/an 11. _____ . The judge agreed.

At one point in the trial, Mr. Wonnell jumped up and argued with the judge; he was told

to be quiet or be held in 12. _____ . Mr. Wonnell feared a stiff

sentence, perhaps even 13. _____ if he were found guilty. Mr.

Wonnell refused to answer some questions about the evidence, claiming his right to avoid

14. _____ . Mr. Wonnell was found guilty of the robberies and

sentenced to ten years in prison, a sentence that was not 15. _____ ,

since it was appropriate for the seriousness of the crime committed.

Lesson 15
Due Process: Civil Law

Objective
- To understand how the concept of due process applies to property rights

Notes to the Teacher
Civil, or noncriminal cases, involve disputes between two individuals, two groups, or between an individual or group and the government. Such cases often involve disputes over property. Property, from a legal viewpoint, refers to ownership and use of land, buildings, or other tangible goods and to intangible property, such as employment, welfare entitlement, or unemployment compensation. Under the Constitution, both state and federal courts are obligated to apply principles of due process in civil proceedings. Cases proceed through either the state or federal court system, depending upon whether state or federal issues are at stake.

Passed during Reconstruction, the Thirteenth Amendment abolished all vestiges of slavery, while the purpose of the Fourteenth Amendment was to solve all problems not solved by the Thirteenth. Many believed the aim of the Reconstruction amendments was to raise African Americans to full legal and social equality and to transform the political landscape of the nation. There was a need to define equal protection under the law as it applied to newly free slaves.

The interpretation of the Fourteenth Amendment is based on intent. Prior to the 1960s, conservatives said that the authors of the amendment did not intend to outlaw segregation; therefore, the amendment could be used as the basis for further legal challenges in an attempt to broaden the rights of some. However, liberals interpreted the amendment to support the idea that the authors did intend to outlaw segregation and that the amendment could be extended beyond its Reconstruction-era intent. Suffragists attempted to remove the words *men* and *male* from the proposed amendment prior to its passage, but failed. Susan B. Anthony attempted to use the Fourteenth Amendment as a defense in her trial for attempting to vote in Rochester, New York, in 1872. Today, the Fourteenth Amendment is used to guarantee the rights of citizenship and equal protection under the law to all Americans.

In this lesson, students are introduced to the basics of property rights and due process. Students define terms associated with civil due process, examine the rights guaranteed in the Fifth and Fourteenth Amendments, and analyze a series of situations associated with civil due process. Students write and share a paragraph explaining the civil protections given to citizens under the Fifth and Fourteenth Amendments.

Procedure
1. Distribute **Handout 29,** and have students complete it for homework. Review students' responses to part A.

    Suggested Responses:

    civil law—*noncriminal proceedings*

    plaintiff—*party initiating legal action*

    defendant—*party being accused or sued*

    federal district court—*lowest court in the federal system*

    federal appellate court—*federal court that hears appeals from federal district courts*

    state appellate court—*a court that hears appeals from lower state or local courts*

    state supreme court—*highest state court*

    eminent domain—*right of the government to purchase private property at a fair price for a public purpose*

    class action suit—*a lawsuit initiated by a group of persons*

    reverse a decision—*action of an appellate court to overturn the decision of a lower court*

    statutory law—*a law made by federal, state, or local legislative bodies*

    constitutional law—*a law resulting from the contents of the Constitution*

2. Explain that the Fifth and Fourteenth Amendments to the Constitution guarantee individuals the right to property, which

may not be taken away from them without due process. Stress that the civil process in the United States is governed by many of the same rules as the criminal process, but the burden of proof in a civil trial is more lenient than that in a criminal trial. A plaintiff in a civil case does not have to prove that the defendant is guilty beyond a reasonable doubt. Review students' responses to **Handout 29,** part B.

Suggested Responses:

Amendment V

capital; crime; indictment; grand jury; cases; militia; war; public danger; subject; twice; jeopardy; himself; life; liberty; property; due process; law; private; public; compensation

Amendment XIV

born; naturalized; jurisdiction; citizens; state; reside; enforce; law; abridge; immunities; deprive; life; liberty; property; due process; law; deny; jurisdiction; equal protection

3. Divide the class into eight groups, and distribute **Handout 30**. Assign one situation to each group. Instruct students that each group is to read the scenario and determine the plaintiff(s), defendant(s), the issue in the case, a probable decision, and a reason for that decision. Each group is to prepare a five-minute presentation on its case. Have students evaluate the constitutionality of the decisions reached by each group.

Suggested Responses:

Situation A

Plaintiff—*group of farmers*

Defendant—*U.S. Department of Transportation*

Issue—*eminent domain*

Probable decision—*against the farmers*

Reason—*Eminent domain places the rights of the many over the rights of the few.*

Situation B

Plaintiff—*citizen group*

Defendant—*automobile company*

Issue—*class action suit over warranty protection on cars*

Probable decision—*some sort of compensation to individuals claiming damages*

Reason—*Government will likely support plaintiffs' claim that warranty protection should provide meaningful coverage.*

Situation C

Plaintiff—*man whose benefits were cut off*

Defendant—*welfare department official*

Issue—*what constitutes property with guarantee of due process*

Probable decision—*in favor of plaintiff*

Reason—*The Supreme Court in recent years has extended the meaning of "property" to include such items as welfare benefits and unemployment compensation.*

Situation D

Plaintiff—*shipping clerk*

Defendant—*employer at brush company*

Issue—*meaning of property and extent to which due process applies in this situation*

Probable decision—*for the plaintiff*

Reason—*Recent Supreme Court decisions have defined employment as a type of property.*

Situation E

Plaintiff—*city butchers*

Defendant—*city slaughterhouse*

Issue—*the rights protecting citizens under the Fourteenth Amendment*

Probable decision—*It would seem that the butchers have the better claim because of the equal protection clause, but the ruling favored the slaughterhouse company and the state of Louisiana.*

Reason—*The butchers believed they were deprived of the privileges and immunities guaranteed to citizens under the Fourteenth Amendment. The Court ruled that the amendment gave no federal protection to the rights associated with state citizenship. Federal protection was distinct from state law.*

Situation F

Plaintiff—*the Lochner brothers*

Defendant—*State of New York*

Issue—*the constitutionality of the due process and privileges and immunities clauses in the Fourteenth Amendment*

Probable decision—*for the plaintiff*

Reason—*The Court applied the idea of liberty of contract, which was considered a fundamental right, and struck down the maximum hours law.*

Situation G

Plaintiff—*West Coast Hotel Company*

Defendant—*State of Washington*

Issue—*minimum wage imposed in the state of Washington*

Probable decision—*in favor of the state of Washington*

Reason—*A prior case ruling stated that the setting of minimum wages for women and minors violated the Fifth amendment's due process clause. The Supreme Court supported the Washington law and forced businesses and corporations to abide by state law.*

Situation H

Plaintiff—*Mrs. Jabrowski and others*

Defendant—*City of Detroit*

Issue—*the right of the city to impose eminent domain for the purpose of development*

Probable decision—*in favor of the city*

Reason—*The Court ruled that the individual had to yield his or her property for the general comfort and protection of the community. The principle of democracy known as majority rule forced the people in the neighborhood, who were in the minority, to give way to the will and benefit of the majority.*

4. Have students write a paragraph on civil law and due process. The paragraph should explain the civil protections given to citizens under the Fifth and Fourteenth Amendments to the Constitution. Have students include all the following terms: *civil law,* *tangible property, intangible property, due process of law, plaintiff, defendant, eminent domain,* and *class action suit.* Select students to share their paragraphs.

Suggested Response:

Civil law concerns noncriminal proceedings, such as those involving conflict over property. Property may be either real, tangible property or intangible benefits, such as welfare entitlement, unemployment compensation, or a job. In recent years, individual plaintiffs and groups bringing class action suits against defendants, involving the extension of the meaning of "property," have often found the Supreme Court supportive of their cause. However, the government retains its constitutional right to purchase private property for a public purpose through its power of eminent domain.

Enrichment/Extension

Have students monitor cases before the U.S. Supreme Court that deal with civil due process and at a later date report on how the Court's ruling has changed the interpretation of the Fifth or Fourteenth Amendment.

The Basics of Property Rights and Civil Due Process

Part A.

Use your textbook or a dictionary to find the meaning of each of the following terms. Write the definitions on a separate sheet of paper.

civil law	federal appellate court	class action suit
plaintiff	state appellate court	reverse a decision
defendant	state supreme court	statutory law
federal district court	eminent domain	constitutional law

Part B.

Read the Fifth and Fourteenth Amendments in your textbook, and fill in the blanks below. Then summarize each amendment in one sentence.

Amendment 5

No person shall be held to answer for a _____, or otherwise infamous _____, unless on a presentment or _____ of a _____, except in _____ arising in the land or naval forces, or in the _____, when in actual service in time of _____ or _____; nor shall any person be _____ for the same offence to be _____ put in _____ of life or limb, nor shall be compelled in any criminal case to be a witness against _____, nor deprived of _____, _____, or _____, without _____ of _____; nor shall _____ property be taken for _____ use without just _____.

Summary: _____

Amendment 14

All persons _____ or _____ in the United States and subject to the _____ thereof, are _____ of the United States and of the _____ wherein they _____. No state shall make or _____ any _____ which shall _____ the privileges or _____ of citizens of the United States, nor shall any state _____ any person of _____, _____, or ____ _____, without _____ of _____; nor _____ to any person within its _____ the _____ of the laws.

Summary: _____

Due Process of Law: Property Rights

Each group has been assigned one of the following situations. Read the situation carefully, and apply the questions that follow to your assigned case. Refer to the Fifth and Fourteenth Amendments. Prepare a five-minute presentation about your case. Listen as each case is presented. Evaluate all the situations, including the one in which you participate.

- Who is the plaintiff?
- Who is the defendant?
- What is the main issue in the case?
- What was the probable decision?
- Why did the court rule as it did?

Situation A

A small group of citizens from Pine Corners organized to prevent the U.S. Department of Transportation from constructing an interstate highway through part of their township. Two farmers will be forced to sell their property to the government. They contend this will ruin their careers as farmers. One objects on the grounds that his family has lived on that property for three generations. The citizens sue the Department of Transportation and claim the highway should be rerouted. The government claims the right of eminent domain.

Situation B

A group of citizens from various states has decided to sue an automobile company. The citizens complain that the company built cars with defective engines that had to be replaced shortly after the cars' warranties expired. The citizens advertised in newspapers and found dozens of other persons wishing to participate in the suit. This action reduced the number of cases to be litigated.

Situation C

A man challenged a welfare official's decision to cut off his welfare benefits for allegedly refusing to accept counseling and rehabilitation for drug addiction. The man argued that he did not use drugs and decided to take his case to court. The public official argued in court that welfare entitlements are not property and, therefore, due process did not apply in this case.

Situation D

A shipping clerk at a brush company is dismissed from his job after a short probationary period. He believes that he lost his job because of his physical handicap—one of his legs is shorter than the other. He sues his employer in court, charging that he has been denied property without due process of law.

Situation E

It is 1869, and the Louisiana state legislature has granted a twenty-five-year monopoly to a company to sell meat to a small exclusive group in the city of New Orleans. Other butchers in the city claim that the monopoly allows the company to sell meat at the expense of all other butchers. They claim that they cannot practice their trade, exercise their livelihood, support their families, or provide meat for a large percentage of the city's population. The city of New Orleans, the state of Louisiana, and the City Slaughter House Company argue that the statute does not block butchers from their trade but merely charges a fee of butchers to use their slaughterhouse.

Situation F

It is 1905, and the Lochner brothers own a New York bakery. Baking requires long hours, seven days a week, in order to produce homemade buns, breads, and other baked goods. Sometimes employees at the Lochners' bakery work twelve to fourteen hours a day, and often as much as sixty to seventy hours a week. The state of New York has passed a law limiting work hours to a ten-hour work day and a sixty-hour week. The brothers were arrested, charged, and convicted under the new law. They want to appeal. The state argues that while workers desire good wages and long hours, they also need reasonable working conditions.

Situation G

It is 1937, during the Great Depression. The owner of the West Coast Hotel Company in the state of Washington knows that the best way of making money from the business is to keep overhead low. His largest expense is employee salaries and benefits, so he tries to keep wages low. The state of Washington has passed a minimum wage law that affects most of his employees, the majority of whom are women or minors. He contested the law as unconstitutional in a local court. He has appealed to the Washington Supreme Court.

Situation H

It is 1980, and Mrs. Jabrowski, an elderly woman, has lived in the same Detroit neighborhood for seventy-five years. Her mother and father also lived there. General Motors and the City of Detroit want to raze her neighborhood in order to build a new factory. The city says that it wants to promote new businesses and increase tax income. City officials defend the action by stating that the new plant would employ over six thousand people and that eminent domain allowed the city to seize the properties. The residents say they cannot place a value on their memories. They argue that eminent domain does not apply in this case, because a private company would benefit from the seizures, rather than the city government, which would benefit only indirectly.

Lesson 16

Equal Protection under the Law: The Civil Rights Act of 1964

Objectives

- To evaluate the Civil Rights Act of 1964 and its legacy

- To determine whether the Civil Rights Act of 1964 achieved its goal of equal protection under the law

Notes to the Teacher

When the Supreme Court announced its decision in *Plessy v. Ferguson* in 1896, the concept of separate but equal, or legal segregation, became the law of the land. Southern states took immediate steps to enact Jim Crow laws. Unfortunately, facilities for African Americans were almost always of inferior quality. In the years after World War II, pressures mounted for change.

In 1954, the decision in *Brown v. Board of Education of Topeka* overturned *Plessy v. Ferguson* and proclaimed that separate educational facilities are inherently unequal and clearly violate the Fourteenth Amendment guarantees of equal protection of the laws. Despite the Supreme Court's proclamation that desegregation of public schools should proceed with all deliberate speed, few schools were desegregated in the ensuing decade. Other public facilities also remained segregated. By the early 1960s, civil rights activists began staging sit-ins, freedom rides, and marches to focus public attention on the injustices of segregation. John F. Kennedy was sympathetic, and proposed major civil rights legislation. In 1964, after President Kennedy's death, Lyndon Johnson secured passage of the Civil Rights Act.

An omnibus bill, the Civil Rights Act dealt with several major issues and provided new methods of enforcement. Major provisions include the following:

- Title I restricted, but did not eliminate, literacy tests as a condition for voting. This portion of the act was further strengthened by the Voting Rights Act of 1965.

- Titles II and III forbade discrimination in public accommodations and public facilities.

- Title IV required public elementary and secondary schools to enforce integration.

- Title V established a Commission on Civil Rights.

- Title VI required nondiscrimination in federally-assisted programs.

- Title VII prohibited discriminatory practices by most employers, employment agencies, and labor unions.

The Equal Employment Opportunity Commission was given the authority to end discrimination in America's workplace. It enforces laws that prohibit discrimination based on race, color, religion, gender, national origin, disability, or age in hiring, firing, setting wages, testing, training, apprenticeship, and all other terms and conditions of employment. The EEOC uses its investigative powers, conciliation programs, lawsuits, and voluntary assistance programs to address the question of fairness. President Lyndon B. Johnson required all executive agencies, when hiring employees, to abide by the criteria set down in the Act.

In this lesson, students assess the success of the Civil Rights Act of 1964, complete a chart on civil rights legislation since 1964, and write a short report on a current application of one of the sections of the act.

Procedure

1. Have students research and define the following terms:

   Plessy v. Ferguson (1896)—*defined the term* separate but equal

   separate but equal—*segregation was acceptable as long as the facilities provided were equal*

   Jim Crow laws—*laws in America's South that created separate facilities for whites and African Americans*

121

Brown v. Board of Education of Topeka (1954)—overturned Plessy v. Ferguson and declared segregation in the South to be unconstitutional

2. Distribute **Handout 31**, and have students read the document silently. Ask them for the main idea in each section. Write the main idea on the chalkboard or on an overhead transparency.

Suggested Responses:

Title I—*did not abolish literacy tests; stated that voter registration requirements must be applied equally to all*

Title II—*outlawed discrimination in places of public accommodation engaged in interstate commerce, such as hotels, motels, restaurants, and theaters (A loophole exempted private clubs.)*

Title III—*ordered the desegregation of public facilities*

Title IV—*authorized the U.S. Attorney General to file suit to desegregate public schools, but did not authorize busing as a means of overcoming de facto segregation*

Title V—*authorized the withdrawal of federal funds from programs that practiced discrimination*

Title VI—*prohibited discrimination in federally assisted programs*

Title VII—*created the Equal Employment Opportunity Commission to review complaints of discrimination in the workplace; outlawed discrimination in businesses that employed more than twenty-five people*

3. Have students examine the results of civil rights acts in America today. Ask students for examples which today reflect federal regulation under the Civil Rights Act of 1964. Have students write a short essay on the following topic: Are the rights of minorities better protected today than in 1964? Explain.

Enrichment/Extension

Have students research and report on the effects today of *Brown v. the Board of Education of Topeka*.

Equality under the Law: The Civil Rights Act of 1964

Part A.

Read the following excerpts from the Civil Rights Act of 1964. Then summarize the main idea of each section in one or two sentences. Give an example of how that section of the act is applied today.

Title I. Voting Rights

(2) No person acting under the color of law shall—

(A) in determining whether any individual is qualified under State law or law to vote in any Federal election, apply any standard, practice, or procedure different from the standards, practices, or procedures applied under such law or laws to other individuals within the same county, parish, or similar political subdivision who have been found by State officials to be qualified to vote. . . .

(C) employ any literacy test as a qualification for voting in any Federal election unless (i) such test is administered to each individual and is conducted wholly in writing. . . .

(3) (b) . . . any person who has not been adjudged an incompetent and who has completed the sixth grade in a public school in, or a private school accredited by, any State or territory, the District of Columbia, or the Commonwealth of Puerto Rico where instruction is carried on predominantly in the English language, possesses sufficient literacy, comprehension, and intelligence to vote in any Federal election.

Title II. Injunctive Relief against Discrimination in Places of Public Accommodation

Sec. 201.　(a) All persons shall be entitled to the full and equal enjoyment of goods, services, facilities, privileges, advantages, and accommodations of any place of public accommodation, as defined in this section, without discrimination or segregation or the ground of race, color, religion, or national origin.

(b) Each of the following establishments which serves the public is a place of public accommodation within the meaning of this title if its operations affect commerce, or if discrimination or segregation by it is supported by State action:

(1) any inn, hotel, motel, or other establishment which provides lodging to transient guests, other than an establishment located within a building which contains not more than five rooms for rent or hire and which is actually occupied by the proprietor of such establishment as his residence;

(2) any restaurant, cafeteria, lunchroom, lunch counter, soda fountain, or the facility principally engaged in selling food for consumption on the premises, including but not limited to, any such facility located on the premises of any retail establishment; or any gas station;

(3) any motion picture house, theater, concert hall, sports arena, stadium or other place of exhibition or entertainment; . . .

(4) (e) The provisions of this title shall not apply to a private club or other establishment not in fact open to the public. . . .

Title III. Desegregation of Public Facilities

Sec. 301.   (a)   Whenever the Attorney General receives a complaint in writing . . . that a person is being deprived of or threatened with the loss of his right to the equal protection of the laws, on account of his race, color, religion, or national origin, by being denied equal utilization of any public facility which is owned, operated, or managed by or on behalf of any State . . . other than a public school or public college . . . and the Attorney General believes the complaint is meritorious . . . [he] is authorized to institute for or in the name of the United States a civil action . . . against such parties. . . .

          (b)   . . . [The Attorney General may intervene] when such person or persons are unable . . . to bear the expense of the litigation or to obtain effective legal representation; or whenever he is satisfied that the institution of such litigation would jeopardize the personal safety, employment, or economic standing of such person or persons, their families, or their property.

Title IV. Desegregation of Public Education

Sec. 401.   (b)   "Desegregation" means the assignment of students to public schools and within such schools without regard to their race, color, religion, or national origin, but "desegregation" shall not mean the assignment of students to public schools in order to overcome racial imbalance.

          (c)   "Public school" means any elementary or secondary educational institution, and "public college" means any institution of higher education or any technical or vocational school above the secondary school level . . . operated wholly or predominantly from or through the use of governmental funds or property, of funds or property derived from a governmental source.

Title V. Commission on Civil Rights

Sec. 104.   (a)   The Commission shall—

          (1)   investigate allegations in writing under oath or affirmation that certain citizens of the United States are being deprived of their right to vote and have that vote counted by reason of their color, race, religion, or national origin . . . ;

          (2)   study and collect information concerning legal developments constituting a denial of equal protection of the laws under the Constitution because of race, color, religion or national origin or in the administration of justice;

          (3)   appraise the laws and policies of the Federal Government with respect to denials of equal protection of the laws under the Constitution because of race, color, religion or national origin or in the administration of justice;

(4) serve as a national clearinghouse for information in respect to denials of equal protection of the laws because of race, color, religion or national origin, including but not limited to the fields of voting, education, housing, employment, the use of public facilities, and transportation, or in the administration of justice;

(5) investigate allegations, made in writing and under oath or affirmation, that citizens of the United States are unlawfully being accorded or denied the right to vote, or to have their votes properly counted, in any election of presidential electors, Members of the United States Senate, or of the House of Representatives, as a result of any patterns or practice of fraud or discrimination in the conduct of such election; . . .

Title VI. Nondiscrimination in Federally Assisted Programs

Sec. 601. No person in the United States shall, on the grounds of race, color, or national origin, be excluded from participation in, be denied the benefits of, or be subjected to discrimination under any program or activity receiving Federal financial assistance. . . .

Title VII. Equal Employment Opportunity

Sec. 703. (a) It shall be an unlawful employment practice for an employer—

(1) to fail or refuse to hire or to discharge any individual, or otherwise discriminate against any individual with respect to his compensation, terms, conditions, or privileges of employment, because of such individual's race, color, religion, sex, or national origin; or

(2) to limit, segregate, or classify his employees in any way which would deprive or tend to deprive any individual of employment opportunities or otherwise adversely affect his status as an employee, because of such individual's race, color, religion, sex, or national origin.

(b) It shall be an unlawful employment practice for any employment agency to fail or refuse to refer for employment, or otherwise discriminate against, any individual because of his race, color, religion, sex, or national origin, or to classify or refer for employment any individual on the basis of his race, color, religion, sex, or national origin.

(c) It shall be an unlawful employment practice for a labor organization—

(1) to exclude or to expel from its membership, or otherwise to discriminate against, any individual because of his race, color, religion, sex, or national origin;

(2) to limit, segregate, or classify its membership, or to classify or fail or refuse to refer for employment any individual, in any way which would deprive or tend to deprive any individual of employment opportunities, or would limit such employment opportunities or

otherwise adversely affect his status as an employee or as an applicant for employment, because of such individual's race, color, religion, sex, or national origin; or

(3)   to cause or attempt to cause an employer to discriminate against an individual in violation of this section. . . .

Part 3
The Legislative Branch

    This section examines the makeup of Congress, the organization and function of each house, the legislative functions of Congress, and its role as a watchdog of government agencies. Lesson 17 examines the composition of Congress as a representative body and evaluates whether the Congress of the United States truly represents the people. Lesson 18 helps students to recognize the differences, in organization and authority, between the House of Representatives and the Senate. Lesson 19 develops an understanding of the role played by the leaders of Congress and gives students an opportunity to research the role played by their congressional representative in the current session of Congress. Lesson 20 develops an understanding of the process by which a bill becomes a law. Lesson 21 evaluates the efficiency of the congressional workload. Lesson 22 analyzes the provisions of the North American Free Trade Agreement. Lesson 23 helps to develop an understanding of the power Congress wields through its right of investigation.

Lesson 17
Our Congressional Representatives

Objectives
- To examine the composition of Congress as a representative governmental body

- To evaluate whether the Congress of the United States is representative of the people

Notes to the Teacher

The basis of our American governmental system is a republic and illustrates the concept of representative democracy. The bedrock of a republican government is a popularly elected legislature. Early in our nation's history, state legislatures kept their constituencies small. Similarly, organization and yearly election assured faithful representation. The federal Constitution radically changed the practice. Article I stipulates that state electors will choose their representatives every two years and elect their senators without a direct vote of the people. Later changes in the Constitution extended the direct election of senators to the people. During the ratification debates, Anti-Federalists were critical of the House of Representatives on four key points: the people were underrepresented by having a large number of people represented by a small number of Congressmen; only the wealthy could be elected; the country was too diverse to be properly represented; and there was a possibility of corruption.

In practice, members of Congress are drawn from an elite segment of the population. Most are white, male, and Protestant. Most are lawyers or businessmen. Regardless of their background, they must be educated in order to deal with issues related to farming, poverty, civil rights, urban development, and foreign affairs—issues that reflect the needs of their constituents or national concerns, rather than their own interests.

In this lesson, students consider whether today's Congress adequately represents the interests of the people. After studying a chart profiling Congress, the jobs of Congressmen, and some typical issues facing Congress, students describe the qualities and characteristics of their ideal Congressman and evaluate the degree to which their own representative exemplifies those ideals.

Procedure

1. Have students review the minimal constitutional requirements for members of Congress. (*Representatives must be at least twenty-five years old, be a citizen of the United States for seven years, and live in the district they represent; senators must be at least thirty years old, be a citizen for at least nine years, and live in the state they represent.*)

2. Divide the class into pairs, and distribute **Handout 32**. Have students read the selections and answer the questions that follow. Review students' responses.

Suggested Responses:

1. *The assembly would not reflect the make-up of the country, which was diverse and had many different classes of people who should have the opportunity to elect individuals who would best represent them. Small numbers of representatives could not fairly represent the citizens. Small numbers of representatives would allow the wealthy to control the assembly and increase a chance of corruption and graft.*

2. *The assembly should be small enough to control and still best represent the interests of the people. It is possible that no two opinions will be the same. The representatives should represent the will of the people. Numbers have nothing to do with obtaining the confidence of the people; that rests with good administration. It is more difficult for corruption to take hold in a large district; in a small district, wealth could more easily influence a representative's vote.*

3. Distribute **Handout 33**. Have students examine and analyze the information contained in the tables. Then have students answer the questions.

Suggested Responses:

1. *Most of the members fall within the forty to fifty-nine age bracket. The percentage of members under the age of forty has fallen by 66 percent.*

129

2. *Events such as the Vietnam conflict, Civil Rights Movement, rise of the Religious Right, tensions and war in the Middle East, and a growing political polarization have resulted in changes in political alignment and how members of Congress approach issues and represent the views of their constituents. The members of Congress are a diverse group with a wide range of experience. Recent changes in rules governing the assignment of powerful committee chairmen have also influenced the actions of Congress. The political party that is in the majority controls the Congress. When a president is a member of the opposition, his plans and legislative agenda can become stalled or even destroyed.*

3. *Typical representatives are male, Protestant, white, Democrats, middle-aged, and lawyers or businessmen.*

4. *that they are well educated*

5. *the Democrats*

6. *Minorities are influential voting blocs. Attracting more of them can be accomplished by formulating party platforms to appeal to minority voters.*

4. Distribute **Handout 34**, and have students complete it as directed. Have students reach consensus on how each congressional representative might vote.

Suggested Responses:

1. *Students should see that party and national pressures may override the desire of constituents that the congressman oppose farm relief.*

2. *Students should see that the congressman would be under strong pressure to vote for a measure that would have direct financial impact on the district.*

5. Have students use the information they have gained in this lesson to answer the following questions:

- After considering the tasks a representative must complete, what are eight skills or qualities a congressman needs in order to do the job well?

- If you could have an ideal representative for your district, what are twelve essential characteristics, qualities, or traits of that person?

Allow time to review students' criteria. Encourage students to justify their choices.

Enrichment/Extension

Have students examine the voting record of local congressional representatives and senators and report on whether their stances on specific issues are consistent with the opinions of their constituents.

Anti-Federalist and Federalist Views of Congress

Read the following selections, and answer the questions.

Anti-Federalist Views

"Brutus"

. . . It must then have been intended, that those who are placed instead of the people, should possess their sentiments and feelings, and be governed by their interests, or, in other words, should bear the strongest resemblance of those in whose room they are substituted. It is obvious, that for an assembly to be a true likeness of the people of any country, they must be considerably numerous.—One man, or a few men, cannot possibly represent the feelings, opinions, and characters of a great multitude. In this respect, the new constitution is radically defective.—The house of assembly, which is intended as a representation of the people of America, will not, nor cannot, in the nature of things, be a proper one—sixty-five men cannot be found in the United States, who hold the sentiments, possess the feelings, or are acquainted with the wants and interests of this vast country. This extensive continent is made up of a number of different classes of people; and to have a proper representation of them, each class ought to have an opportunity of choosing their best informed men for the purpose; but this cannot possibly be the case in so small a number.

Delegates of the Pennsylvania Ratification Convention

Thus it appears that the liberties, happiness, interests, and great concerns of the whole United States, may be dependent upon the integrity, virtue, wisdom, and knowledge of twenty-five or twenty-six men—How unadequate and unsafe a representation! Inadequate, because the sense and views of three or four millions of people diffused over so extensive a territory comprising such various climates, products, habits, interests, and opinions, cannot be collected in so small a body; and besides, it is not a fair and equal representation of the people even in proportion to its number, for the smallest state has as much weight in the senate as the largest. . . .

Melancton Smith

Besides, the influence of the great [the wealthy] will generally enable them to succeed in elections. . . .

In so small a number of representatives, there is great danger from corruption and combination. A great politician has said that every man has his price. I hope this is not true in all its extent—But I ask the gentlemen to inform, what government there is, in which it has not been practised? . . .

Federalist Views of Congress

Robert R. Livingston

. . . It is agreed, that the representative body should be so small, as to prevent disorder inseparable from the deliberations of a mob; and yet sufficiently numerous, to represent the interests of the people; and to be a safe depository of power. There is, unfortunately, no standard, by which we can determine this matter. . . . Indeed, these effects depend so much upon contingency, and upon circumstances totally unconnected with the idea of number; that we ought not to be surprized at the want of a standing criterion. On so vague a subject, it is very possible that the opinions of no two gentlemen in this assembly, if they were governed by their own original reflections, would entirely coincide. I acknowledge myself one of those who suppose the number expressed in the constitution to be about the proper medium. . . . Some gentlemen suppose, that to understand and provide for the general interests of commerce, and manufactures, our legislatures ought to know how all commodities are produced, from the first principle of vegetation to the last polish of mechanical labour; that they ought to be minutely acquainted with all the process of all the arts. . . .

Alexander Hamilton

. . . It is the fortunate situation of our country, that the minds of the people are exceedingly enlightened and refined: Here than we may expect the laws to be proportionably agreeable to the standard of perfect policy; and the wisdom of public measures to consist with the most intimate conformity between the views of the representative and his constituent. If the general view of the people be for an increase, it undoubtedly must take place: They have it in their power to instruct their representatives; and the State Legislatures, which appoint the Senators, may enjoin it also upon them. . . .

It was remarked yesterday, that a numerous representation was necessary to obtain the confidence of the people. This is not generally true. The confidence of the people will easily be gained by a good administration. . . .

. . . The author reckons in the aristocracy, all governors of states, members of Congress, chief magistrates, and all officers of the militia—This description . . . is ridiculous. . . . Does the new government render a rich man more eligible than a poor one? No. It requires no such qualification. It is bottomed on the broad and equal principle of your state constitution. . . .

There is an advantage incident to large districts of election, which perhaps the gentlemen, amidst all their apprehensions of influence and bribery, have not adverted to. In large districts, the corruption of the electors is much more difficult:—Combinations for the purposes of intrigue are less easily formed: Factions and cabals are little known. In a small district, wealth will have a more complete influence; because the people in the vicinity of a great man, are more immediately his dependants. . . .

1. What do the Anti-Federalists regard as the greatest problem with the congressional structure?

2. How did the Federalists counter the Anti-Federalists' claims?

Profiling Congress

Use the following tables to help you answer the questions at the end of the handout.

Table 1. Members of Congress: Gender, Ethnicity, and Marital Status, 1971–2001

The House of Representatives

Congress	Female	African American	Hispanic	Not Married
92nd (1971)	12	12	5	26
95th (1977)	18	16	5	56
97th (1981)	19	16	6	86
100th (1987)	23	22	11	64
102nd (1991)	29	25	10	—
105th (1997)	51	37	18	—
107th (2001)	59	36	19	—

The Senate

Congress	Female	African American	Hispanic	Not Married
92nd (1971)	1	1	1	3
95th (1977)	0	1	0	9
97th (1981)	2	0	0	7
100th (1987)	2	0	0	11
102nd (1991)	2	0	0	—
105th (1997)	9	1	0	—
107th (2001)	13	0	0	—

Source: *Vital Statistics on American Politics, 2001–2002,* Harold W. Stanley and Richard G. Niemi (Washington, D.C.: Congressional Quarterly, 2001), 203.

Table 2. Age of Congressional Representatives, 1971–2001

The House of Representatives

Congress	Under 40	40–49	50–59	60–69	70–79	Over 80
92nd (1971)	40	133	152	86	19	3
95th (1977)	81	121	147	71	15	0
97th (1981)	94	142	132	54	12	1
100th (1987)	63	153	137	56	24	2
102nd (1991)	39	153	133	86	20	4
105th (1997)	47	145	147	82	10	2
107th (2001)	36	118	175	78	26	0

The Senate

Congress	Under 40	40–49	50–59	60–69	70–79	Over 80
92nd (1971)	4	24	32	23	16	1
95th (1977)	6	26	35	21	10	2
97th (1981)	9	35	36	14	6	0
100th (1987)	5	30	36	22	5	2
102nd (1991)	0	22	47	24	5	2
105th (1997)	2	21	39	26	12	1
107th (2001)	0	17	43	31	7	2

1. Is there a trend from the 92nd Congress to the 107th regarding age?

2. How might the events of the past fifty years have affected the political leadership of the Congress?

Source: "Congress of Relative Newcomers Poses Challenge to Bush, Leadership," Julie Hirschfield, *Congressional Quarterly Weekly* (20 January 2001), 178–82.

Table 3. Occupations, 107th Congress (2001)

Occupation	The House of Representatives		
	Democrat	Republican	Total
Actor/Entertainer	0	1	1
Aeronautics	0	1	1
Agriculture	8	17	25
Artistic/Creative	0	1	1
Business/Banking	56	103	159
Clergy	1	1	2
Education	53	38	92
Engineering	1	8	9
Health Care	3	1	4
Homemaker/Domestic	1	1	2
Journalism	1	7	8
Labor	1	1	2
Law	84	71	155
Law Enforcement	7	3	10
Medicine	6	8	14
Military	0	2	2
Professional Sports	0	3	3
Public Service/Politics	70	56	126
Real Estate	2	22	24
Secretarial/Clerical	0	2	2
Technical/Trade	1	2	3
Miscellaneous	1	5	6

Note: Totals do not include Bernard Sanders (I-Vermont, journalist) or Virgil H. Goode Jr. (I-Virginia, attorney).

Source: "Congress of Relative Newcomers Poses Challenge to Bush, Leadership," Julie Hirschfield, *Congressional Quarterly Weekly* (20 January 2001), 178–82.

The Senate

Occupation	Democrat	Republican	Total
Actor/Entertainer	0	1	1
Aeronautics	1	0	1
Agriculture	1	5	6
Artistic/Creative	0	0	0
Business/Banking	8	16	24
Clergy	0	1	1
Education	8	8	16
Engineering	0	0	0
Health Care	0	0	0
Homemaker/Domestic	1	0	1
Journalism	1	6	7
Labor	0	1	1
Law	28	25	53
Law Enforcement	0	0	0
Medicine	0	3	3
Military	0	1	1
Professional Sports	0	1	1
Public Service/Politics	18	10	28
Real Estate	2	2	4
Secretarial/Clerical	0	0	0
Technical/Trade	0	0	0
Miscellaneous	0	0	0

3. Based on the information contained in the tables, what are four characteristics of a typical Senator? of a member of the House of Representatives?

4. What do the members' occupations suggest about them as a whole?

5. Which party has the best minority representation over time?

6. Why is it worthwhile for political parties to make an effort to attract more minority voters to their ranks? How might that be accomplished?

Source: "Congress of Relative Newcomers Poses Challenge to Bush, Leadership," Julie Hirschfield, *Congressional Quarterly Weekly* (20 January 2001), 178–82.

Name_____

Date_____

If You Were the Congressman

Congressional representatives constantly face conflicting pressures in voting. They must represent their constituents, satisfy their party, do what is best for the country as a whole, and still act in a manner their conscience tells them is right. Read the following situations, and then decide how you would vote if you were the representative.

1. You are a congressional representative from a large northern city. You are confronted with a vote on farm relief sponsored by your own party. The president is of the opposite party and opposes farm relief. Would your vote be based primarily on the wishes of your constituents, national interest, party pressures, or your conscience? Explain your vote.

2. You are a congressional representative from a rural area. You are confronted with a vote on a defense contract for a large corporation that is planning to build a factory in your district. Your party is split on the issue. Would your vote be based primarily on the wishes of your constituents, national interests, party pressures, or your conscience? Explain your vote.

Lesson 18
The House of Representatives and the Senate

Objective
- To recognize the differences, in organization and authority, between the House of Representatives and the Senate

Notes to the Teacher

The bicameral Congress of the United States was created to balance the interests of the people with those of the states. The Constitutional Convention of 1787 brought together some of the greatest minds on political philosophy, thought, and action. Bankers, gentlemen farmers, lawyers, politicians, and merchants—they were, for the most part, very wealthy and well educated.

One of the main topics of discussion was the structure of the legislative body under the new Constitution. The first days of the convention focused on debating the merits of the Virginia Plan. James Madison and other supporters, those of the three largest states (Pennsylvania, Virginia, and Massachusetts) as well as three southern states (Georgia, South Carolina, and North Carolina) wanted representation in the Congress based on population. They supported a representation plan in which the more citizens a state had, the more representatives it sent to Congress, with slaves counting as three-fifths of a person. Five smaller states (New Jersey, Maryland, New York, Delaware, and Connecticut) feared domination by the large states who had consistently outvoted them under the Articles of Confederation.

William Paterson, a delegate from New Jersey, moved for an adjournment in order to craft an alternate plan. The supporters of the New Jersey Plan demanded three things: a revision of the Articles of Confederation which retained individual state sovereignty; a new centralized government which would act equally on the interests of the small and large states; and a provision for an upper house based on equal representation.

After much debate, supporters of both plans reached a compromise, which melded components of both plans into an acceptable structure. The plan contained proportional representation for the lower house and an equal representation in the upper house. Today 435 members of the House of Representatives are elected biennially from districts that are determined by the population figures established every ten years by the U.S. Census. Each state sends two senators to serve, regardless of the size of its population.

In this lesson, students read a selection about the Constitutional Convention of 1787 and compare the New Jersey Plan and the Virginia Plan. To conclude, they complete a chart contrasting the organization and authority of the House of Representatives and Senate and analyze reasons for the differences between the two houses of Congress.

Procedure

1. Have students review the organization and special duties of the House of Representatives and the Senate. Distribute **Handout 35**, and have students complete it individually or in small groups. Review students' responses.

Suggested Responses:

Part A.

1. *435; 100*

2. *two; six*

3. *determined by population of state; two*

4. *twenty-five; thirty*

5. *seven; nine*

6. *one hundred; thirty-three and one-third*

7. *always elected by the people; chosen by state legislatures until adoption of the Seventeenth Amendment, which gave the vote to the people*

8. *districts of approximately 500,000 people; entire state*

9. *Speaker of the House; Vice President of the United States*

10. *impeachment, introduces all revenue bills; approves or rejects treaties, approves or rejects presidential appointments, tries cases of impeachment*

Part B.

1. *A senator's term is longer; requirements to be a senator are stricter; they are fewer in number, they have additional and important responsibilities not assigned to the House.*

2. *Representation in the House must reflect the relative population of the states; thus, the Constitution provides for a census every ten years in order to reapportion seats fairly.*

3. *With few exceptions, a representative is elected from a smaller district than a senator. Thus, most people feel closer to their representative.*

4. *They recalled the colonial complaints against British taxation without representation and sought to insure that the people's representatives would have authority in taxation.*

5. *The House is based on population while each state is represented by two senators.*

6. *Senators were elected directly by the people instead of by state legislatures.*

2. Distribute **Handout 36**, and have students read the excerpts and answer the questions. Review students' responses.

Suggested Responses:

1. *cannot know precise number of representatives in the future; corruption is lessened by a check of federal and state governments against each other, the will of the people and the number of representatives; the president represents all the people*

2. *examine the qualities of representatives; wealthy will be in control; combinations and corruption probable; too small a number of representatives; need more middle class representatives*

3. *The confederation is a compact with each member having an equal vote; small states are reluctant to sign the Constitution because the confederation is a collective, it destroys the balance of equality, the power of the large states is usurped, and the rights of states are destroyed.*

4. *Being a citizen of the United States is just as good as being a citizen of a state; citizens look to national government to solve problems now; could create worse objectionable minority; no plan against foreign wars or state projects that would harm other states and cannot be controlled by the federal government.*

3. Have students select a bill currently before Congress and use the following criteria to evaluate the bill:

- Is it relevant?
- Is it timely?
- Is it costly?
- Is it a pork barrel package?
- Does it fulfill a particular need?
- If you were a member of Congress, would you try to kill it in committee, vote for the bill, vote against the bill, or revise it?
- Is this bill in the interest of the people?

Provide class time to discuss students' evaluations.

Enrichment/Extension

Have students write a paragraph on how the criticisms leveled by the two parties at the structure of government reflect on the government today. Have selected students read their paragraphs aloud. Have students try to reach consensus on whether the criticisms of the plans were valid.

The House of Representatives and Senate

Part A.

Complete the following chart by selecting the best term from the word bank. Answers may be used more than once.

Topic	House of Representatives	Senate
1. Number of members		
2. Term of office (years)		
3. Number per state		
4. Age requirement		
5. Citizenship requirement		
6. Percent elected every two years		
7. Method of selection		
8. Size of constituency		
9. Presiding officer		
10. Special duties		

Word Bank

100

Speaker of the House

always elected by the people

nine

twenty-five

seven

districts of approximately 500,000 people

introduces all revenue bills

six

one hundred

determined by the population of the state

tries cases of impeachment

thirty-three and one-third

435

Vice president of the United States

chosen by state legislatures until adoption of the Seventeenth Amendment, which gave the vote to the people

thirty

entire state

approves or rejects presidential appointments

impeachment

two

Part B.

Use the chart in part A to answer the following questions.

1. Give three reasons why senators seem to have more prestige than representatives.

2. Refer to Article 1, Section 2, Clause 3 of the Constitution. What relationship exists between the census and the distribution of seats among the states in the House of Representatives?

3. What evidence in your completed chart suggests that the House of Representatives was intended to reflect the interests of the people, rather than the states?

4. How does your answer to question 3 help you to understand why the Founding Fathers required all revenue bills to originate in the House of Representatives?

5. How does the chart reflect the compromise between large and small states?

6. How did the Seventeenth Amendment to the U.S. Constitution create a more democratic Senate?

The Structure of Congress: A Constitutional Debate

Read the following excerpts, and answer the questions. Make a list of the criticisms each side levels at the other.

The Virginia Plan

The Constitutional Convention was to begin in May 1787. Because of poor transportation and communication, many delegates were late arriving in Philadelphia. Representatives of both the large and small states had their own agendas. James Madison and his supporters from other large states devised the Virginia Plan, fifteen resolutions which greatly expanded the original purpose and plans of the Convention itself, which was to create a new national government with a bicameral legislature, develop a plan for proportional representation, and establish a relatively weak executive, who was to be elected by the legislature to a seven-year term. Nearly all of the fifteen resolutions proposed by Madison passed. However, the small states were threatened by this plan and devised one of their own.

Defense of the Virginia Plan

. . . I agree that there should be a broad democratic branch in the national legislature. But . . . it is impossible, in the first instance to be precise and exact with regard to the number; and it is equally impossible to determine to what point it may be proper in the future to increase it. . . . In all their reasoning upon the subject, there seems to be this fallacy:—They suppose that the representative will have no motive of action, on the one side, but a sense of duty; or on the other, but corruption:—They do not reflect, that he is to return to the community; that he is dependent on the will of the people, and that it cannot be his interest to oppose their wishes. . . .

. . . In these, the will of the people makes the essential principle of the government; and the laws which control the community. . . . If the general view of the people be for an increase, it undoubtedly must take place: They have it in their power to instruct their representatives. . . .

. . . But I ask him, why will not ninety-one be an adequate and safe representation? This at present appears to be the proper medium. Besides, the President of the United States will be himself a representative of the people. . . .

Does the new government render a rich man more eligible than a poor one? No. It requires no such qualification. . . .

. . . In large districts, the corruption of the electors is much more difficult:—Combinations for the purposes of intrigue are less easily formed: Factions and cabals are little known. In a small district, wealth will have a more complete influence; because the people in the vicinity of a great man, are more immediately his dependants, and because this influence has fewer objects to act upon. . . .

. . . This balance between the national and state governments ought to be dwelt on with peculiar attention, as it is of the utmost importance.—It forms a double security to the people. If one encroaches on their rights, they will find a powerful protection in the other. . . . .

—Alexander Hamilton

Criticism of the Virginia Plan

To determine whether the number of representatives proposed by this Constitution is sufficient, it is proper to examine the qualifications which this house ought to possess, in order to exercise their powers discreetly for the happiness of the people. . . .

Besides, the influence of the great will generally enable them to succeed in elections. . . . [I]t appears that the government will fall into the hands of the few and the great. This will be a government of oppression. . . . Those in middling circumstances, have less temptation—they are . . . more temperate, of better morals and less ambition than the great. . . . The great consider themselves above the common people—entitled to more respect—do not associate with them—they fancy themselves to have a right of preeminence in every thing. . . .

In so small a number of representatives, there is great danger from corruption and combination. A great politician has said that every man has his price. I hope this is not true in all its extent. . . . Can the liberties of three millions of people be securely trusted in the hands of 24 men? Is it prudent to commit to so small a number the decision of the great questions which will come before them? Reason revolts at the idea.

—Melancton Smith

The New Jersey Plan

By mid-June 1787, most of the provisions of the Virginia Plan had been passed with few changes. The small states felt threatened by the proposed plan and William Paterson, a delegate from New Jersey, moved to adjourn the convention in order to allow time for the small states, led by New Jersey, New York, Connecticut, and Delaware, to craft an alternative plan. They proposed the following: The Articles of Confederation were to be revised in order to preserve the sovereignty of the states, and each state was to have an equal vote. Paterson voiced the opinion that a strong national government would hurt the interests of the small states. While the convention voted down the plan submitted by Paterson, its key plank, equal voting power for the states, served as the basis for the structure of the upper house as it appears in the Constitution.

Defense of the New Jersey Plan

. . . The confederation is in the nature of a compact; and can any State, unless by the consent of the whole, either in politics or law, withdraw their powers? . . .

And although it is now asserted that the larger States reluctantly agreed to that part of the confederation which secures an equal suffrage to each, yet let it be remembered, that the smaller States were the last who approved the confederation. . . .

When independent societies confederate for mutual defence, they do so in their collective capacity; and then each State, for those purposes, must be considered as *one* of the contracting parties. Destroy this balance of equality, and you endanger the rights of the *lesser* societies by the danger of usurpation in the greater.

—William Paterson

Criticism of the New Jersey Plan

. . . Why should a National Government be unpopular? Has it less dignity? Will each Citizen enjoy under it less liberty or protection? Will a Citizen of *Delaware* be degraded by becoming a Citizen of the *United States*? Where do the people look at present for relief from the evils of which they complain? Is it from an internal reform of their Governments? No, Sir. It is from the National Councils that relief is expected. . . .

—James Wilson

Proceeding to the consideration of Mr. Paterson's plan, he stated the object of a proper plan to be twofold. 1. To preserve the Union. 2. To provide a Government that will remedy the evils felt by the States both in their united and individual capacities. Examine Mr. Paterson's plan, and say whether it promises satisfaction in these respects.

1. Will it prevent those violations of the law of nations and of Treaties which if not prevented must involve us in the calamities of foreign wars? The tendency of the States to these violations has been manifested in sundry instances. . . . A rupture with other powers is among the greatest of national calamities. It ought therefore to be effectually provided that no part of a nation shall have in its power to bring them on the whole. The existing Confederacy does not sufficiently provide against this evil. . . . It leaves the will of the States as uncontrolled as ever. . . .

. . . The plan of Mr. Paterson, not giving even a negative on the acts of the States, left them as much liberty as ever to execute their unrighteous projects against each other.

—James Madison

1. What are the main points of Alexander Hamilton's rebuttal in the debate against Melancton Smith?

2. What are the concerns expressed by Smith in the same debate?

3. What ideas does William Paterson assert about the New Jersey Plan?

4. What is the criticism brought by James Wilson and James Madison against the New Jersey Plan?

Lesson 19
Leadership in Congress

Objectives
- To understand the role of various leaders in the Senate and House of Representatives
- To research the roles congressional representatives play in the current session of Congress

Notes to the Teacher
The need to work through several thousand bills in Congress each year requires a division of labor. The main legislative work of Congress is accomplished in standing committees and subcommittees that have jurisdiction over specific subjects in each house. Each bipartisan committee roughly reflects the relative strength of each party in the whole House. Committee chairmen are always members of the majority party in the House or Senate. At the beginning of each new Congress, party leaders in each House assign freshmen representatives to standing committees. Since powerful committee chairmanships are usually determined by seniority in the committee, few experienced representatives wish to change their committee assignments unless they can move to substantially more powerful committees. Thus, representatives, by repeated assignment to the same committee, develop considerable expertise on matters related to their committee.

Committees or subcommittees frequently hold open hearings on proposed legislation, but decision making is done in executive sessions with no outsiders allowed. Committees have much influence over legislation through their power to kill a bill, amend it, pigeonhole it for weeks, or approve it and send it on to the full House or Senate for debate. If the subcommittee rules favorably on the bill, chances are good that the entire committee and then the whole House or Senate will pass it. Congressional representatives respect the expertise and considered judgment of their colleagues on subcommittees. Equally important, they hesitate to overrule a subcommittee for fear of reciprocity at a later date.

In this lesson, students research and prepare reports on congressional representatives and senators who hold positions of leadership in the current Congress.

Procedure
1. Discuss the structure and purpose of congressional committees. Students should understand the possible actions a committee may take on proposed legislation.

2. Distribute **Handout 37**, and have students complete it either individually or in small groups. Review students' responses.

Suggested Responses:

Part A.

1.	k	10.	c
2.	a	11.	d
3.	j	12.	e
4.	m	13.	f
5.	l	14.	i
6.	n	15.	o
7.	h	16.	p
8.	b	17.	q
9.	g	18.	r

Part B.

1.	c	4.	b
2.	a	5.	d
3.	a		

Part C.

1. *to provide expertise on complicated matters and divide the labor in Congress*

2. *Committee chairmen are chosen because they are the ranking members of the majority party with the longest service on their committees.*

3. *eliminates controversy*

4. *often means that conservative and perhaps less-qualified individuals serve as powerful chairmen of committees*

5. *Students might cite intelligence, ability to compromise, ability to communicate, salesmanship, courage, practicality, and ability to be reelected many times from their state or district.*

6. Students might suggest aggressive lobbying with direct communication, negotiation, playing pragmatic politics, or being a tough player with a reputation as a hard worker.

3. Distribute **Handout 38**, and have students research the current holders of congressional committee leadership positions as listed. Current textbooks and almanacs are good sources of information. Review students' responses to parts A and B. Allow class time for the presentations assigned in part C.

Enrichment/Extension

Have students evaluate their congressional representative. Instruct them to use the criteria they developed in question 5 in part C of **Handout 37**.

Congressional Leadership

Part A.

The following list includes important positions of leadership in Congress. Use your textbook or other reference material to match the lettered positions with the numbered descriptions of the tasks each job involves.

a. Vice President

b. Senate Majority Leader

c. Senate Minority Leader

d. Senate Majority Whip

e. Senate Minority Whip

f. House Majority Leader

g House Minority Leader

h. House Majority Whip

i. House Minority Whip

j. President Pro Tempore

k. Speaker of the House

l. Chairman of House Ways and Means Committee

m. Chairman of House Appropriations Committee

n. Chairman of Senate Commerce Committee

o. Chairman of Senate Foreign Relations Committee

p. Chairman of House Foreign Affairs Committee

q. Chairman of House Judiciary Committee

r. Chairman of Senate Armed Services Committee

_____1. I have the most powerful position in the House of Representatives. I assign bills to committees and appoint, select, and conference committee members.

_____2. I serve as president of the Senate. Although I cannot participate in debates, I can vote in case of a tie.

_____3. I preside over the Senate in the absence of the vice president. The caucus of the majority party chose me for this post.

_____4. The seniority system allowed me to become chairman of the House committee that has power over all federal spending.

_____5. I am chairman of the House committee that has power over taxation.

_____6. My seniority in the Senate has given me the chairmanship of the committee that specializes in transportation, communication, and interstate commerce.

_____7. As majority party leader in the House of Representatives, I exert pressure on party members to vote with the party. I am responsible for getting my party's program enacted into law.

_____8. In the Senate, I am responsible for passage of the majority party's programs. I inform and pressure party members to vote for programs, and I determine the order in which bills are to be debated.

_____9. I am the leader of the minority party in the House of Representatives. I am responsible for informing party members and organizing resistance to programs submitted by the majority.

_____10. I am the leader of the minority party in the Senate. I am responsible for resisting programs submitted by the majority.

_____11. I aid the majority leader in keeping party members informed and supportive of programs in the Senate.

_____12. I am the minority party leader in the Senate who informs members when important bills are scheduled for a vote. My usual goal is to oppose majority bills.

_____13. I have control of the dominant party in the House of Representatives, and I am responsible for enactment of our party's program.

_____14. I am the party leader in the House of Representatives. I inform members and assist the minority leader in resisting some of the majority party's programs.

_____15. The seniority system has allowed me to become chairman of the powerful committee in the Senate that handles matters relating to other nations.

_____16. I am chairman of the less powerful committee in the House of Representatives that handles matters with other countries.

_____17. I am chairman of this powerful committee in the House of Representatives that deals with impeachment charges.

_____18. I am chairman of the Senate committee that supervises expenditures of the department of government with the largest budget.

Part B.

Read each of the following statements and decide the House or Senate committee to which each issue would most likely be assigned. Write the letter of your choice in the space to the left. One answer is used more than once.

a. House Appropriations Committee

b. Senate Armed Services Committee

c. Senate Commerce Committee

d. Senate Foreign Relations Committee

_____1. If someone wanted to construct a new transcontinental railroad, what Senate committee would most likely handle the request for congressional aid?

_____2. A representative for a group of businessmen presents the group's views before this House committee in hopes of securing funds for a new bridge across the Cuyahoga River.

_____3. A group concerned with the effects of smoking seeks to convince this House committee to add a tax on cigarettes; the group believes such a tax would reduce smoking and would increase funds for cancer research.

_____4. This Senate committee works closely with the president to raise defense spending in proportion to increases in the cost of living.

_____5. The president would have to work closely with this committee to approve any treaty in the Middle East.

Part C.

Answer the following questions.

1. Why are the houses of Congress divided into standing committees?

2. What is the meaning of the seniority system in the committees?

3. What is one advantage of the seniority system?

4. What is one disadvantage of the seniority system?

5. List six qualities a member of Congress needs in order to be an effective leader.

Name_____

Date_____

Who Has the Power?

Part A.

Use an almanac and other references to identify the person who holds each important congressional leadership position during the current Congress.

1. Vice President _____

2. Senate Majority Leader _____

3. Senate Majority Whip _____

4. Senate Minority Leader_____

5. Senate Minority Whip _____

6. President Pro Tempore _____

7. Chairman of Senate Commerce Committee _____

8. Chairman of Senate Foreign Relations Committee_____

9. Chairman of Senate Armed Services Committee _____

10. House Majority Leader _____

11. House Majority Whip _____

12. House Minority Leader _____

13. House Minority Whip_____

14. Speaker of the House _____

15. Chairman of House Ways and Means Committee _____

16. Chairman of House Appropriations Committee _____

17. Chairman of House Foreign Affairs Committee _____

18. Chairman of House Judiciary Committee_____

Part B.

Identify your congressional representatives and the committee positions they hold.

1. Senator _____

    Committees _____

2. Senator _____

    Committees _____

3. Representative_____

    Committees _____

Part C.

Select one individual listed in part A or B, and prepare a two- to three-minute biographical sketch of that person for presentation to the class.

Lesson 20
The Legislative Obstacle Course: A Bill Becomes a Law

Objective
- To understand the process by which a bill becomes a law

Notes to the Teacher
The majority of both houses of Congress must pass a bill in exactly the same form in order for it to become law. Most bills today are introduced by the executive branch. Most die in committee before they are considered by Congress. Each house follows similar procedures when considering legislation, although there are significant variations. The powerful House Rules Committee decides the order of debate for each bill under consideration and whether amendments may be attached to the bill. The chairman of this committee wields enormous power. At the end of a congressional session, when time is limited, the committee determines which bills will be considered by the House. When the House of Representatives and the Senate produce two different bills on the same topic, a conference committee, made up of members of both the House and the Senate, must agree on a compromise bill, which must be passed by both houses without further changes.

Passage by both Houses does not guarantee enactment of a law. If the president vetoes the bill, it must be passed by a two-thirds vote in each house to override the veto. Between 1913 and April 1980, Congress sustained 1,337 vetoes while overriding only fifty-nine. Normally, if the president does not sign a bill, it becomes law without his signature in ten days. However, if Congress adjourns during the period given the president to take action on the bill, his failure to sign a bill, called a pocket veto, prevents its passage.

To transform a good bill into law is the essence of politics itself and requires a large degree of political acumen and the ability to compromise. Bills do not become laws merely because they are good ideas. Usually, a group of legislators works together to answer the needs of constituents.

The most controversial bills—those which deal with topics such as abortion, gun control, campaign finance reform, health care, and social security reform—can be the source of bitter rivalry and partisan political acrimony. Congressional representatives must often put aside their personal feelings and deal with issues important to their constituencies. They must move beyond political infighting and craft viable legislation.

In this lesson, students analyze the process of moving a bill through the House of Representatives and the Senate toward a vote. Students examine the main parts of a bill and develop a strategy for moving the bill through Congress. They conclude by examining reasons why so few bills actually become law.

Procedure
1. Review the process necessary for a bill to become law. Distribute **Handout 39**, and have students complete the chart as directed. Review students' responses. See the Teacher Resource Page on page 155 for a completed diagram.

2. Explain that laws are not always easily made. Explain that considerable public pressure was needed to convince Congress to pass the Civil Rights Bill in 1964. Ask students how a concerned citizen might demonstrate his support, or disapproval, of a bill under consideration in Congress.

Suggested Responses:
- *writing letters to congressional representatives before the floor vote*
- *writing letters to influential newspapers or television stations*
- *participating in demonstrations to support, or oppose, the bill*
- *joining and/or making contributions to groups strongly concerned with the bill's passage*
- *calling the White House or sending telegrams during the period when the president must take action on the bill*

3. Divide the class into groups of four or five. Explain that one of the most controversial topics today involves laws that permit the carrying of a concealed weapon. Explain that each group is a committee that has been given the task of preparing a bill, either permitting or prohibiting the carrying of a concealed weapon, for presentation to the whole assembly. Remind students that the bill must be clear and concise. Allow adequate time for students to prepare the bills.

4. Have groups present their bills. Have the class vote on whether to accept the bill for discussion or to send it back to committee. Allow students to discuss the merits of each bill. Have the class try to reach consensus on what should be contained in the bill.

5. Have students list six ways in which their bill might suffer defeat. (*It might be defeated in the subcommittee of either House; it might fail to gain approval in the full committee of either House; it might die on either calendar for lack of time; it might be defeated in either House after the floor debate; Congress might fail to override a presidential veto; or the president might use a pocket veto at the end of the session.*)

Enrichment/Extension

Have students research and report on amendments to the U.S. Constitution that have been proposed during the last year.

Suggested Responses, Handout 39

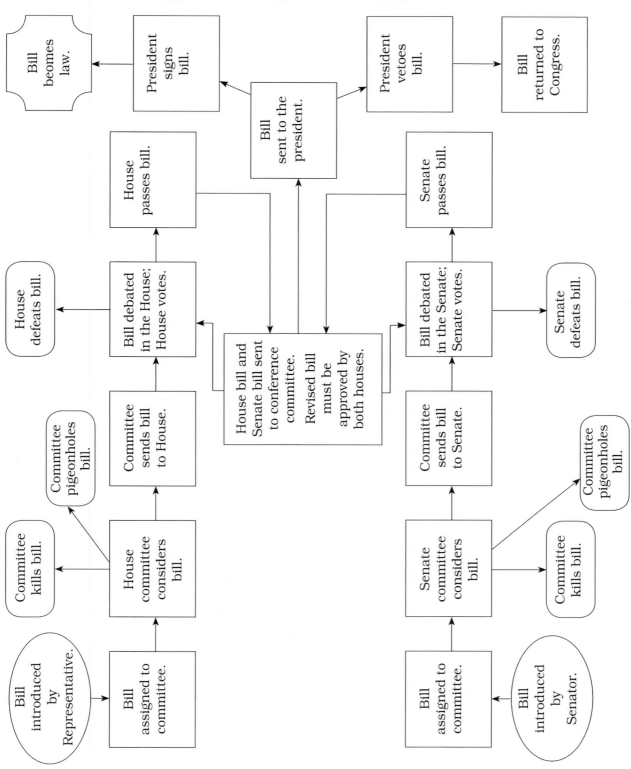

How a Bill Becomes a Law

Use your textbook and other references to complete the following chart

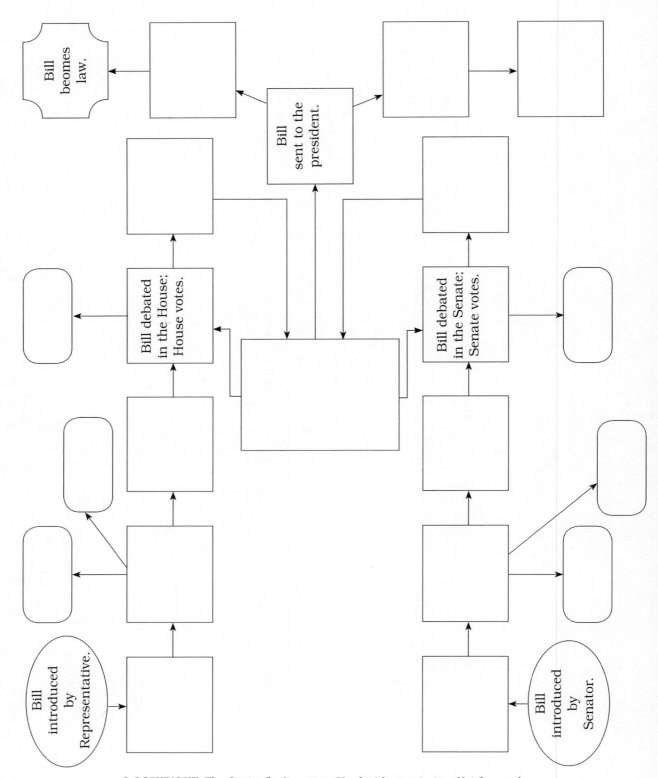

Lesson 21
Congressional Gridlock

Objective
- To evaluate the efficiency of the congressional workload

Notes to the Teacher
Congressional gridlock is a reality in modern American politics. For legislators who have come to Washington to make good policy decisions for constituents back home, it is a political conundrum and a legislative nightmare. Gridlock on the highway means bumper-to-bumper traffic, with no movement in sight, for drivers who only want to get home and deal with more important matters. Congressional gridlock is similar. As bill after bill becomes stalled in committee or on the floor, impatient lawmakers grow angry. The passage of a bill into law requires political acumen. Veteran lawmakers know how to make deals. Some are savvy strategists, who are adept at compromise and conciliation. Unfortunately, even these dealmakers cannot prevent gridlock.

A variety of political situations can result in gridlock: A president and a Congress from different political parties can fail to agree on legislation or to make the concessions and compromises needed to pass a bill on the legislative agenda. A party with a slim majority in either the House of Representatives or the Senate can fail to compromise in order to craft policy acceptable to the other party and independents. The minority party can obstruct the majority with filibusters. The majority rule can cause acrimony among members of the minority, resulting in gridlock. Sometimes, when legislators reach an impasse that prevents them from moving legislation along, the congressional leadership or even the president will choose to sell their ideas directly to the American people.

In this lesson, students analyze a gridlock scenario. They respond by writing a letter to their congressional representative or senator on how to avoid gridlock or dissolve gridlock.

Procedure
1. Review the process during which a bill becomes a law (Lesson 20).

2. Read aloud the following information about the shutdown of the federal government in November 1995.

> The shutdown occurred because Congress has not completed action on all of the measures to provide funding for the government during the current fiscal year, which began on October 1. A short-term funding measure, called a continuing resolution (CR), was passed in September and gave Congress until November 14 to enact spending bills. But by that date only three of the thirteen appropriations bills had been signed into law.
>
> Congress and the President have not been able to agree to extend the CR. The congressional leadership attached a number of provisions to the second continuing resolution, including an increase in Medicare premiums. President Clinton objected to these provisions, and vetoed the measure. . . . Congress then passed a continuing resolution that would keep the government open until December 5 and called for balancing the budget in seven years. However, President Clinton also vetoed this measure.
>
> On November 14, some 800,000 of the federal government's two million civilian employees were furloughed. Many federal government offices were closed, including national parks and museums. New applications for federal benefits, such as Social Security, could not be processed, though payment of Social Security and Medicare benefits continued. The Agriculture and Energy Departments remained open because their funding had been approved. In addition, employees

157

vital to the safety and health of the public, such as air traffic controllers and guards in federal prisons, were kept on duty, as were those on active duty in the military.[1]

Ask students what the problem is. (*The Republican-controlled Congress and President Bill Clinton could not agree on a spending bill.*) What was the result? (*Gridlock resulted, and the government was shut down.*)

3. Distribute **Handout 40**, and have students read the information and answer the questions. Review students' responses.

   Suggested Responses:

   1. *To some, it is only a symbol of America, while to others, it is a national treasure representing all that is good in America.*

   2. *Some see flag burning as free speech that is protected under the First Amendment. Others think the flag is a revered symbol, one that should be protected by a constitutional amendment. There are also the issues of how often flag burning occurs and whether burning the flag dishonors veterans.*

   4. *Members of Congress must reach consensus through compromise and conciliation in order to pass the bill.*

4. Assign the role of Democrat, Republican, or Independent to each student. Have students from each group meet in a party caucus. Distribute **Handout 41**, and have students develop a strategy to prevent congressional gridlock. Have students share their strategies and then develop a consensus list of strategies that might be used by a legislative body to avoid gridlock.

5. Have students write their congressional representative a letter containing examples of how to prevent, avoid, or solve gridlock.

Enrichment/Extension

Have students explore and report on other issues that have become the subject of legislative gridlock, such as appointments to the federal court.

[1]Representative Lee H. Hamilton, 104th Congress, 1st sess., *Congressional Record* 141 (29 November 1995): E 2258.

Name_____

Date_____

Burning the Flag

Read the following information, and answer the questions.

Congress has tried and failed to pass an amendment to the Constitution that would prohibit the burning of the American flag. The Supreme Court has ruled that the burning of the flag is considered to be protected speech. During the 107th Congress, a bill that sought to give Congress the power to prohibit the physical desecration of the flag was introduced. Some senators, like Edward M. Kennedy, D-Mass., stated that the act of flag burning was rare and was not the basis for changing the First Amendment. Others stated that the burning of the flag was an aggressive and provocative act against a symbol of our country and an insult to all those who had defended our nation in the past.

Forty-nine legislatures, with the exception of Vermont, have passed resolutions urging Congress to pass a ban. When polled, the majority of Americans support a ban against flag burning.

1. If it is true that most Americans want a flag-burning amendment, why do you think it has not become law?

2. What position does each side take in the debate?

3. Do you believe the Constitution should be amended to prevent the burning of our national symbol?

4. What steps would have to be taken to avoid gridlock on this issue?

Name_____

Date_____

Battling Gridlock

You have been assigned the role of a Democrat, Republican, or Independent. Caucus with the other members of your party, and consider what compromises your group must reach in order to solve the following dilemma. What deal-making strategy could you employ to avoid gridlock? What will result if an agreement is not reached? Prepare a possible solution to the crisis, and be prepared to present it to the class.

> The president and the majority of Congress belong to different political parties. The president has submitted his budget to Congress. The majority party has produced a spending bill that is at odds with the president's proposals. The president has threatened to veto any bill Congress passes which he feels attacks the "little guy." The majority party has promised to balance the budget, but in seven years, has not done so. While the president feels that the budget needs to be reduced, he believes that the cuts proposed by Congress affect programs that help the middle class, such as student loans. The responsibility for solving this problem rests with the president and Congress.

Lesson 22
International Legislation: The North American Free Trade Agreement, 1994

Objectives

- To analyze the provisions of the North American Free Trade Agreement (NAFTA)

- To examine and analyze the effects of NAFTA on U.S. trade

- To examine and analyze U.S. trade with Mexico

Notes to the Teacher

James Madison, who had a broad background on the structure and history of government, was convinced of the need for a new document that would replace the Articles of Confederation. Under the Articles, each state had the right to negotiate treaties, both with foreign nations and with America's Native American people. Madison believed that states repeatedly broke agreements and treaties. The new nation needed a mechanism that would place the negotiation and signing of treaties in the hands of a federal government.

Since its earliest days, the United States has worked to establish agreements with other foreign powers. Colonial assemblies tried to negotiate changes in Great Britain's mercantile practices and the Continental Congress arranged for economic and military aid from France during the American Revolution. A treaty with the Netherlands granted formal recognition of the United States as a sovereign nation. Over time, Congress became occupied with affairs in the western and northern hemispheres, involving such actions as the settlement of territorial disputes with Great Britain, Mexico, and Spain; the purchase of Louisiana from France and Alaska from Russia; the establishment of the principles of the Monroe Doctrine, which sought to prevent the expansion of European nations into the lands of the western hemisphere; the Spanish-American War; the Cuban Missile Crisis; and the invasion of Iraq.

While military engagement with other nations has moved to other areas of the world, in the western hemisphere economic and trade matters have moved to the forefront of American foreign policy. Our nation now seeks to make agreements that will be the most advantageous to our economy. In 1994, Canada, Mexico, and the United States formed the North American Free Trade Agreement, a comprehensive plan for free trade among the three nations. Each year the United States and Canada exchange more goods and services than any two other countries in the world. They are each other's largest trading partners and share the world's longest unprotected border. Mexico has also been a huge importer of goods from its neighbors to the north.

With the passage of NAFTA, tariffs and other barriers to free trade were eliminated. Increased economic growth, lower prices, expanded employment, and enhanced competitiveness in the world marketplace have resulted.

NAFTA affects all areas of a nation's production of goods and services, from agriculture to textiles. Its creation is widely popular among some, while others believe it causes the outsourcing of jobs and the movement of businesses from the United States to areas where manufacturing costs are lower. Under the terms of the agreement, the treaty may be adjusted to adapt to changing market conditions. Proponents of the treaty argue that fewer regulations will spur the economies of all three countries to higher growth rates, increased efficiency, and improved competitiveness.

In Canada, the power to enter into an international agreement rests in the hands of the prime minister and his Cabinet, but the Canadian Parliament, a bicameral legislature, alone has the power to approve proposed agreements. In the United States, the president engages in economic and political talks with other nations, but the Senate must ratify any agreement reached by the Executive Branch. Treaties may be ratified quickly, using a process in which the Senate agrees to accept all or none of the agreement. In Mexico, the bicameral National Congress passes the recommendation of the Executive Branch, which negotiates treaties, into law.

In this lesson, students analyze the basic provisions of NAFTA. They create thematic maps illustrating the economic production of Canada, Mexico, and the United States. Students construct a bar graph depicting the effects of NAFTA on the economy of Mexico and conclude by discussing the merits and problems of NAFTA based on the handouts.

Procedure

1. Indicate the similarities and differences in the legislative processes of Canada, Mexico, and the United States. Review basic information about why nations trade. Students should be familiar with the following terms:

   GATT—the General Agreement on Tariffs and Trade

   tariff—a tax on imports

   quota—a portion of a particular item which is guaranteed

   reciprocal—an agreement in which both sides agree to apply the same rules to all participants

   customs—the process of regulating goods that enter a country

2. Divide the class into groups of three or four. Have students use the almanac and other sources, such as the Internet, atlases, and encyclopedias, to find ten relevant facts about the geography, economic production, and trade of one of the following countries: Canada, Mexico, or the United States. Instruct students to use the ten facts to create a map highlighting imports, exports, manufactured goods, raw materials, etc. Tell students that a good map should contain all the following elements: a date; a compass indicator; a grid or legend; a scale to tell relevant distance; a title; the name of the creator of the map; a source for the information contained on the map. Allow students sufficient time to complete this assignment. Have groups share their maps at a later date. Maps will vary depending on the statistical information used.

3. Distribute **Handout 42**, and have students complete the chart in part A. Review students' responses.

Suggested Responses:

Agriculture—*Tariffs on all farm products will be eliminated over fifteen years. Price supports will continue provided they do not distort trade.*

Automobiles—*By 2002, 62.5 percent of the value of an automobile must be manufactured in North America in order to qualify for duty-free status. By 2004, tariffs on automobiles are to be phased out.*

Banking—*Canada and the United States may purchase interest of up to 8 percent in Mexican banks. All limits on ownership will end in 2004.*

Disputes—*Special panels of judges will resolve disagreements within strict timetables.*

Energy—*U.S. and Canadian companies may bid on contracts offered by Mexican oil and electricity producers.*

Environment—*A nation's or state's environmental, health, or safety laws will take precedence over the terms of the treaty.*

Immigration—*Restrictions on the movement of businessmen and professionals must be eased.*

Jobs—*U.S. barriers to Mexican immigration will remain.*

Patent and Copyright Protection—*Mexico agreed to strengthen laws providing protection to intellectual property.*

Tariffs—*Tariffs on an estimated 10,000 manufactured goods are to be eliminated by 2009. One half of all U.S. exports to Mexico are to be duty free by 1999.*

Textiles—*Duty-free garments must be made with yarns or fabrics produced in North America. Most tariffs will be phased out by 1999.*

Trucking—*Trucks will have free access to cross borders, but the United States retained the right to impose restrictions of Mexican trucks.*

4. Have students complete parts B and C of **Handout 42**. Review students' responses. Consider asking students to update part B with more recent information, and to compare and contrast that data with the information given on the handout. Graphs will vary depending on the statistical information used.

5. Use the following questions as a basis for a whole-class discussion.

   • Give examples of protection of policies contained in the agreement (*environment, jobs, patent and copyright protections*)

   • Why does the United States want to be more restrictive regarding jobs, immigration, and trucking? (*The United States is wary of illegal immigration, threats to job security, and potential terrorist threats.*)

   • What effect has NAFTA had on how much the United States exports to and imports from Canada? (*Exports have increased, and imports have increased dramatically.*)

   • How has this affected our trade balance with Canada? (*experienced a steady negative trade imbalance*)

   • What trend has occurred regarding exports to Mexico? (*Overall, exports have increased.*)

   • How can the United States decrease its negative trade balance with Mexico? (*by exporting more goods to Mexico*)

   • What conclusions can you draw about NAFTA's effects on the trade relationships among Canada, Mexico, and the United States? (*Overall, Canada and Mexico have increased their exports to the United States since the passage of NAFTA.*)

Enrichment/Extension

1. Have students research and report on trade policies in Europe under the Economic Union and compare and contrast them with the terms of NAFTA.

2. Have students research and report on the outsourcing of jobs and its effects on American employment figures.

The North American Free Trade Agreement, 1994

Part A.

Use an almanac, your textbook, and other sources to gather information about the North American Free Trade Agreement (NAFTA). Write a one-sentence summary of how NAFTA applies in each of the following areas.

Areas Governed by NAFTA	Application
Agriculture	
Automobiles	
Banking	
Disputes	
Energy	
Environment	
Immigration	
Jobs	
Patent and Copyright Protection	
Tariffs	
Textiles	
Trucking	

Part B.

Interpret the following table. Use the information to create a bar graph illustrating Mexico's exports to the United States.

Mexican Exports to the United States in 2001

Miscellaneous manufactured articles	15.16%
Fuels	7.77%
Goods by material	6.64%
Others	4.40%
Food and live animals	3.44%
Chemicals	1.39%
Beverages and tobacco	1.07%
Crude materials	0.57%
Animal and vegetable oils	0.02%
Machinery and vehicles	59.55%

Part C.

Use a variety of resources (including almanacs and Web sites) to find information on exports from Canada to the United States. Prepare a bar graph illustrating your data.

Lesson 23
The Impact of Congressional Investigations

Objective
- To understand the power Congress wields through its right of investigation

Notes to the Teacher
Recalling the abuse of executive power they had suffered under the British, the Founding Fathers wrestled with the problem of controlling the government in the new Republic. James Madison in *The Federalist Papers*, number 51, stated the problem this way:

> But the great security against a gradual concentration of the several powers in the same department consists in giving to those who administer each department the necessary constitutional means and personal motives to resist encroachments of the others. The provision for defence must in this, as in all other cases, be made commensurate to the danger of attack. Ambition must be made to counteract ambition. The interest of the man must be connected with the constitutional rights of the place. It may be a reflection on human nature that such devices should be necessary to control the abuses of government. But what is government itself but the greatest of all reflections on human nature? If men were angels, no government would be necessary. If angels were to govern men, neither external nor internal controls on government would be necessary. In framing a government which is to be administered by men over men, the great difficulty lies in this: you must first enable the government to control the governed; and in the next place oblige it to control itself.

To help the government control itself, the U.S. Constitution established a system of checks and balances designed to split and check the power to govern. In this regard, Congress has three vital powers: the power to authorize war, the power to control spending, and the power to investigate.

Congress, through its power to investigate, has played a particularly invaluable role in exposing domestic problems in the government. Originally, Congress used the power of special committees to investigate a specific problem. More recently, congressional standing committees have exercised their power to investigate as a prelude to proposing protective legislation.

In 1792, the Senate investigated the conduct of General Arthur St. Clair, who lost more than seven thousand men when his fort was attacked by Native Americans in the Northwest Territory. The investigating committee received conflicting evidence and eventually dropped the inquiry. St. Clair urged the Senate to reconsider the investigation after complaining that his reputation had been damaged by the charges. The investigation was never resumed.

In 1832, Sam Houston, a close friend of President Andrew Jackson, was investigated by a House Select Committee. Houston had allegedly received a lucrative contract to serve as an agent for Indian Affairs, even though his bid for the contract was much higher than other bids. Houston responded violently to the accusations. He attacked Ohio Representative William Stanberry, who was his chief critic, with a walking stick. Stanberry obtained a bench warrant for Houston's arrest, and Houston was fined $500, which President Jackson paid after Houston complained that he was only defending his honor. The committee, which was packed with Jacksonian Democrats, acquitted Houston.

More recently, hearings for independent counsel investigations and congressional committee hearings have exposed unethical and illegal practices.

In this lesson, students read and summarize eight congressional investigations from the impeachment trial of President Andrew Johnson to the impeachment of President William Jefferson Clinton. To conclude, they compose a paragraph on the appropriate and inappropriate uses of the congressional power of investigation.

Procedure

1. Discuss the power delegated to Congress which allows for the investigation of U.S. domestic problems.

2. Distribute **Handout 43**, and have students complete part A either individually or in small groups. Review students' responses.

Suggested Responses:

Johnson's Impeachment Trial—*When the House of Representatives impeached President Johnson on purely political grounds, the Senate failed to convict him.*

Teapot Dome—*The Senate Public Land Committee's investigation of the dealings of Secretary of the Interior Albert Fall revealed the need for stricter regulation of executive departments in order to protect the public interest.*

The Dies Committee—*This committee did irreparable damage to many people's reputations.*

The Truman Committee—*This committee did a responsible inquiry into waste, racial discrimination in hiring, and corruption in defense spending during U.S. preparations for World War II.*

The Watergate Inquiry—*The Watergate Committee exposed a pattern of deception that toppled a presidency and put new restrictions on the powers of the office.*

The Iran-Contra Affair—*An unconstitutional Executive Branch covert foreign policy plan was exposed; members of President Reagan's staff were punished for their abuse of the law.*

The Keating Five—*A corrupt savings and loan industry and unethical ties between bankers and senators who gave political favors for campaign donations were revealed; some senators were censured and did not seek reelection.*

Clinton's Impeachment Investigation—*The unethical behavior of President Clinton, who lied in a civil deposition and knowingly misled his Cabinet and constituents,*

was revealed; he was impeached but not removed from office.

Examples of good uses of the power to investigate are as follows: Teapot Dome; Truman Committee; Watergate Inquiry; Iran Contra; Keating Five.

Examples of questionable uses of the power of investigation are as follows: Johnson's Impeachment Trial and the Dies Committee.

3. Review the writing process for developing a good paragraph:

   • Develop a topic sentence.

   • Write four sentences giving evidence in support of your topic sentence.

   • Complete the paragraph by drawing a conclusion.

4. Assign part B of **Handout 43**. Review students' responses.

Suggested Responses:

Students might point out that congressional investigations have exposed an assortment of both real and imagined abuses in the executive branch. Students could cite evidence from any combination of investigations in the lesson. They might conclude that Congress has considerable power to check inappropriate uses of power in the executive branch but that Congress also has the power to damage people's reputations unjustly if the inquiries are not conducted responsibly.

Enrichment/Extension

Have students research and report on other congressional investigations and their outcomes. Examples include the Whitewater investigations and investigations into the abuse of prisoners in Iraq.

The Impact of Congressional Investigations

Part A.

Read the following descriptions of congressional investigations. Write a one-sentence summary of the problem and result in each investigation. Then determine which instances represent an appropriate, responsible use of the power of congressional investigation and which instances represent an inappropriate, irresponsible use of the power of investigation.

Andrew Johnson's Impeachment Trial, 1867

During the Civil War, President Abraham Lincoln assumed extraordinary powers to deal with the crisis between the North and the South. Lincoln's successor, Tennessee Democrat Andrew Johnson, proposed a conciliatory reconstruction plan that would have further increased the power of the president at the expense of Congress. Radical Republicans, hoping to prolong their control of Congress, pushed for harsher terms regarding the reentry of southern states into the Union. In 1867, Congress passed two laws, the Tenure of Office Act and the Command of the Army Act, which aimed to reduce the power of the president. When President Johnson tested the constitutionality of these acts by removing Secretary of War Edwin Stanton from office without congressional approval, the House of Representatives instituted impeachment proceedings against the president and approved eleven articles of impeachment. In the Senate trial, President Johnson was acquitted by a vote of thirty-five to nineteen, one vote short of the two-thirds majority needed for conviction and removal from office.

Teapot Dome, 1924

After an investigation, the Senate Public Land Committee charged that Secretary of the Interior Albert Fall had leased government oil lands in Teapot Dome, Wyoming, to Harry Sinclair and in Elk Hills, California, to Edward Doheny. In return, Secretary Fall received nearly half a million dollars in "loans" to ease his private financial problems. The Senate investigation forced President Calvin Coolidge to establish a special counsel to prosecute Fall and Sinclair. Both men were found guilty of criminal conspiracy and given jail sentences. Sinclair later appealed his conviction to the Supreme Court. In its statement on the issue, the Court stated that Congress may investigate, as in this instance, in order to understand the effect of its own laws.

The Dies Committee, 1938

Congressman Martin Dies of Texas, founding chairman of the House Committee on Un-American Activities, took the lead in trying to protect his ideal of "American purity" from dilution by immigrants, Catholics, African Americans, and Jews. The strongly antiunion Dies attempted to use the committee to make these groups scapegoats for the Great Depression and link them with the New Deal in order to slander it. The committee struck fear in both liberals and moderates and even aroused the concern of President Franklin D. Roosevelt when it manipulated publicity to reveal the political associations of individuals who had unorthodox political views. By threatening the career of each witness, the committee exerted tremendous power. Refusal to answer the committee's questions was regarded as an admission of guilt, and unjustly ruined many professional careers.

The Truman Committee, 1941

Senator Harry Truman, a Democrat from Missouri, became concerned about the waste, favoritism, and lack of direction in the World War II defense program. Defense contracts were awarded to Eastern businesses rather than to companies in the Midwest. On February 10, 1941, Senator Truman spoke on the Senate floor about scandals in the defense program. Of particular concern were possibilities for corruption and the administration's economic injustices in assigning defense contracts. Truman's investigative committee served as a watchdog of defense industries and exposed waste, chicanery, and racial discrimination in hiring. The inquiry, often considered a model of responsible, restrained investigation, served primarily to arouse public support for fair employment practices, an end to the duplication of programs, and the creation of a War Production Board to coordinate the war effort.

The Watergate Inquiry, 1973–74

In June 1972, five members of the Committee to Re-Elect the President broke into the Democratic Party headquarters in the Watergate Apartments in Washington, D.C. Both President Richard Nixon and Attorney General John Mitchell denied any knowledge of the break-in. James McCord, one of the defendants, implicated high administration officials in his testimony. The administration attempted one cover-up after another, with each further damaging the credibility of the president and his administration. The Senate Watergate Committee exposed the deception and political sabotage carried out by officials in the highest positions in the administration. The hearings resulted in a grand jury indictment of the president's closest associates—Robert Haldeman, John Erlichman, and John Mitchell—on charges of conspiracy, obstruction of justice, and perjury. The president himself was named as an unindicted coconspirator. President Nixon had tapes of White House conversations edited before he turned them over to the House Judiciary Committee, which was investigating the legality of the affair. Using the principle of executive privilege, Nixon withheld other tapes completely, a step that prompted the committee to take its case for the tapes to the Supreme Court and to make preparations for impeaching the president. When the Supreme Court ordered Nixon to turn over his files, and with no support in government and very little support among the American people, Nixon became the first president to resign from office to avoid impeachment and conviction. Vice President Gerald Ford assumed the presidency and later pardoned former President Nixon for all offenses against the United States.

The Iran-Contra Affair, 1986–87

In 1984, Congress passed the Boland Amendment, which prohibited U.S. military support for a group of rebels in Nicaragua fighting against the leftist Sandinista government. One of the legacies of the Carter administration was the seizure of hostages by Iran. In 1985, reports began to surface that the administration of President Ronald Reagan had secretly engaged in illegal covert actions involving the Contras and the hostages in Iran. When the operation was exposed by the media, the White House immediately denied the allegations. Eventually, it was acknowledged that some staff had engaged in illegal activity. A bipartisan committee led by Daniel Inouye, D-Hawaii, sought to determine how much the president knew, whether there were impeachable offenses, and if there had been the misuse of funds. The investigation revealed that both Secretary of Defense Caspar Weinberger and Secretary of State George P. Schultz had opposed the plan. The hearings exonerated President Reagan but led to the conviction of National Security Advisors Dexter Poindexter and Bud McFarlane and presidential advisors John Secord and Colonel Oliver North.

The Keating Five, 1989–91

During the 1980s, Congress deregulated the savings and loan industry. As a result, several savings and loans managers profited from unsecured business loans and risky large commercial real estate loan schemes. Hundreds of millions of dollars were paid to investors in a government bailout. A Senate Ethics Committee investigated five senators: Don Reigle, D-Mich., Dennis de Concini, D-Ariz., Alan Cranston, D-Calif., John McCain, R-Ariz., and John Glenn, D-Ohio. They allegedly intervened on behalf of Charles Keating, a California banker, to prevent an investigation of Lincoln Savings and Loan by federal investigators. At issue was whether the senators acted on behalf of Keating or his interests in exchange for cash campaign contributions. After two years of hearings, the committee agreed to exonerate McCain and Glenn. On the recommendation of the committee, the Senate mildly rebuked Reigle and de Concini and severely reprimanded Cranston, who had clearly helped Keating. Only McCain still serves in the Senate.

William Jefferson Clinton's Impeachment Investigation, 1998–99

In response to allegations that White House mailroom staff were improperly fired, as well as an alleged mishandling of an Arkansas real estate transaction, Independent Counsel Kenneth Starr was appointed to determine the innocence or guilt of President William Jefferson Clinton, First Lady Hilary Rodham Clinton, and members of the White House staff. The investigation uncovered evidence that President Clinton had engaged in efforts to impede testimony of female witnesses who charged the president with sexual harassment during his service as governor of Arkansas and as president. Evidence mounted that the president had discouraged several female staff members from making statements against him and had lied in a civil deposition about his sexual relationship with Monica Lewinsky, a White House intern. The issue raised was twofold. Had the president obstructed justice by making misleading statements under oath in the civil deposition, and were these impeachable offenses? The Republican-dominated House of Representatives voted to impeach. In bipartisan action, the Senate refused to convict the president but did criticize him publicly. In the course of the impeachment proceedings, two House speakers resigned when their own extramarital affairs were exposed.

Part B.

Write a short paragraph discussing the appropriate and inappropriate use of congressional power. Remember to develop a topic sentence, write four sentences giving evidence to support your topic sentence, and complete the paragraph by drawing a conclusion about the topic.

Part 4
The Executive Branch

This section deals with the executive branch and covers the many roles of the president, and the checks and balances on the powers of the president as exercised by the Congress and the Supreme Court. The range of activities the national government controls today, including the Cabinet and executive departments, are also explored. Lesson 24 examines the varied and complex roles of the president of the United States. Lesson 25 investigates the influence of various presidents on Congress. Lesson 26 evaluates the effectiveness of checks on the powers of the president. Lesson 27 develops an understanding of the cautions of the Founding Fathers about the abuse of presidential power and examines past and contemporary presidents in light of these cautions. Lesson 28 develops an understanding of the range of responsibilities of each Cabinet member and department as well as the relationship between individual Cabinet members and the president. Lesson 29 discusses how the vice presidency has evolved from a position of limited constitutional responsibility to one of active participation in the administration of the day-to-day operations of the national government.

Lesson 24
The Roles of the President

Objective
- To examine the varied and complex roles of the president of the United States

Notes to the Teacher

While President George Washington had an unprecedented popularity as president, those who followed fell prey to bitter partisan party politics. The Founding Fathers did not envision an especially powerful role for the president. Most state constitutions gave little or no power to the governor. Ratification debates between Federalists and Anti-federalists pessimistically expressed the fear that a president with all his powers, and no limits on time served, could become a tyrannical monarch. One of the most famous opponents of a strong executive branch was the Anti-Federalist Cato. Scholars now speculate that Cato was possibly New York Governor George Clinton. Cato wrote letters published in the *New York Journal* quoting French philosopher Baron de Montesquieu in warning against a powerful presidency: "he therefore fancies that he may be great and glorious by oppressing his fellow-citizens, and raising himself to permanent grandeur on the ruins of his country."

Despite these fears, the presidency has not become a monarchy. Strong presidents such as Washington, Thomas Jefferson, Andrew Jackson, and Abraham Lincoln enhanced the power of the presidency, while weaker presidents such as Ulysses S. Grant, Warren Harding, and Calvin Coolidge diminished presidential power. As years have passed, the powers of the presidency have greatly expanded. However, the man makes the office, and while some have been trapped by the legislative motives of Congress, others have sought to polish the prestige of office by establishing a strong legislative agenda in both domestic and foreign affairs. Some presidents, like Franklin D. Roosevelt, affected the time in which they lived. Others were forced to lead the nation in the face of incredible peril and strife, such as Lincoln during the Civil War.

The sources of presidential power are mixed and, in some cases, without clear definition. The Constitution explicitly delegates to the president the roles of commander-in-chief and chief executive. Other powers stem from congressional statutes, such as legislation that created an executive branch to support the president. The Employment Act of 1946 assigned the president responsibility for maintaining a stable and prosperous economy. Still other sources of authority and influence have accumulated through two centuries of custom and experimentation. The president has a role as leader of his political party and in fulfilling the obligations the American public imposes in the event of national emergencies. Together, these sources of power, influence, and authority make the American presidency the foremost seat of power in the world.

Moreover, the American political system, unlike that of the British, concentrates the duties as ceremonial head of state and actual leadership of the government in one person. Also, the executive branch, headed by the president, is distinct from the legislature and judiciary, while the prime minister of Great Britain is also a member of Parliament, Britain's bicameral legislature. In Britain, the reigning monarch assumes many ceremonial responsibilities as the symbolic head of the government and thus frees the prime minister to concentrate on policy-making duties. The American president, on the other hand, combines the time-consuming role of ceremonial head of state with many other demanding leadership roles.

In this lesson, students match the roles of the president with some of the responsibilities that flow from each role. They consider qualifications for the American presidency and discuss the implications of the expectations of the American public and the need to find individuals competent to perform the many duties of the office.

Procedure
1. Distribute **Handout 44**, and have students provide examples from history of the roles of the president. Have them complete the handout either individually or in small groups. Review students' responses.

Suggested Responses:

1.	c	6.	b
2.	g	7.	d
3.	h	8.	j
4.	i	9.	a
5.	e	10.	f

2. Ask students to name eight qualities that a president must possess in order to be an effective leader. Review students' responses.

Suggested Responses:

- *intelligence*
- *wide range of knowledge*
- *ability to compromise*
- *patience*
- *ability to communicate*
- *ability to motivate*
- *salesmanship*
- *good judgment*
- *courage*
- *innovation*
- *practicality*
- *ability to read the will of the people*
- *compassion*
- *skill in negotiation*
- *ability to plan*

3. Have students assume the persona of a presidential advisor. Tell students to select a presidential role and develop a seven-point checklist of whether the current president is performing well, according to their valued judgment. Have students spend a week evaluating the president on his performance in the role they selected. For example, as protector of the peace, has the president supported police and fire-fighters or helped defend the country against outside attack?

Enrichment/Extension

1. Have students research the accomplishments of a past president of their choice. Instruct students to write an editorial about why they esteem this president and his accomplishments. *The White House* (http://www.whitehouse.gov) is a helpful resource.

2. Have students search the Internet, magazines, newspapers, and television news programs for examples of the current president enacting two of his roles. Have students share with the class a brief explanation of what the president has done.

The Roles of the President

Match the lettered descriptions of ten roles the American people expect their president to perform with the numbered statements and quotations. Write the letter of the role in the space provided.

a. Chief of State—serves as the ceremonial head of government at public functions

b. Chief Executive—oversees the operation of government agencies; appoints Cabinet members, agency heads, and other officials; sees that laws are properly enforced

c. Commander-in-Chief—heads the military branches

d. Chief Diplomat—represents the country in foreign affairs

e. Chief Legislator—initiates possible legislation and works with Congress to achieve the administration's goals

f. Chief of Party—heads chosen political party

g. Voice of the People—represents the wishes of the general public

h. President of the West—acts as spokesman for the Free World

i. Protector of the Peace—preserves order in times of national emergency

j. Manager of the Prosperity—engineers economic controls to maintain a stable economy

_____1. " . . . George W. Bush lives by a simple code. The military needs hardware? Send it to them. U.S. allies are hesitant to engage? Go it alone. Iraq, Iran, and North Korea are rogue nations encouraging terrorism? Condemn them as an 'axis of evil.'"[1]

_____2. "What I'd really like to do is go down in history as the president who made Americans believe in themselves again."—Ronald Reagan

_____3. "Many Americans identified with him as the symbol of their own aspirations both for their country and for themselves. . . . More were captivated by his chic, his wit, his glamour. Above all, John F. Kennedy appealed to a sense of upward mobility, individual and national."[2]

_____4. "On October 14, [1962,] high administration officials expressed their disbelief that the Soviets and Cubans would try to install offensive, ground-to-ground missiles [in Cuba], particularly after President Kennedy had expressly warned against any such attempt in mid-September. . . . At 7 P.M. on October 22, the President broke the well-kept secret to the American people. Because the Soviets were building bases in Cuba 'to provide a nuclear strike capability against the Western Hemisphere,' . . . the United States would 'regard any nuclear missile launched from Cuba against any nation in the Western Hemisphere as an attack by the Soviet Union on the United States, requiring a full retaliatory response upon the Soviet Union.' . . . On . . . October 28 . . . sixteen Soviet ships sailing toward Cuba turned around in midocean to return to Russian ports. The crisis was over."[3]

_____5. "Unlike previous presidents, he proposed laws regulating the economy and pushed them through Congress—a ban on railroad rebates to big shippers, railroad rate regulation, inspection of meatpacking plants, the Food and Drugs Act. And he promoted conservation as no other president had, establishing many new national parks and national monuments."[4]

[1]Kenneth T. Walsh, "W, as in War," *U.S. News and World Report* (25 February–4 March 2002): 43.
[2]Godfrey Hodgson, *America in Our Time* (Garden City, N.Y.: Doubleday and Company, 1976), 5.
[3]Walter LaFeber, *America, Russia, and the Cold War 1945–1984* (New York: Alfred A. Knopf, 1985), 225–26.
[4]Michael Barone, "A Big Stick," *U.S. News and World Report* (25 February 25–4 March 2002): 55–6.

_____6. "The White House' in FDR's time, meant fewer than one hundred people. Even late in the Eisenhower administration, 'the Executive Office of the President,' complete with the Council on Economic Advisers and their staff, with the Office of Defense Mobilization and the NSC staff as well as the Bureau of the Budget and the President's own assistants and helpers, totaled only some twelve hundred. By the second Nixon administration, 'the White House' meant well over five thousand people."[5]

_____7. " . . . Clinton said that the United States had to lead on Bosnia, for humanitarian reasons if no other. . . . So the President took a number of decisions: to become directly involved in humanitarian action (this led to U.S. airdrops of food into Muslim-held areas of Bosnia.) . . . "[6]

_____8. [According to James A. Baker III,] "We had seven and a half years of sustained, noninflationary growth; we took six million poor Americans off the tax rolls; it was the longest peacetime expansion in the history of this country. Why? Because of supply-side economics. People say, 'Well, yes, instead of tax and spend, it was borrow and spend.' My answer to them is, Baloney!"[7]

_____9. In 1803, for pennies on the acre, Thomas Jefferson tripled the size of the American nation with the purchase of Louisiana from the French. "Whilst the property and sovereignty of the Mississippi and its waters secure an independent outlet for the produce of the Western States, and an uncontrolled navigation through their whole course, free from collision with our powers and the dangers to our peace from that source, the fertility of the country, its climate and extent, promise in due season important aids to our Treasury, an ample provision for our posterity, and a wide spread for the blessings of freedom and equal laws."[8]

_____10. In 1964, Democratic President Lyndon B. Johnson made several supportive phone calls to the home as well as posed with him in White House Oval office photos to be used for postcard political mailings, of the young Democratic congressional hopeful John A. Young, inspired to serve in politics by the youthful example of John F. Kennedy, who was running a reform campaign against an entrenched well-financed incumbent Republican candidate in Allegheny Pennsylvania. Like other presidents before him, Johnson hoped to sweep the young candidate of his party into office on the coattails of his presidency.

[5]Hodgson, *America in Our Time*, 108.
[6]Elizabeth Drew, *On the Edge: The Clinton Presidency* (New York: Touchstone, 1994), 146.
[7]Deborah Hart Strober and Gerald S. Strober, *Reagan: The Man and His Presidency* (Boston: Houghton Mifflin, 1998), 132.
[8]Thomas Jefferson, *The Life and Selected Writings of Thomas Jefferson*, ed. Adrienne Koch and William Peden (New York: Modern Library, 1972), 335–36.

Lesson 25
The President's Influence on Congress

Objective
- To investigate the influence of various presidents on Congress

Notes to the Teacher
Although the Constitution charges Congress with the responsibility for enacting legislation, the president has often been called the chief legislator because of the formal and informal influence he has in the legislative process. The president's annual State of the Union address and budget and economic messages to Congress announce his legislative agenda for the year. The effectiveness of the president in securing congressional approval for his programs depends upon many factors, including his personal popularity among congressmen, his success in building public support, and his skill in the use of patronage, personal lobbying, and political bargaining. A presidential veto—or even the threat of one—often proves persuasive. In the past, only about 3.5 percent of presidential vetoes have been overturned by Congress.

In this lesson, students read, contrast, and evaluate examples of the styles of two presidents in dealing with Congress. Students assume the role of a presidential advisor and select and research a problem currently confronting the American people. Lastly, students prepare a white paper outlining four steps the president should take to encourage Congress to pass a piece of proposed legislation.

Procedure
1. Ask students to give examples of current problems facing our nation (*the economy and joblessness, taxes, homeland security, better health care, social security*). List the examples on the chalkboard or on an overhead transparency for reference later in the lesson.

2. Divide the class into groups of three or four, and distribute **Handout 45**. Have students complete it as directed. Review students' responses.

Suggested Responses:
1. *unwillingness to cooperate and compromise with the opposition party; ineffective communication with the public; failure to consult Congress in the early planning stages of a program*

2. *work with opposition leaders; deal with congressmen on a personal level; communicate public concerns to Congress; understand and work through the committees in Congress; use outside influences to support one's position; announce plans in public in advance of congressional approval*

3. Have each group assume the role of a presidential advisor and select a problem from the list generated in procedure 1. Allow several days for students to gather information from print media and the Internet regarding their selection. Have students analyze the information gathered and research any legislation currently under consideration on the topic. Have each group prepare for the president a white paper in which they present four steps that may be taken to move this legislation successfully through Congress.

4. Have students present their white paper. Have the class reach consensus on the viability of each presentation and make suggestions on how the proposal might be changed to gain passage in Congress. Ask students what steps a president might take to gain passage of a bill. (*Students might mention the need to cooperate with the opposition; the need to work through individual congressmen; the need to enlist outside support groups and public endorsements; and the need to understand and communicate the public will to Congress, and perhaps understand the importance of, at times, creating public support for an idea.*)

Enrichment/Extension
Have selected students research, prepare, and present a short play on clashes between Congress and the president.

The President's Relations with Congress

Read the two selections, and then answer the questions.

Woodrow Wilson and the League of Nations

During World War I, President Woodrow Wilson authored the Fourteen Points, a plan for permanent world peace, and gained a popular following on both sides of the Atlantic. Determined to trust no one else with his program, Wilson headed the American delegation to the peace conference at Versailles in 1919. Seemingly unconcerned about the need for Senate ratification of the treaty, Wilson, a Democrat, selected negotiators to represent the United States without regard for political affiliation and snubbed powerful senators and opposition Republicans. In the long months of bargaining after the war, America's allies were determined to impose a vengeful peace on postwar Germany, and they forced Wilson to bargain away most of his Fourteen Points in return for acceptance of his beloved League of Nations.

When Wilson returned to the United States, he faced a Republican-controlled Senate and the bitter opposition of key senators. Isolationists, such as Senator William Borah, opposed any measure that might limit American independence or congressional authority to declare war. Henry Cabot Lodge, the chairman of the Senate Foreign Relations Committee and a moderate on the League of Nations, was bitterly hostile to Wilson. Lodge tried to humiliate the president and protect American sovereignty by promising to accept the League of Nations only if the agreement included a long list of reservations that Wilson contended would cripple the organization as an instrument of world peace.

Unable to persuade the Senate to accept his version of the treaty, Wilson embarked on a nationwide speech-making tour to convince a public disillusioned by World War I that international cooperation offered a better prospect for world peace than a return to isolationism. Midway through the tour, Wilson collapsed and suffered a stroke. The president's long recuperation in the White House isolated him from Congress. Wilson remained adamantly opposed to compromise and urged his supporters to reject the Treaty of Versailles and Lodge's reservations. Wilson's proposal failed, and the Senate rejected his version of the treaty. A second vote on the Lodge amendments failed to gain the two-thirds vote necessary for passage. At that point, Wilson urged the American people to view the election of 1920 as a referendum on the League of Nations. A vote for James M. Cox of Ohio was to be a vote for the League of Nations. Instead, Republican Warren G. Harding won the election, the Treaty of Versailles became a dead issue, and the United States never joined the League of Nations.

Lyndon B. Johnson and the Great Society

In the months after the assassination of John F. Kennedy, President Lyndon B. Johnson urged Congress to pass key proposals, focusing on civil rights and poverty programs, as a memorial to the late president. Public awareness of pressing economic and social problems had developed in the early 1960s. Johnson interpreted his huge electoral victory in 1964 as a mandate for reform. Subsequently, he pushed hard for enactment of his far-reaching Great Society programs. During the Johnson presidency, Congress became a tool of the chief executive as he forged the necessary coalitions needed to secure passage of his proposals.

Johnson had risen through the ranks of the House of Representatives and Senate and understood well the inner workings of Congress and the committee system. His close ties with individuals in both houses gave him credibility among congressmen, and he began by developing a wide variety of ideas and opinions on a broad range of issues. He read major newspapers and newsmagazines, watched television, kept in daily contact with congressmen, met with government leaders and specialists, and read his mail from both friends and enemies, the informed and the uninformed. Johnson believed that his job was to know the problems of each state and the temperament of each congressman in order to apply the right mix of persuasion, pressure, patronage, and punishments. As a former Senate majority leader, Johnson had paid attention to strategic details, cultivated individual personalities in Congress, and spent hours calling key congressmen in the final days before a crucial vote in order to accumulate the votes needed for passage. The Johnson strategies proved highly successful. During Johnson's five years in office, more than two hundred bills were enacted to create sweeping social and economic reforms in such areas as education, urban renewal, voting rights, immigration policy, welfare, public transportation, housing, and law enforcement.

1. List and explain three major mistakes President Woodrow Wilson made in trying to secure Senate approval for the League of Nations.

2. List five major ways that President Lyndon B. Johnson influenced the legislative process.

Lesson 26
Checks on Presidential Power

Objective
- To evaluate the effectiveness of checks on the powers of the president

Notes to the Teacher
The president of the United States has limited powers, which are kept in check by a series of checks and balances. According to the Constitution, the president may approve or veto bills submitted by Congress. However, Congress may override a presidential veto by a two-thirds vote. Congress may exercise considerable authority over the president by approving or withholding funds for specific projects. Moreover, the House of Representatives may vote impeachment charges against the president, who may be convicted and removed from office by the Senate. Finally, the Supreme Court may declare an action of the president to be unconstitutional.

Informal checks also limit the president's power. The president must work with his own political party during the election campaign and with both parties during the legislative process. The voters can turn an incumbent president out of office or defeat his party at the next election. The media, through their powers of investigating, reporting, and editorializing, can affect the president's public support and political strength in Congress. Even foreign countries and organizations abroad at times influence the president's foreign policies. In addition, the precedents of previous administrations act as a powerful guide to the president.

Within these constitutional and informal limits, presidents have considerable latitude in interpreting the extent of their powers. Like Congress, the president may view his powers in a narrow or broad perspective. William Howard Taft saw his role as little more than being chief executive. On the other hand, Theodore Roosevelt attempted to use all the power and influence of his office to lead the nation toward his vision of progressive reform. Presidents considered to be great by later generations usually have chosen a broader view of their powers.

In this lesson, students identify the various restraints on the actions of the president. They then evaluate the adequacy of these limitations and discuss how individual citizens play a role in shaping the boundaries within which an individual president may operate.

Procedure
1. Distribute **Handout 46**, and have students complete it either individually or in pairs. Have students summarize the view of the presidency as presented by Taft and Roosevelt. Review students' responses.

   Suggested Responses:

   Part A.

   Taft took a narrow interpretation of the powers of the presidency and considered it wrong to take any action not specifically listed in the Constitution or logically implied from such a grant of power.

   Roosevelt vastly broadened the powers of the presidency when he considered himself the "steward of the people" with the right to take any action not specifically prohibited to the president by the Constitution or Congress.

   Part B.

   1. Roosevelt

   2. Roosevelt

   3. Roosevelt

   4. Both presidents

2. Distribute **Handout 47**, and have students complete it as directed. Review students' responses.

   Suggested Responses:

   1. Supreme Court ruled an act of the president unconstitutional.

   2. Senate must approve treaties negotiated by the president.

   3. The threat of removal from office restricts the powers of the president.

183

4. *The power to override vetoes—and even the threat of overrides—restricts the president.*

5. *Presidents must take into account the views of powerful lobbies.*

6. *The precedents of previous presidents are often influential; soon after Franklin Roosevelt defied this long-established tradition, Congress initiated a constitutional amendment to make the restriction law.*

7. *The president cannot act independently of the members of his party.*

8. *The Supreme Court overrode an action of the president.*

9. *The Senate must approve presidential appointments.*

10. *The people can defeat a candidate—or at least his party—in the next election.*

11. *The president must listen to the voice of voters and powerful lobbying groups.*

12. *The president cannot make the voters respond to his wishes.*

13. *The Supreme Court overrode an action of the president.*

14. *The media adversely affected the president's public support.*

15. *The Congress failed to enact legislation to accomplish the desired presidential action.*

3. Have students categorize the checks on the president into two or three kinds of restrictions. Then have them write one sentence that summarizes the checks on the president of the United States. (*Constitutional and political restrictions, as well as the precedents of previous presidents, act as checks on the power of the president.*) Ask students what responsibilities each citizen has to keep the president's powers in check. (*Citizens need to be informed on current issues and their implications, to vote, to write letters to the editor, to speak out on current concerns, and to become involved in or otherwise support watchdog agencies.*)

Enrichment/Extension

Have students research and report on how Congress has used the system of checks and balances to control the power of the executive branch.

Checks on Presidential Power

Part A.

Read the two contrasting concepts of the presidency, and summarize each in your own words.

> The true view of the executive functions is, as I conceive it, that the president can exercise no power which cannot be fairly and reasonably traced to some specific grant of power or justly implied and included within such express grant as proper and necessary to its exercise. Such specific grant must be either in the federal Constitution or in an act of Congress passed in pursuance thereof. There is no undefined residuum of power which he can exercise because it seems to him to be in the public interest. . . .
>
> —William Howard Taft

> The most important factor in getting the right spirit in my Administration, next to the insistence upon courage, honesty, and a genuine democracy of desire to serve the plain people, was my insistence upon the theory that the executive power was limited only by specific restrictions and prohibitions appearing in the Constitution or imposed by the Congress under its Constitutional powers. My view was that every executive officer, and above all every executive officer in high position, was a steward of the people bound actively and affirmatively to do all he could for the people, and not to content himself with the negative merit of keeping his talents undamaged in a napkin. I declined to adopt the view that what was imperatively necessary for the Nation could not be done by the President unless he could find some specific authorization to do it. . . . Under this interpretation of executive power I did and caused to be done many things not previously done by the President and the heads of the departments. I did not usurp power, but I did greatly broaden the use of executive power. . . .
>
> —Theodore Roosevelt

Part B.

Determine to which president each listed role could be applied.

Role	Taft	Roosevelt
1. Chief Legislator		
2. Manager of the Prosperity		
3. President of the West		
4. Chief Executive		

Presidential Power

Presidents can wield considerable power. There are, however, limits on their powers. Read the following statements. On a separate sheet of paper, explain who checks the powers of the president and how the powers are checked.

1. By an 8–0 vote, the Supreme Court directed Richard Nixon to turn over the Watergate tapes to the Special Prosecutor and the House Judiciary Committee. President Nixon had claimed executive privilege in refusing to surrender the tapes.

2. Woodrow Wilson proposed the creation of a League of Nations as the first step in maintaining world peace. Because the Senate refused to ratify the Treaty of Versailles in 1919, the United States never joined the League of Nations.

3. In 1868, the House of Representatives impeached Andrew Johnson, but the Senate failed by one vote to convict him. In 1974, Richard Nixon resigned the presidency rather than face certain impeachment and removal from office.

4. Congress has overridden almost one hundred of the more than 2,800 presidential vetoes to date.

5. The American Medical Association exerted such strong pressure against John F. Kennedy's Medicare proposal that Kennedy did not push the measure because he knew he could not win.

6. Until Franklin Roosevelt, no president had served more than two terms. The two-term limit had been considered binding since Washington's time.

7. Republican leaders met with President Richard Nixon to recommend Gerald Ford to replace Spiro Agnew as vice president. Nixon agreed.

8. President Harry Truman's attempt to seize control of American steel mills during the Korean Conflict was declared unconstitutional.

9. Richard Nixon nominated Clement Haynesworth and Harold Carswell to the Supreme Court, but the Senate refused to confirm either nominee.

10. Gerald Ford was voted out of office in 1976 after two years as president. Jimmy Carter lost his bid for reelection in 1980.

11. When the Carter administration proposed minor cuts in Social Security, the elderly reacted so strongly that no one in Congress would even introduce the bill.

12. In 1938, Franklin Roosevelt actively campaigned against congressional representatives who opposed his New Deal programs. In almost every instance, voters returned the congressional representatives to office in the election.

13. In 1935, the Supreme Court declared the National Recovery Act, a key part of Franklin Roosevelt's New Deal to end the Great Depression, to be unconstitutional. Roosevelt was forced to dismantle the program.

14. In March 1968, Lyndon Johnson announced he would not seek reelection to the presidency. This, he cited, was due to his lack of popularity and the public's unhappiness with the public's course of the Vietnam War, which had intensified into a full-scale conflict during his administration.

15. Following his reelection in 1936, Franklin Roosevelt tried to increase the number of justices on the Supreme Court to fifteen. These new justices would counter those already on the Court who opposed Roosevelt's New Deal legislation. Congress refused to increase the Court's size despite its having been increased six times since 1789.

Lesson 27
The Imperial Presidents: Andrew Jackson and Richard Nixon

Objectives

- To understand the cautions of the Founding Fathers about the abuse of presidential power

- To examine past and contemporary presidents in light of these cautions

Notes to the Teacher

Many of the Founding Fathers were skeptical of the role of president and assumed the worst: that a presidency would lead to self-aggrandizement and thus exploit the good will of the people. These fears were demonstrated in the ratification debates contrasting the new presidency to a monarchy. It should be noted that the Founding Fathers were the most talented, educated, propertied men of the nation. They took a dim view not only of human nature, but also (more practically) of their fellow citizens—yeomen farmers, tradesmen, and sailors. They were, after all, the product of aristocratic principles like primogeniture and the propertied vote for gentlemen only. Some, like Alexander Hamilton, preferred some type of aristocratic rule. Gouverneur Morris desired some type of property qualification as a qualification for voting, while others thought that such action would disenfranchise many. Benjamin Franklin, the voice of the common man, reminded the assembly of the great virtues of citizens which shone during the Revolutionary War.

Given their political philosophy regarding human nature and their experience in governance, it is easy to understand why the Founding Fathers cautioned their political peers to take heed of a too powerful presidency. George Mason proposed an executive office composed of three persons. Others warned against the unchecked power and ambition of talented presidents and cited specific power of veto, pardons, and appointments that easily could lead to abuse.

In the world of the twentieth century, with its urgent domestic and foreign perils, the president has assumed some powers formerly reserved for Congress. The need for immediate remedies in economic and foreign crises has frequently prompted the American people to look to their president for quick solutions. Thus, the potential exists for the president to become more imperial and less democratic.

In America's past, there have been charges of abuse of power, or the Constitution, by the president. Thomas Jefferson, a strict constructionist, opposed increased power for the federal government, yet purchased a piece of land that doubled the size of our fledgling nation with taxpayers' money and without the consent of Congress. Out of government funds came expenses to hire a crew of explorers led by Meriwether Lewis and William Clark. Later, Andrew Jackson was strongly criticized for flaunting the rulings of the Supreme Court and trampling on the powers of Congress, earning for himself the nickname "King Andrew." In 1986, the attempts of Ronald Reagan's administration to trade arms for hostages and divert funds to the Contras led to a Senate investigation of whether the president had violated the letter and spirit of the Constitution.

Many presidents have been accused of abusing their power. During the Great Depression and World War II, Franklin D. Roosevelt vastly increased the power and authority of the presidency when he proposed solutions for America's economic problems and later in coordinating the Allied war effort. Roosevelt used the radio to keep the people informed about his programs. However, when his court-packing proposal threatened the basic principle of checks and balances, Congress refused its assent.

In the same vein, Lyndon Johnson wielded considerable power in the first months of his administration as he worked closely with Congress to enact wide-ranging Great Society programs. In the end, he submitted to the public will by abandoning his bid for reelection when it became apparent that Congress and the general public no longer supported his Vietnam policies.

Richard Nixon remains the one president who so violated the public trust that he was threatened with certain impeachment and removal from office. Nixon tried to thwart Congress, the Supreme Court, and the public in a manner many considered inconsistent with the democratic process. His imperial presidency ended when he resigned in 1974, rather than face removal from office.

In this lesson, students analyze two political cartoons on the Jackson and Nixon presidencies and then write a paragraph showing how Nixon so violated the public trust that he was forced to resign. In preparation for this lesson, consider having students research the meaning of the following issues crucial to understanding the cartoons:

- the constitutional crisis over the Watergate tapes, where Nixon tried to invoke executive privilege in defense of his refusal to turn over tape recordings of critical Watergate conversations in the White House

- Nixon's secret authorization of bombing raids on supply depots in Cambodia in 1970 during the Vietnam War

- the Cooper-Church Amendment to the 1971 Foreign Aid bill, which specified that the president could not use funds in Indochina except to withdraw all U.S. forces (This Senate move to impose legislative restrictions on the president's authority in war-making was narrowly defeated by a forty-seven to forty-four margin.)

Procedure

1. Review the powers vested in the president by the Constitution. Distribute **Handout 48**, and read the selections aloud. Conduct a whole-class discussion using the following questions as a guide:

   - What type of presidency did George Mason suggest? (*a three person presidency*)

   - How would this triumvirate be chosen? (*from three different regions*)

   - What would such a style of presidency prevent? (*cabals and intrigues*)

   - What role did Patrick Henry believe the president should assume? (*if he is ambitious and able, that of monarch or king*)

- How would the president's role be affected if he were guilty of a crime? (*He would increase his power and not listen to the court.*)

- What concerns about elections did Cato have? (*no specific concerns*)

- What were Cato's concerns regarding the influence of appointments and pardons? (*The president could select or pardon whomever he wants.*)

- What did Cato believe could ruin the United States? (*presidential ambition and unrestricted presidential power*)

2. Distribute **Handout 49**, and have students read the biographical sketches of Andrew Jackson and Richard Nixon in part A. Ask students the following questions:

   - How would you characterize Jackson's presidency? (*He tried to act on behalf of citizens and acted responsibly to keep the union together during the nullification crisis.*)

   - What are some of Jackson's actions that led to his being called King Andrew? (*Jackson ignored states' rights; he seemed to ignore the ruling of the Supreme Court in the case of* The Cherokee Nation v. Georgia, *causing a philosophical crisis about the interpretation and enforcement of the Constitution; he imposed his policy for removing Native Americans from their lands on the states; he opposed those who supported the National Bank. Jackson challenged the existence of the bank and attempted to destroy it.*)

   - What actions of Richard Nixon caused him to be regarded as an imperial president? (*He condoned breaking the law, when he approved of the Watergate burglary and the burglary of Daniel Ellsberg's psychiatrist's office. He refused to turn over tapes as evidence, and when he did, they were edited and incomplete.*)

3. Consider preparing an overhead transparency of the cartoons in part B of **Handout 49** to facilitate discussion. Have students analyze the cartoons as a whole-group activity. Ask students to explain the significance of the hydra in Cartoon 1 in depicting the

Bank of the United States and the use of the sword by Jackson. (*The bank's state representatives were all connected. Killing one will only grow another head.*) Ask whether students believe that Jackson had an imperial presidency. Opinions will vary, but students should be able to support their answer. Have students identify the following symbols in Cartoon 2:

- crown (*royalty*)

- dome (*capitol building*)

- scepter and eagle (*imagined royal American power*)

- scroll (*proclaims President Nixon to be king*)

- court attendant (*Spiro T. Agnew, vice president*)

Have students summarize the main idea of the cartoon. (*Nixon imagines himself as a king rather than an elected official.*)

4. Have students develop a paragraph analyzing the concept of the imperial presidency as depicted in the cartoons. The first sentence should state the thesis. Students should be able to write at least three sentences with supporting evidence for the main idea. Finally, in a concluding sentence, students should state the effects of the imperial presidency on American government.

Suggested Response:

Students may state that the cartoonists illustrate Jackson's and Nixon's disregard for the public's right to information about the conduct of his administration, and a defiance of the federal courts. Students might conclude that the men's actions threatened democratic government. Americans must be vigilant to regulate the power of the presidency as a result of abuses by past administrations.

Enrichment/Extension

1. Ask selected students to research other examples of imperial leadership and prepare short reports to be presented to the class. Topics might include Ronald Reagan's arms-for-hostages deal with Iran, William Clinton's assignment of U.S. troops to Bosnia and Somalia, and George W. Bush's invasion of Iraq.

2. Conduct a class debate on the following topic: Resolved: The Constitution of the United States should be amended to restrict the president's use of armed forces without a declaration of war by Congress.

The Imperial Presidency

Read each of these short excerpts. Be prepared for class discussion.

. . . If the Executive is vested in three Persons, one chosen from the northern, one from the middle, and one from the Southern States, will it not contribute to quiet the Minds of the People, & convince them that there will be proper attention paid to their respective Concerns? Will not three Men so chosen bring with them, into Office, a more perfect and extensive Knowledge of the real Interests of this great Union? Will not such a Model of Appointment be the most effectual means of preventing Cabals and Intrigues between the Legislature and the Candidates for this Office?

—George Mason

If your American chief, be a man of ambition, and abilities, how easy is it for him to render himself absolute: The army is in his hands, and, if he be a man of address, it will be attached to him. . . . If ever he violates the laws, one of the two things will happen: He shall come to the head of his army to carry every thing before him; or, will he give bail, or do what Mr. Chief Justice will order him. If he be guilty, will not the recollection of his crimes teach him to make one bold push for the American throne? . . . Away with your President, we shall have a King: The army will salute him Monarch. . . .

—Patrick Henry

. . . [T]he first section of the second article is vague and inexplicit, and leaves the mind in doubt as to the election of a president . . . after the expiration of the election for the first term of four years. . . . [H]is power of nomination and influence on all appointments, . . . the unrestrained power of granting pardons for treason, which may be used to screen from punishment those whom he had secretly instigated to commit the crime, and thereby prevent a discovery of his own guilt, his duration in office of four years . . . if the president is possessed of ambition, he has power and time sufficient to ruin his country.

—Cato

Presidential Power Abused

Part A.

Read the biographical sketches of Andrew Jackson and Richard Nixon, and be prepared for class discussion.

King Andrew

Andrew Jackson, whose nickname was "Old Hickory," was born in South Carolina in 1767. He was the first president to be born in a log cabin. Though he was poorly educated, he became a lawyer. Jackson was most famous, though, for his service as a military leader. He led American forces in New Orleans during the War of 1812 and served briefly as military governor of the Louisiana Territory. He was also known for his leadership during a series of wars against the Creeks and Seminoles in the southeastern United States.

In 1824, Jackson ran in the presidential election against John Quincy Adams. This was the election that was famous for the "corrupt bargain." Henry Clay allegedly gave his electoral votes to Adams in exchange for an appointed office, resulting in Jackson's defeat. In 1828, Jackson ran again against the incumbent, John Quincy Adams, and was elected.

Jackson's supporters began to call themselves Democrats. His election marked a new era in American politics. Jackson was a man of the west and prided himself on representing the people. He had been poor most of his life and was an orphan and a self-made man. When he became president, one of the first things he did was fire 10 percent of the workers on the federal payroll and replace them with his own people. This was the beginning of the "spoils system."

Jackson believed that he was the only government official, except for the vice president, who had been elected by all the people. It is ironic that this man of the people was accused of assuming the powers of a king.

In 1830, Jackson became involved in a dispute between the state of Georgia and the Cherokee Nation. The U.S. government had regarded most of the Indian tribes as sovereign nations. They had their own laws and, in many cases, elected leaders and assemblies. The Cherokee Nation was one of the most advanced of the Eastern tribes. They had assumed the trappings of a white society and lived peacefully with their white neighbors. The U.S. Congress passed the Indian Removal Act, which confiscated Native American land and gave the government the right to relocate the Indians of the Southeast west into unoccupied land. When gold was discovered on Cherokee lands, the state of Georgia attempted to use the Indian Removal Act to force the Cherokees to leave their ancestral home. The Cherokee Nation sued the state of Georgia. The case was ruled on by the U.S. Supreme Court. Chief Justice John Marshall wrote the majority opinion, which stated that only the federal government had the right to move the Cherokees off their lands. Marshall stated that Georgia had no right to apply its laws to the Cherokee Nation, which was just that, a separate and sovereign nation. Jackson, who had no love for the Native Americans of the Southeast, openly defied the Court and refused to enforce Marshall's ruling. The forced removals were allowed to continue.

Jackson next came into conflict with his vice president, John C. Calhoun. A South Carolinian, Calhoun had been a vocal opponent of a federal tariff that he believed unfairly taxed the southern economy. Calhoun referred to this tariff as the "Tariff of Abominations." The conflict between Calhoun and Jackson resulted in Calhoun's resignation and would eventually lead to the Nullification Crisis. Calhoun would defy Jackson and lead South Carolina in a fight to "nullify" laws that the state felt were in their best interest.

During Jackson's campaign for reelection in 1832, the fate of the Second Bank of the United States became an important issue. Jackson had always hated banks. He believed that banks took money from those who could least afford to lose it, the poor farmer. When he was elected to a second term, Jackson set out to destroy the bank. Jackson withdrew federal money from the Second Bank of the United States and deposited in state banks, creating what came to be known as "pet" banks. When the director of the bank, Nicholas Biddle, could not cover the withdrawals, he began to call in loans. Biddle's action brought the nation to the brink of financial panic. Eventually, the state banks began to lend the money deposited by Jackson to farmers. A land boom resulted, causing Jackson to believe that his action in dismantling the national bank was justified. Jackson had acted without the consent of Congress, which had created the bank. One of Jackson's last actions before leaving office was to issue the Specie Circular. Jackson was worried that the state banks were issuing money, which had little gold or silver to back it, resulting in an unstable national economy. The Specie Circular declared that buyers could no longer use paper money to purchase federal land but had to use gold or silver. Because few people had gold or silver available, land sales plunged. Businesses closed their doors, and a bank panic spread when the government refused to accept paper money from the state banks. By the time Jackson left office, America's economy was floundering. Soon a full-scale bank panic occurred. It would take years before the U.S. economy recovered.

Richard Nixon and Watergate

In November 1968, Richard Nixon was elected president of the United States. Nixon, who had served as vice president under Dwight D. Eisenhower, took office at the height of protests against the Vietnam War. Nixon had always had questions about the intelligence-gathering capabilities of the United States. In July 1970, he approved a plan, which he later rescinded, to expand the domestic intelligence gathering by the FBI and other agencies.

In June 1971, *The New York Times* published the Pentagon Papers, the Defense Department's secret history of the Vietnam War. Daniel Ellsberg, a Defense Department employee, had leaked the files to a reporter at the *Times*. In September 1971, a group of White House "plumbers" burglarized the office of Ellsberg's psychiatrist to plug any leak that might affect the administration. One year later, five men were arrested when they tried to install bugging equipment in the office of the Democratic National Committee at the Watergate Hotel and office complex. A Republican security aide is among those arrested, as well as another individual who claimed to be a member of the CIA.

In August 1972, a cashier's check in the amount of $25,000, drawn on money given as contributions to Nixon's reelection campaign, was found to have been deposited in the bank account of one of the Watergate burglars. The money was traced to a secret fund administered by John Mitchell, Nixon's former attorney general. An investigation by FBI agents uncovered a massive campaign of political spying and sabotage conducted by the Committee to Re-Elect the President (CREEP).

In November 1972, Richard Nixon was reelected in a landslide victory. Shortly after Nixon was inaugurated for his second term, two former White House employees, G. Gordon Liddy and James W. McCord Jr., were convicted on charges of conspiracy, burglary, and illegal wiretapping in the Watergate incident. In April 1973, two of Nixon's aides, H. R. (Bob) Haldeman and John Ehrlichman, and Attorney General Richard Kleindeinst resigned. White House counsel John Dean was fired.

In May 1973, the Senate Watergate Committee began nationally televised hearings. Archibald Cox was named as special prosecutor. In June 1973, John Dean told Watergate investigators that he had discussed a cover-up of the Watergate incident at least thirty-five times with the president. A memo from Ehrlichman detailing the plans to break into the office of Ellsberg's psychiatrist surfaced. In July, Alexander Butterfield, a former presidential appointments secretary, testified before Congress that all conversations in the Oval Office were tape-recorded. Five days later, Nixon ordered the taping system to be dismantled.

Nixon refused to turn over the presidential tape-recordings to the Senate Watergate Committee or to the special prosecutor. In October 1973, Nixon fired Cox as special prosecutor and abolished the office. Attorney General Elliot Richardson and Deputy Attorney General William Ruckelshaus resigned in protest.

Members of the House of Representatives began to discuss a possible impeachment vote. In December 1973, the White House was called upon to explain an eighteen-and-a-half-minute gap in one of the subpoenaed tapes. In April 1974, the White House released twelve hundred pages of edited transcripts of presidential tapes to the House Judiciary Committee. Members of the committee then ordered Nixon to turn over the actual tapes. Nixon appealed to the Supreme Court on the grounds that the tapes were protected by the principle of executive privilege. The Supreme Court rejected Nixon's argument and ordered in a 8–0 ruling that Nixon must surrender the tapes of sixty-four conversations.

On July 24, 1974, the House Judiciary Committee passed the first of three articles of impeachment, charging the president with obstruction of justice. On August 8, 1974, Nixon became the first president to resign from office because of the threat of impeachment. Vice President Gerald R. Ford became president and later pardoned Nixon of any charges associated with Watergate.

Part B.

Analyze the following cartoons, and be prepared for class discussion.

Fig. 27.1.

Fig. 27.2.

Fig. 27.1. President Andrew Jackson destroying the Bank of the United States. Lithograph cartoon, 1828. The Granger Collection, New York.

Fig. 27.2. "Thou mayest announce to the assembled multitudes that my governmental reorganization is complete." Hugh Haynie, *Louisville Courier-Journal,* 1972.

Lesson 28
The Cabinet and Executive Departments

Objectives
- To understand the range of responsibilities of each Cabinet member and his or her department

- To understand the relationship between individual Cabinet members and the president

Notes to the Teacher
The Cabinet, which was not mentioned in the Constitution, has evolved by custom and usage from the earliest days of the Republic. President George Washington recognized the need to delegate power for administering various governmental departments. His Cabinet included four positions: secretary of state, secretary of the treasury, secretary of war, and attorney general. Over the years, the Cabinet has grown to include the heads of fourteen executive departments, including the Department of Homeland Security.

In the early days of the nation, the selection of Cabinet members was based on their prior knowledge and experience in a specific field. Washington's Cabinet was a group from a wide-ranging political spectrum. Secretary of the Treasury Alexander Hamilton was a supporter of a strong federal government, while Secretary of State Thomas Jefferson leaned toward state sovereignty. Washington used the expertise of his Cabinet to make decisions for the nation. When the Bank of the United States was created, Washington sought to determine its constitutionality. Hamilton believed that the law creating the bank was constitutional under the "necessary and proper clause." Jefferson, on the other hand, stated that nowhere in the Constitution was Congress given the power to create banks or corporations. This was a right of the states alone.

Presidential Cabinets have been divided more often than not. Under John Adams, the members of the Cabinet believed that the executive branch was ruled by committee and that they had an equal vote with the president in making decisions for the good of the nation. When Adams tried to dismiss Timothy Pickering, his secretary of state, for undermining the president's authority, Pickering refused to leave office.

Sometimes Cabinet members become embroiled in controversies with the other branches of the government. Cabinet members serve in two capacities. They administer the department they head and they act, to the extent the president wishes, as his policy-making advisers. Some presidents, such as John Kennedy, have consulted their Cabinets infrequently. Others, including Dwight Eisenhower and Ronald Reagan, relied heavily on the advice of Cabinet members. Under President Reagan, a Cabinet council, including the ambassador to the United Nations, the director of the Central Intelligence Agency, the director of the Office of Management and Budget, and White House counsel, helped integrate executive department heads into the decision-making process at the highest levels. The real power of the Cabinet depends, to a large extent, on a president's willingness to delegate authority. The department heads are obligated to serve the public and to contribute to a positive image of honesty, integrity, and efficiency for the administration they serve.

In this lesson, students categorize administrative tasks under the appropriate executive departments. Students examine the responsibilities of the Cabinet departments, analyze the selection of Cabinet members, and assess members' performances.

Procedure
1. Review the history and responsibilities of the president's Cabinet. The Notes to the Teacher section provides guidance for such a review.

2. Distribute **Handout 50**, and have students complete it either individually or in small groups. Review students' responses.

Suggested Responses:

1. Department of State
   a. *Passport and Visa Office*
   b. *Foreign Service*
   c. *Bureau of African Affairs*

2. Department of Defense
   a. *Department of the Navy*
   b. *Joint Chiefs of Staff*

3. Department of the Interior
   a. *Bureau of Indian Affairs*
   b. *National Park Service*

4. Department of Commerce
   a. *National Bureau of Standards*
   b. *Bureau of the Census*
   c. *Patent and Trademarks Office*

5. Department of Health and Human Services
   a. *Social Security*
   b. *Public Health Service*

6. Department of the Treasury
   a. *Customs Service*
   b. *Internal Revenue Service*
   c. *Secret Service*
   d. *Bureau of Engraving and Printing*

7. Department of Justice
   a. *Antitrust Division*
   b. *Civil Rights Division*
   c. *Drug Enforcement Administration*
   d. *Federal Bureau of Investigation*

8. Department of Agriculture
   a. *Forest Service*
   b. *Food Safety and Inspection Service*
   c. *Soil Conservation Service*

9. Department of Labor
   a. *Occupational Safety and Health Administration*

10. Department of Housing and Urban Development
    a. *Agency for Community Planning and Development*

11. Department of Transportation
    a. *Federal Aviation Administration*
    b. *National Highway Traffic Safety Administration*

12. Department of Education
    a. *Assistant Secretary for Elementary and Secondary Education*
    b. *Title I*
    c. *Head Start*

13. Department of Energy
    a. *Environmental Protection Agency*
    b. *Fossil Energy*

3. Distribute **Handout 51**, and have students complete it individually, in small groups, or in a large group. Review students' responses.

Suggested Responses:

1. *Transportation*
2. *Interior*
3. *State*
4. *Agriculture*
5. *Justice*
6. *Commerce*
7. *Health and Human Services*
8. *Transportation*
9. *State*
10. *Defense*
11. *Justice*
12. *Housing and Urban Development*
13. *Agriculture*
14. *Interior*
15. *Health and Human Services*
16. *Commerce*

4. Have students write and share a short essay on the following topic: Explain the need for the president to consider a variety of factors in selecting members of his Cabinet.

Suggested Responses:

Cabinet members should reflect the following characteristics: loyalty to the president; same political philosophy; administrative skill; diversity of race, gender, or ethnic background.

The following factors are important in creating a strong Cabinet: implement the president's policies; help the president in policymaking; must have a political philosophy consistent with that of the chief executive; must be able to administer the department skillfully and reflect creditably on the president.

The Cabinet should reflect the diversity of the country. A Cabinet department can enhance or detract from the effectiveness in carrying out the president's agenda and providing efficient service to the public. Students should provide examples from recent administrations.

Have selected students share their essays.

Enrichment/Extension

Have students research and report on areas in which they believe a Cabinet position should be created. Have them write an editorial explaining the reasons for their choice.

Name_____

Date_____

Responsibilities of the Executive Departments

Use your textbook or other reference materials to complete the outline by categorizing each of the following agencies under the executive department to which it is responsible.

Antitrust Division

Customs Service

Civil Rights Division

Agency for Community Planning and Development

Drug Enforcement Administration

Bureau of Indian Affairs

Department of the Navy

Forest Service

National Bureau of Standards

Federal Aviation Administration

Passport and Visa Office

Federal Bureau of Investigation

Foreign Service

Occupational Safety and Health Administration

Social Security

Bureau of the Census

Assistant Secretary for Elementary and Secondary Education

Environmental Protection Agency

National Highway Traffic Safety Administration

Secret Service

Public Health Service

Patent and Trademarks Office

Soil Conservation Service

Bureau of African Affairs

Bureau of Engraving and Printing

Joint Chiefs of Staff

Fossil Energy

National Park Service

Title I

Head Start

Food Safety and Inspection Service

Internal Revenue Service

1. Department of State

    a. _____

    b. _____

    c. _____

2. Department of Defense

    a. _____

    b. _____

3. Department of the Interior

    a. _____

    b. _____

4. Department of Commerce

    a. _____

    b. _____

5. Department of Health and Human Services

    a. _____

    b. _____

6. Department of the Treasury

    a. _____

    b. _____

    c. _____

7. Department of Justice

    a. _____

    b. _____

    c. _____

    d. _____

8. Department of Agriculture

    a. _____

    b. _____

    c. _____

9. Department of Labor

    a. _____

10. Department of Housing and Urban Development

    a. _____

11. Department of Transportation

    a. _____

    b. _____

12. Department of Education

    a. _____

    b. _____

    c. _____

13. Department of Energy

    a. _____

    b. _____

    c. _____

Identifying Executive Departments

For each statement, identify the executive department that has responsibility for the individual's concern. Write the name of the department in the space to the left.

_____ 1. Mr. Adams, after rescuing a railroad from bankruptcy and making it profitable, now seeks permission to sell it in the private sector.

_____ 2. A coalition of Native Americans appealed for assistance in improving public health services on their reservations.

_____ 3. Mrs. Pulaski appealed to this department for a visa to Poland.

_____ 4. Mrs. Smith asked this department to check a local food processor for improperly grading meats.

_____ 5. Mr. Oprita asked a bureau of this department to check on a neighbor for housing a criminal.

_____ 6. Miss Jones applied to this department for a patent on a new type of hair curler.

_____ 7. Dr. Johanni asked this department to investigate an epidemic of skin rashes in the area.

_____ 8. Ohio Shipbuilding Corporation asked this department to investigate the possibilities of enlarging the St. Lawrence Seaway.

_____ 9. Secretary Hall sought the release of American hostages being held by Iraqi terrorists.

_____ 10. President Reagan used this department to protect American interests in Grenada.

_____ 11. During the 1960s, blacks asked a division of this department for help with voter registration problems.

_____ 12. The mayor of Houston announced the city's receipt of a block grant to rehabilitate declining neighborhoods.

_____ 13. Mr. Black received advice on the best methods of maintaining ground moisture in the semiarid region of Nebraska.

_____ 14. Mr. Moxley wrote to this department for information about camping in the national park system.

_____ 15. Mr. and Mrs. Dare were distraught by this department's announced intention to reduce their retirement income.

_____ 16. Every ten years Mr. Schofield has been visited for the purpose of counting him and his family in the census.

Lesson 29

The Transformation of the Vice Presidency

Objective
- To understand how the vice presidency has evolved from a position of limited constitutional responsibility to one of active participation in the administration of the day-to-day operations of the national government

Notes to the Teacher
The presidential election of 1800 resulted in a tie in the Electoral College. The Twelfth Amendment was added to the Constitution to provide for the election of the president and vice president on separate ballots. In practice, a presidential nominee usually chooses a running mate who balances and strengthens the ticket in terms of geography, gender, religion, and ethnicity.

While the actual duties of the vice president are few, the vice president must swear to uphold and defend the Constitution. Article II, Section 1 of the Constitution indicates that the vice president will assume the duties of the president in the event of his death, resignation, or incapacitation. The Twenty-Fifth Amendment clarifies the process by which this transfer of power will take place. Other than presiding over the Senate, early vice presidents had few responsibilities. Several vice presidents, including John Adams and Thomas Jefferson, commented on the insignificance of the office. Undoubtedly, Republican leaders had a similar role in mind when Theodore Roosevelt became vice president in 1900. They saw this as a way to remove the reformer from a position of leadership where he could alienate party conservatives; little did they realize that an assassin's bullet would elevate him to the presidency a few months later.

In recent years, vice presidents have become better informed and more active in their office. Harry Truman's assumption of the presidency, after being given only minimal briefings on the affairs of state, pointed to the need for well-informed vice presidents. John F. Kennedy's assassination reinforced the idea that the vice president must be well informed on the workings of government and prepared to assume the presidency on a moment's notice. Dwight D. Eisenhower used his vice president, Richard Nixon, as an envoy to foreign nations and made him acting president on several occasions when Eisenhower was very ill. In spite of the recent evolution of the office, the duties of the vice president depend on the willingness of the chief executive to delegate authority.

In this lesson, students examine possible roles for the vice president and evaluate the role of the vice presidency in the modern world.

Procedure
1. Review the requirements for the role of vice president as set out in the U.S. Constitution (*thirty-five years of age, a resident of the United States for fourteen years, and a native-born citizen*).

2. Distribute **Handout 52**, and have students read the excerpts in a large-group session and indicate how each characterizes the role of the vice president. Review students' responses.

   Suggested Responses:

   Document A—*position of insignificance*

   Document B—*more than one in four chance that the vice president will eventually become president*

   Document C—*carry the home state in the election*

   Document D—*everybody's best friend in the administration*

   Document E—*to influence public opinion*

   Document F—*most influential vice president in history*

   Document G—*a shadow president who influenced policy decisions and Cabinet appointments*

3. After students have identified the roles of the vice president, have them answer the four questions at the end of **Handout 52**. Review students' responses.

201

Suggested Responses:

1. *The documents suggest new and increasingly important tasks are being assigned to modern vice presidents.*

2. *The increased demands on the president and the strong possibility that the vice president will become president, perhaps on very short notice, require a competent and well-informed vice president. Vice presidents in recent years have assumed numerous duties not envisioned in the original delegation of authority in the Constitution.*

3. *The vice president must be well-informed on both domestic and foreign affairs because the chances are good that he may, at some point, become president.*

4. Ask students to give examples of the role of the vice president in the current administration.

Enrichment/Extension

Have students research and report on vice presidents who became president.

The Transformation of the Vice Presidency

Read the following excerpts about the vice presidency, and indicate how each characterizes the roles of the vice president. Then, on a separate sheet of paper, answer the questions that follow.

Document A

Before his first term ended, John Adams wrote that "my country has in its wisdom contrived for me the most insignificant office that ever the invention of man contrived or his imagination conceived."

Document B

To date, thirteen of forty-five vice presidents have, at some point, assumed the presidency of the United States either as a result of the death or resignation of the president or their own eventual election to the office.

Document C

Often the primary responsibility of the second man [in an election campaign] was simply to carry his home state. [Chester A.] Arthur organized the Republican effort in New York in 1880. He never left that state nor did he make a single major campaign speech.

Document D

In 1965, Lyndon Johnson made the following comment about his vice president, Hubert Humphrey:

. . . I guess if we had a man-of-the-year poll . . . the Vice President would be voted the one person in the Government that is everybody's best friend. If the Secretary of State, Defense, or Labor or any of them had a peculiar and particular and delicate situation on their hands, I imagine they would want to talk to him—and they usually do—to get not only sympathy and understanding, but to get some energy and some effort and some constructive leadership. I know that is true of the Cabinet. It is particularly true with me. In a very wide range of fields, and complex subjects, I find the Vice President specializes in practically all of them.

Document E

The *Washington Post* commented

> Vice President Lyndon Johnson has been speaking out on civil rights issues with increasing frequency, force, and clarity. He is doing a great deal to shape public opinion and alter public outlook. Frequently he gets to the gist of the matter with a directness and vigor that pierces the fog of legal dispute into which we so frequently become mired. . . . The Presidency always has been known as a great platform from which to appeal to the mind and heart of America. . . .

Document F

> [Vice President] Gore didn't lose many such arguments. Clinton rarely overruled him. He was the most influential Vice President in history. He and Clinton had established and maintained a remarkably close and even amazing relationship. . . .
>
> Gore . . . had negotiated the arrangements for Gore's Vice Presidential role with Clinton . . . : an office in the West Wing; his Chief of Staff would be an assistant to the President as well; authority to attend any Clinton meeting, unless it was a personal one; specific Presidential authority for Gore in his dealings with the Cabinet. . . . In return, Gore would take on such things as attending fundraising and other events, to keep them off the President's schedule. . . .
>
> And Gore was utterly loyal. . . . Gore knew that his future was tied to Clinton's success.

Document G

> After the 2000 presidential election, Vice President Richard Cheney was seen as a shadow president, the man behind the curtain, who pulled the strings in the selection of Cabinet members. Cheney was alleged to have streamlined decision making within the Bush administration, and helped to craft and implement a realign energy policy more in line with his administration's views. After the events of September 2001, Cheney was rarely seen in public, either formally or informally.

1. How do these documents suggest a changing role for the vice president?

2. What factors make the vice presidency important today?

3. What is the importance of an informed vice president in the world today?

4. Give two examples of activities of the current vice president, and identify the roles represented.

Sources: *The Modern American Vice Presidency: The Transformation of a Political Institution*, Joel K. Goldstein (Princeton, N.J.: Princeton University Press, 1982), and *On the Edge: The Clinton Presidency*, Elizabeth Drew (New York: Simon and Schuster, 1994).

Part 5
The Judicial Branch

This section deals with the federal courts, beginning with an overview of the structure of the courts and their responsibilities. Lesson 30 examines the organization and authority of the courts within the federal court system. Lesson 31 examines the scope of the Supreme Court's jurisdiction. Lesson 32 explores ways in which the president and the Supreme Court check each other. Lesson 33 traces the changing philosophies of juvenile justice in this country.

Lesson 30
The Structure of the Federal Court System

Objective
- To examine the organization and authority of courts within the federal court system

Notes to the Teacher
The Constitution established the Supreme Court and empowered Congress to create such inferior federal courts as it deemed necessary. The federal court system forms a pyramid. At the bottom of the pyramid are the ninety-one federal district courts and a number of specialty courts, such as the U.S. Claims Court, Bankruptcy Court, and Tax Court, which hear specific types of cases. Thirteen appeals courts review cases from the federal district and specialty courts, and the U.S. Supreme Court, the highest court in the pyramid, acts as a court of last resort for federal cases. Federal judges are nominated by the president and confirmed by the Senate, after a hearing by the Senate Judiciary Committee. Federal judges serve for life, subject to good behavior.

Federal courts deal primarily with issues of constitutional law, real damages over $10,000, and issues involving more than one state or residency. District courts, which have original—or first—jurisdiction in federal cases, sometimes use a grand jury to indict and a petit jury to convict. The thirteen appellate courts hear appeals from lower federal courts. The Supreme Court selects the cases it wishes to hear. In only rare instances—all of them listed in the Constitution—does the Supreme Court have original jurisdiction. These are cases involving two or more states, the United States and a state government, or foreign ambassadors or diplomats. Most cases before the Supreme Court involve appeals from lower courts or cases the justices believe involve significant constitutional issues. The Court's chief justice and eight associate justices render decisions by a majority vote. Minority justices often write dissenting opinions to explain the rationale for their differing opinions. The Supreme Court relies heavily, but not exclusively, upon past legal practice as a basis for its decisions.

In this lesson, students learn the basic structure of the federal court system. They then determine which federal court would have jurisdiction over specific cases. Students should bring issues from newspapers and newsmagazines to class for the concluding activity.

Procedure
1. Explain that the U.S. court system has its roots in English common law and acts as a check on the powers of the executive and legislative branches of government.

2. Distribute **Handout 53**, and have students complete it either individually or in small groups. Review students' responses.

Suggested Responses:

Part A.

1. *lowest court's authority over an issue*
2. *authority over appeals from the lower courts*

Part B.

Top—Supreme Court; court of last resort; decides constitutional issues

Next tier—Federal Appeals Court; court of appellate jurisdiction; decides appeals and constitutionality of lower court rulings

Next tier—Federal District Court; court of original jurisdiction

Bottom—Specialty Courts: U.S. Claims Court, Bankruptcy Court, Tax Court; courts of original jurisdiction

Part C.

1. *b; relates to federal law*
2. *d; next step up the pyramid from federal district court*
3. *a; The issue of an appeal was not a federal case initially.*
4. *a; would be the next higher authority on the state level*
5. *b; The case involves a federal issue.*

6. *a; No federal issue is involved.*

7. *b; The case involves a federal issue.*

8. *b or c (U.S. Court of Claims), depending upon the wishes of the plaintiff's lawyer*

9. *e; She has no place to go except the U.S. Supreme Court.*

10. *a; This is not a matter for federal courts; it would go to state or local courts.*

11. *b; the status of the Justice Department*

12. *b; likelihood of involving federal legislation and individuals of several states*

13. *c or b; If she chooses to go to court before paying, she would go to Tax Court; an alternative would be to pay the amount in dispute and then sue for a refund in U.S. Court of Claims or a federal district court.*

14. *b; nature of the issue*

15. *c; The farmers could seek relief by suing the U.S. government.*

Part D.

1. *Federal courts are specified in the Constitution and deal with issues whose nature is beyond the state and local level or are of a national concern or interest.*

2. *In appellate courts, lower court decisions may be challenged.*

3. *The Supreme Court interprets the Constitution and settles disputes between states or ones in which foreign governments or citizens may be involved.*

3. Have students research an issue in editions of a local paper or a newsmagazine. Have students find as many cases as possible that have come before the federal courts recently. Compile the list on the chalkboard or on an overhead transparency. Encourage students to follow the progress of cases not yet settled in court.

Enrichment/Extension

Have student volunteers prepare a bulletin board of current cases before the federal district court in the local area.

The Structure of the Federal Court System

Part A.

The following terms are essential to understanding the federal court system. Use your textbook and other reference material to define them.

1. original jurisdiction

2. appellate jurisdiction

Part B.

The federal court system forms a pyramid. Create a diagram showing the four levels of the court system, and place the following terms on the appropriate level.

Bankruptcy Court

Court of appellate jurisdiction

Court of last resort

Court of original jurisdiction

Courts of original jurisdiction

decides appeals and constitutionality
    of lower court rulings

decides constitutional issues

Federal Appeals Court

Federal District Court

Specialty Courts

Supreme Court

Tax Court

Supreme Court

U.S. Claims Court

Part C.

For each scenario, write in the blank the letter of the court to which you believe the case should be assigned. Be prepared to give a reason for your choice.

a. State or local (not federal) court

b. Federal district court

c. Specialty courts: U.S. Court of Claims, Tax Court, Bankruptcy Court

d. U.S. Court of Appeals

e. Supreme Court

_____1. Employees of Chester Carpet Company sued their employer for failing to make pension contributions as required by the Employee Retirement Income Security Act.

_____2. David Steigerwald appealed his conviction in a federal district court for kidnapping a twenty-three-year-old woman.

_____3. Paul Frankiewicz was tried and convicted of burglary in a municipal court and appealed the decision by challenging the validity of eyewitness accounts.

_____4. The state appeals court refused to overturn the murder conviction of David Jenkins. He appealed to a higher court based on new DNA evidence.

_____5. Seamus Riley is being deported for lack of a proper visa and has sued the Department of Immigration.

_____6. Donald Miller believed he was unfairly terminated by his employer, Rose Foods, and sued for back pay.

_____7. Edward Ruiz, 70, sued a hotel that refused to employ him because of his age.

_____8. Joe Running Eagle represented a tribe of Native Americans who were denied mineral rights for their reservation, as provided in an agreement with the Bureau of Indian Affairs, and who sued for compensation in the name of the tribe.

_____9. Harriet Fulton felt that she was discriminated against by the U.S. Civil Service Commission. She sued in a federal district court but lost her case. She then sued in the federal court of appeals to overturn the district court's decision.

_____10. John Davis and his family sued a nearby restaurant, where they believe they were served tainted food.

_____11. The Justice Department brought suit against several supermarket chains for conspiracy to fix prices of grocery and meat products.

_____12. Arnold Wilson sued several manufacturers of asbestos, claiming that he had contracted asbestosis as a result of direct exposure to their products.

_____13. Lisa Jones challenged the Internal Revenue Service's disallowance of a tax deduction she considered legitimate.

_____14. The attorney general of the state of California initiated a class action suit against a leading woolen manufacturer and charged the company with conspiracy to fix the prices of certain blankets and items of clothing.

_____15. A group of farmers sought damages because they claimed that the Army Corps of Engineers built dams in rivers that caused floods on their property, resulting in a reduced crop harvest and loss of income.

Part D.

Answer the following questions.

1. Why does the United States need federal courts?

2. Why does the United States need appellate courts?

3. Why does the United States need a Supreme Court?

Lesson 31
The Supreme Court in Operation

Objective
- To examine the scope of the Supreme Court's jurisdiction

Notes to the Teacher

Today many people believe that the Supreme Court has always been a venerable institution that meticulously renders legal decisions based on the Court's interpretation of the Constitution and legal precedent. In historical reality, the Supreme Court's role as the ultimate legal arbiter—the actual practice of its legal jurisdiction—evolved over time.

The greatest influence on the establishment of the role the Court would play in American life was John Marshall. In two landmark cases, *Marbury v. Madison* (1803) and *McCulloch v. Maryland* (1819), Marshall, through the use of judicial review, established the Supreme Court as a powerful branch of the federal government. Marshall's opinions demonstrated that he saw the Constitution not only as a means to limit the power of the federal government, but also as a guide in its actions. He believed the Founders' intent was to rely on the powers that could be reasonably implied from what was expressly stated.

Jurisdiction for the Supreme Court was not always clear. Marshall took his cue from the relationship between the Court and Congress, from the Constitution's direct powers and what was implied. In the early years of our nation, state governments gave grants, exclusive contracts, and monopolies to ambitious individuals who sought to develop businesses using the roads and rivers of America. A conflict arose when two men, Thomas Gibbons and Aaron Ogden, both wanted to ply their trade on the Hudson River. The state of New York had granted a state navigation license to Ogden, while Gibbons had been granted a federal license. The question was, which of the two licenses would have precedence? The ruling in the case established the Supreme Court's right to settle disputes between the states and the federal government.

The Supreme Court has two kinds of authority: original jurisdiction and appellate jurisdiction. The Constitution specifically states instances where original jurisdiction must begin and end. A dispute involving an ambassador from a foreign country constitutes such a case. More often, the Supreme Court rules on appeals from a state supreme court or a federal appeals court. Justices may also decide to grant a writ of certiorari under the rule of four. If four justices believe that a petitioner has a case involving a significant constitutional issue or one having broad application to the judicial process, they may grant a writ of certiorari and commit the Court to review the case. Since the Supreme Court has far more requests for review than it can handle, it must select carefully those on which the justices wish to rule. Seldom does the Court hear in detail more than a small percentage of the several thousand cases presented to it for review in a given year.

Supreme Court decisions require a majority rather than a unanimous vote. In the event of a tie, the lower court decision stands. Although the Supreme Court stands as the court of last resort, members never consider their decisions the final word on an issue. Later courts may—and often do—reverse, revise, or clarify earlier rulings. For example, *Brown v. Board of Education* (1954) overturned *Plessy v. Ferguson* (1896).

In this lesson, students distinguish between original and appellate jurisdiction and learn under what circumstances the Supreme Court is likely to hear appeals from lower courts. To conclude, students research and report on cases currently under consideration by the Supreme Court.

Procedure
1. Review the operation of the Supreme Court. Review the meaning of *original jurisdiction* (*the authority of the lowest state or federal court over an issue*), and *appellate jurisdiction* (*the authority of higher courts to review the decision of a lower court*). Explain that most Supreme Court cases involve appellate jurisdiction.

2. Distribute **Handout 54**, and review the criteria for determining whether or not the Supreme Court would be likely to hear a case. Have students complete the handout individually. Review students' responses.

Suggested Responses:

Part A.

1. not personally injured by the law

2. use the recall or election process instead

3. too broad a question

4. question of fact, not law

5. trivial

6. could be denied as moot [a dead issue], political, or perhaps even trivial

Part B.

1. person bringing suit must be personally and substantially injured

2. protection of valuable legal rights

3. substantial federal issue

4. protection of valuable legal rights

5. person bringing suit must be personally and substantially injured

6. specific constitutional issue

7. person bringing suit must be personally and substantially injured

3. Distribute **Handout 55**, and have students read the background of *Gibbons v. Ogden* (1824) and answer the questions. Review students' responses.

Suggested Responses:

1. Did the state or federal government have jurisdiction over licenses on the Hudson River? Conflict arose when two men had licenses issued by two different jurisdictions.

2. The New York legislature gave permission to grant licenses, and that state's court had ruled in favor of Thomas Gibbons, who had a state license. Why would a federal court become involved in a state matter?

3. Answers should include the following points: history of conflicts between states; states needed a higher judicial authority to settle disputes between states; waters crossed state boundaries; trade, commerce, and transportation issues affect people from other states; to settle an interstate conflict; to help unify citizens in a federal system.

4. Article I, Section. 8 of the Constitution, the Commerce clause; Article VI regarding the supremacy of the national law; basically national over states in matters of commerce and transportation, state law was divisive and impeded trade with its barriers.

5. Trade was intermingled, and trade between states could not stop at the boundary line of each state; therefore, trade disputes would necessarily become a federal issue.

6. The Supreme Court ruled in favor of the plaintiff, Ogden, who was a federally licensed navigator, because of previous historical state disputes involving commerce; a definition of commerce included transportation because that is how goods are moved from a supplier to a buyer; stating that the commerce clause "should comprehend all foreign commerce and all commerce among the States."

7. They had lived under the Articles of Confederation for so long, that they did not want to give up their states' rights position.

8. It allowed tradesmen, artisans, and shop owners in Virginia to ply their trade in Pennsylvania, Massachusetts, and New York. It opened up new markets and expanded old ones.

9. A definite benefit is a more diverse array of types of goods sold on the market, such as food, farm products, and clothes. There is a tangential benefit of cross-cultural trade in ideas and trends in music and the arts.

10. Positive—removes financial barriers such as added cost to goods that decrease the profit of the seller and increase cost to buyer; provides a wider selection of goods for consumers

    Negative—results in homogenization of taste, ideas, and trends; lax standards in quality of goods; force of competition, or the drive to compete in market, could reduce enforcement of important environmental and health regulations, especially in underdeveloped countries

4. Have students research and report on cases currently before the Supreme Court. Discuss students' findings, and encourage them to follow the progress of such appeals.

Enrichment/Extension

1. Have students monitor the decisions issued throughout the year by the Supreme Court, beginning when the new term opens in October. Have students prepare a display examining the rulings that they believe to be most important.

2. Have students research, prepare, and share a time line of Supreme Court decisions that have influenced American society.

The Operation of the Supreme Court

Part A.

The Supreme Court receives far more cases for consideration than it can handle in a year. Therefore, the justices use the criteria listed below to select the cases they will review each year. Read the criteria, and then decide why each case was rejected for review. Write your reasons for rejection on a separate sheet of paper.

Criteria for Determining Supreme Court Authority in Cases

a. Before the Supreme Court will consider a particular issue or dispute officially, a definite case or controversy under constitutional statute must exist. It may involve the protection or enforcement of valuable legal rights, or the punishment, prevention, or redress of wrongs. The Supreme Court will not render an opinion on the constitutionality of government actions in the absence of a case or controversy.

b. The person bringing the suit must be personally and substantially injured by the law or action he or she protests.

c. The person bringing suit must have a specific constitutional issue relating to a narrow and specific provision of the Constitution.

d. All remedies in the lower federal courts and/or state courts must have been exhausted.

e. The federal question at issue must be substantial rather than trivial to the dispute.

f. Generally, the Court hears only questions of law, not questions of fact.

g. The Court generally avoids political disputes.

h. The Supreme Court does not check against inept, unwise, emotional, or unrepresentative legislators whom voters may remove at the polls through the use of recall or the election process.

i. The Supreme Court will not rule on the constitutionality of a law or action for an individual who has benefited from its use but decides to challenge the constitutionality of the law or action anyway.

j. A law or executive action may be unwise, unjust, unfair, undemocratic—even tyrannical or stupid—but still be constitutional in the eyes of the Supreme Court.[1]

Cases

1. In 1943, Dr. Wilder Tileson challenged the Supreme Court's prohibition on the distribution of birth control devices.

2. A group of African Americans in an urban congressional district appealed to the Supreme Court to remove their white congressman, who failed to respond to their concerns, because of his racist views.

[1]Adapted from *The Judicial Process*, 3rd edition, Henry J. Abraham (New York: Oxford University Press, 1975), 354–70.

3. John Jones appealed to the Supreme Court to overturn his conviction on the grounds that his Fifth Amendment rights had been violated.

4. A student seeking admission to a university was denied the reduced tuition rate granted to residents in his state. The student asked the Supreme Court to verify his residency.

5. A fraternity asked the Supreme Court to review the college trustees' new policy that required the fraternity chapter to set deadlines for removing racial and religious requirements for membership or lose campus privileges.

6. In 1980, President Jimmy Carter withdrew the United States from Olympic competition to protest the Soviet invasion of Afghanistan. Disgruntled athletes appealed to the Supreme Court for redress against a decision that denied them the right to earn a gold medal.

Part B.

Using the criteria in part A, determine why each of the following cases was accepted for review. Write your reasons on a separate sheet of paper.

1. J. W. worked for a machinery company but he quit when his old job was eliminated and he was transferred to making gun turrets for tanks. He claimed that his religious convictions prevented him from working on war materials. He asked the Supreme Court to decide whether he was entitled to unemployment compensation.

2. The Supreme Court was asked to decide whether congressional districts must have population equity based on the census figures.

3. The Supreme Court was asked to decide whether Congress could place limits on the amount of money people gave to candidates running for office.

4. The Supreme Court was asked to decide if school officials had the power to censor material printed in student-produced school newspapers.

5. Lawyers for a New Jersey teenager asked the Supreme Court to decide if her suspension, which resulted from a questionable search of her purse, was legal.

6. The Supreme Court agreed to hear a challenge to a law requiring that the names of sex offenders be posted publicly.

7. A divided Supreme Court decided that defendants must have a lawyer present even for misdemeanor charges; unless constitutional rights of a defendant are knowingly and voluntarily waived, the state must provide a lawyer.

Part C.

If, as a Supreme Court member, you wished to avoid deciding an issue, which of the preceding criteria might allow you the greatest opportunity to sidestep the issue? Explain the reasons for your choices.

Gibbons v. Ogden, 1824

Gibbons v. Ogden was a landmark Supreme Court decision for two reasons: it further established the Court's jurisdiction, and it defined the role of Congress in regulating commerce and transportation. Read the following selection, and answer the questions.

During the 1820s, America was a bustling, energetic young nation that was rapidly expanding its commercial activity. New opportunities were available for the infant nation's ambitious citizens. Competition was welcomed. Few understood the part the new federal government would play in the areas of trade, navigation, and transportation on the nation's roads, canals, and waterways.

After the ratification of the Constitution, the New York state legislature continued to allow the partnership of Robert Livingston and Robert Fulton to issue licenses to all steam-powered transportation on the navigable waters within the state's borders. Livingston and Fulton had been granted, in effect, a monopoly to issue licenses. Monopolies were regarded as being in the interest of the greater public good. Livingston and Fulton issued a state navigation license to Aaron Ogden. He, like other aggressive and imaginative businessmen, saw money to be made in America's expanding markets.

A rival navigator, Thomas Gibbons, had been granted a federal navigation license, and demanded the right to operate his steamboat on the Hudson River. Livingston and Fulton insisted that he apply and pay for a license issued under the terms set down by the state of New York. The legal battle began in the New York courts, which agreed with Livingston and Fulton. They ruled that Gibbons needed a state license. When he refused to apply for a state license, his steamboat operations were halted.

Gibbons took his case to the federal court. Many asked why a federal court was interfering in the internal affairs of the state of New York, since the case had been settled when the New York Court ruled in Ogden's favor.

The plaintiff's lawyers—William Wirt, the attorney general of the United States, and the great orator Daniel Webster—laid out a sound argument, based on their understanding of John Marshall's previous rulings and their understanding of federal versus state law. Webster strongly supported the federal government and understood that the Court was keen to unify the states and the people under a federal system, which recognized the imperatives of a national power. Their opponent was James Kent, a formidable legal scholar.

Webster began by quoting Article I, Section 8 of the Constitution, which granted the power to regulate commerce with foreign nations and among the states to Congress. Webster argued that this power was complete and entire, and that the states, in ratifying the Constitution, had yielded control over commerce to the national government. Then Webster argued that the congressional statute authorizing the navigation of the Hudson River was based on the constitutional principle of the supreme law of the land. Next, William Wirt argued that the state laws, like those in New York, were divisive and placed barriers on a free movement of goods and services. He cited prior disagreements between states on commerce and trade.

The question that was to be answered was this: What was commerce? Did it include transportation? Or should it be narrowly defined only to include the trading, buying, or selling of goods?[1]

[1]Adapted from *It Is So Ordered: A Constitution Unfolds*, Warren E. Burger (New York: William Morrow and Co., 1995), 105–10.

1. What is the key problem regarding the licenses and navigation on New York waters?

2. Why is the jurisdiction of the Supreme Court questioned?

3. Why do you think the federal court had jurisdiction? Why was it important for the federal court to make a ruling?

4. What were the key arguments of the plaintiff?

5. How did John Marshall define *commerce*?

6. How do you think the Supreme Court ruled? Why?

7. Why might this new jurisdiction have been difficult for lawyers, judges, and political leaders to follow?

8. What impact do you think the ruling had on commerce and trade?

9. What benefits were there to having a common market in America?

10. Today, in the larger world market, how do new treaties, like the General Agreement on Tariffs and Trade (GATT), the North American Free Trade Agreement (NAFTA), and the European Union (EU), affect regulations that govern trade between countries?

Lesson 32
Presidential Relations with the Supreme Court

Objective

- To examine ways in which the president and Supreme Court check each other

Notes to the Teacher

In the early years of the Republic, the Supreme Court appeared to be the weakest branch of the new government. In 1803, the Supreme Court handed down a landmark decision in *Marbury v. Madison* when, under the leadership of Chief Justice John Marshall, the Supreme Court declared unconstitutional a portion of the Judiciary Act of 1789. In doing so, the Court set a precedent for the right of judicial review. The Supreme Court ruled also unconstitutional, and thus unenforceable, decisions made by the president, and has the potential for exercising enormous power in its relations with both the Congress and the president.

Marbury v. Madison and other cases established judicial review of national and state legislation and set a precedent for acting on disputes between states and between states and Congress. *McCulloch v. Maryland* (1819) strengthened a growing economy by limiting the power of the states to tax a federal service and permitted the establishment of a national bank. *Gibbons v. Ogden* (1824) helped to establish a common market in America through its definition of the Constitution's commerce clause.

The Supreme Court may check the president by reviewing the constitutionality of laws he has sponsored, as well as the constitutionality of executive orders and other actions. Franklin D. Roosevelt, in response to the Great Depression, submitted several acts to Congress under his New Deal programs. He proposed sweeping legislative reforms in order to feed the hungry, provide work for the unemployed, and assist impoverished farmers. Roosevelt felt these actions were constitutional, but the Supreme Court ruled that the National Industrial Recovery Act (NIRA) and the Public Works Act were not. He greatly expanded federal authority and the power of the executive branch. However, conservative legal scholars have argued that most of Roosevelt's actions were unconstitutional.

The chief executive nominates individuals to fill vacancies on the Supreme Court. Although these appointments are subject to Senate confirmation, the justice, once confirmed by the Senate, serves for life. Presidents try to influence the philosophy of the Supreme Court by selecting individuals who share their political philosophy. Frequently, presidents have been surprised by the independence of justices they have chosen for the Court. Depending upon the number of appointments a president makes during his time in office, he can substantially alter the direction of the Court. The president has considerable influence on the enforcement of the Court's decisions through his control of the executive branch. Some presidents, like Andrew Jackson, have had little enthusiasm for specific Supreme Court decisions and have found ways to delay enforcement.

One method used by Congress to check the president's power over the judiciary is through the confirmation process. Sometimes a presidential appointee is never confirmed. During the presidency of William J. Clinton, about 80 percent of his nominees to the federal bench were confirmed. A partisan Senate Judiciary Committee can delay or derail a nominee. Sometimes the process becomes increasingly parsimonious and partisan, especially when controversial issues such as abortion, privacy, or civil rights are involved. The backgrounds of nominees are vigorously investigated and sometimes result in the withdrawal of the nomination.

Ronald Reagan appointed the first woman to the Supreme Court: Sandra Day O'Connor, an appeals court judge from Arizona. O'Connor's nomination, though opposed by some conservatives, was supported by many powerful Republicans, and she was eventually confirmed. The nomination of Clarence Thomas by George H. W. Bush proved to be one of the most controversial. His nomination process was overtaken by his alleged sexual harassment of a coworker, Anita Hill, while employed as legal counsel at the Equal Employment Opportunity Commission. Thomas was eventually confirmed. Bush's second nomination, David Souter, was less controversial. Souter, a Harvard graduate and a Rhodes scholar, had been a state supreme court justice and had served as a judge in the First Circuit Court. Clinton wanted to take a centrist approach to his Supreme Court nominations. His first appointment was Justice Stephen Breyer, a former Harvard law professor, who had served on the U.S. Court of Appeals. Breyer was conservative in his views on business practices and a centrist on the regulation of the country's economy. Breyer had served as a chief counsel of the Senate Judiciary Committee and had the backing of powerful senators from both sides of the aisle. He was easily confirmed. Clinton's next appointment, Ruth Bader Ginsberg, a graduate of Cornell Law School, was also a centrist. She had voted conservatively on business regulation and criticized *Roe v. Wade* for its reasoning.

In this lesson, students examine ways the chief executive and Supreme Court check each other. Also, students interpret a political cartoon about Franklin Roosevelt's court-packing plan of 1937. To conclude, they interpret in a structured paragraph the significance of the checks operating between the two branches.

Procedure

1. Review the checks and balances system. Explain the each branch of government has the power to check the other two branches.

2. Distribute **Handout 56**, and have students complete it either as a small-group or large-group activity. Review students' responses.

Suggested Responses:

Part A.

- *The president checks the Supreme Court by nominating justices when vacancies occur and enforcing Supreme Court rulings.*

- *The Supreme Court checks the president by ruling unconstitutional either actions of the president or laws suggested to Congress by the president.*

Part B.

1. *Franklin Roosevelt*

2. *Congress*

3. *six Supreme Court justices*

4. *because of their opposition to his New Deal legislation*

5. *He wanted to add six justices to those already on the Court in order to insure a majority for his New Deal proposals.*

6. *Congress rejected his proposal.*

7. *Congress, even though it was of the same party as the president, acted quickly to stop an action that appeared to threaten the independence of another branch.*

8. *Congressional rejection of the plan prevented the chief executive from taking control of the Supreme Court and, thus, upsetting the long-standing principle of checks and balances.*

3. Instruct students to write a brief paragraph containing at least five facts about the relationship between the president and the Supreme Court. Provide class time for students to share completed paragraphs.

Suggested Responses:

Students might cite the following facts:

- *The president influences the Supreme Court through his right to fill vacancies on the Court.*

- *The president has some control over decisions of the Supreme Court by the enthusiasm with which he enforces its decisions.*

- *The Supreme Court may rule unconstitutional laws that a president considers essential to his presidential program.*

- *The Supreme Court may rule actions of the president unconstitutional.*

- *Franklin Roosevelt tried to pack the Supreme Court with supporters of the New Deal in 1937.*

- *Congress refused to grant Roosevelt's request to increase the number of justices on the Supreme Court when it appeared that he wanted to control the Court.*

Both the president and the Supreme Court have ways of checking each other. A conclusion might be that when the system of checks and balances itself was threatened, Congress took swift action to preserve the separation of powers.

Enrichment/Extension

1. Direct students to examine the relationship between the current president and the Supreme Court. Then have students report their findings to the class.

2. Have students research and report on the checks imposed on the president by the Supreme Court in the past. Examples might include Andrew Jackson (*Worcester v. Georgia*), Harry Truman (*Youngstown Sheet and Tube Co. v. Sawyer*), and Franklin D. Roosevelt (*Korematsu v. United States*).

Presidential Relations with the Supreme Court

Part A.

Read the following examples of relations between the president and the Supreme Court. Then complete the chart; show how each checks the other.

1. In 1937, President Franklin D. Roosevelt appointed Hugo Black to the Supreme Court because of Senator Black's pro-New Deal views.

2. In *Worcester v. Georgia* (1832), the Supreme Court ruled that Georgia laws did not apply to Cherokee lands. President Andrew Jackson was reported to have asserted: "John Marshall has made his decision, now let him enforce it." Jackson had his administration officials renegotiate treaties with the Cherokees, forcing them out of Georgia.

3. In *United States v. Nixon* (1974), the Supreme Court ruled that President Richard Nixon's sweeping claims of executive privilege when he withheld presidential communications that covered up criminal evidence exceeded his authority as president. The Court required that the president give to the Watergate special prosecutor tapes of conversations in his office.

4. In 1981, President Ronald Reagan appointed Sandra Day O'Connor to become the first woman justice on the Supreme Court.

5. In 1935, the Supreme Court ruled unconstitutional the National Recovery Act, a key part of Roosevelt's New Deal to end the Great Depression. The disappointed president was forced to dismantle the National Recovery Administration that carried out the program.

6. In 1952, the Supreme Court ruled unconstitutional President Harry Truman's attempt to take over the steel mills during a strike at the height of the Korean War.

Ways the President Checks the Supreme Court	Ways the Supreme Court Checks the President
a.	a.
b.	b.

Part B.

Interpret the political cartoon by answering the questions that follow.

Fig. 32.1.

1. Who is the quarterback?

2. Who is the referee?

3. What players does the quarterback want to replace?

4. Why does he want to replace these players?

5. Why is the strategy he attempted called "court-packing"?

6. What is the response of Congress?

7. What conclusion can you draw about the likelihood of one branch effectively undermining the authority of another branch?

8. How did congressional action in this case maintain the system of checks and balances?

Fig. 32.1. "The Ingenious Quarterback!" in *The Capitol: Symbol of Freedom* (Washington D.C.: Government Printing Office, 1973), 102.

Lesson 33
Juvenile Justice

Objective
- To trace the changing philosophies of juvenile justice in this country

Notes to the Teacher
American courts trace their roots to the three-hundred-year-old English system of common law, which meted out harsh physical punishments and the death penalty even for juvenile offenders. During the Progressive Era, reforms were promoted. These reforms recognized children as a distinct class of citizens who needed protection from extended workdays and oppressive conditions. With the advent of a new status for minor children came child labor laws, mandatory schooling, reform school, and the establishment of curfews.

Judge Ben Lindsey of Colorado broke long-established traditions when he introduced a new approach to the treatment of juveniles in his Denver courtroom. After he had sentenced a young boy to the state reform school for stealing coal, the boy's mother put up such a protest in the courtroom that Lindsey stopped the proceedings and set out to investigate the circumstances of the youth's criminal behavior. When he found that the boy had been trying to provide heat for the tenement apartment where his father lay dying from lead poisoning, Judge Lindsey became convinced that young offenders were victims of their home and neighborhood environment and needed rehabilitation far more than they needed confinement in the city's jail. Lindsay led a movement to reform the juvenile justice system and deal with young offenders in a more sympathetic and humanitarian manner. Reformers sought to rehabilitate children while sheltering them from hardened criminals.

By the late 1960s, concern developed that children were not receiving the due process protection afforded adults and were not being rehabilitated in the detention homes and reformatories where they were sent after their hearings. The landmark case *In Re Gault* (1967) established the right of juveniles to the same due process given to adults and set the stage for the present code of juvenile justice. Later cases have expanded the guarantees in *In Re Gault* to include protection from confinement for a longer period than adults would be incarcerated for the same crime, protection from double jeopardy in a juvenile hearing and then a trial in criminal court, and protection against illegal searches and seizures. Today judges attempt to balance the needs of society with those of the child while upholding the dignity of the law and the public's faith in the judicial system.

In this lesson, students examine the changing philosophies of juvenile justice and how the present system tries to balance the concerns of the public with the welfare of the child.

Procedure
1. Discuss the changes proposed by Judge Lindsey in dealing with juvenile justice. Distribute **Handout 57**, and have students complete it in a large-group session. Review students' responses.

   ### Suggested Responses:
   1. *whether the child could tell right from wrong*
   2. *fourteen*
   3. *true*
   4. *Change the child's environment by altering conditions in his home or neighborhood.*
   5. *protecting the rights of the juvenile, protecting the community in which he lives, and maintaining respect for the law*

2. Explain that the juvenile justice system has changed dramatically from what it was in the nineteenth century. Distribute **Handout 58**, and have students complete part A. Review students' responses.

   ### Suggested Responses:
1. *true*	6. *true*
2. *false*	7. *true*
3. *false*	8. *false*
4. *true*	9. *true*
5. *false*	10. *false*

3. Have students complete part B of **Handout 58**. Review students' responses.

Suggested Responses:

1. *j*	6. *h*
2. *h*	7. *f*
3. *b*	8. *e*
4. *d*	9. *c*
5. *i*	10. *a*

4. Explain that California has passed a law that authorizes the arrest of the parents of a minor who commits a serious offense. A parent may be held responsible for his or her child's actions. Stress that in most instances assistance in determining sentencing might involve school counselors and mental health or youth services. Have students complete part C of **Handout 58**. Review students' responses.

Suggested Responses:

1. *c*

2. *a*

3. *b; The appeals court attempted to alter his environment rather than punish.*

4. *b*

5. *b*

6. *either b or c; Changing the environment of the child has been used for years and is still used today.*

5. Distribute **Handout 59**, and have students read it either individually or in small groups. Have students write a short paragraph explaining how the Supreme Court decision in *In Re Gault* defined the rights of a juvenile in the criminal justice system in America. Provide class time to share completed paragraphs.

Suggested Response:

The In Re Gault *case gives the juvenile the same protections of due process that he or she would receive if tried in a criminal court. What will be best for the child is still an important consideration of the justice system. Students should indicate basic rights recently guaranteed juveniles by the courts.*

Enrichment/Extension

1. Have students research and report on Supreme Court cases that have dealt with the rights of juveniles.

2. Make arrangements with a local attorney to speak to the class about the legal rights of juveniles.

Juvenile Justice: A Historical Perspective

Read the following selection, and answer the questions.

Until the late nineteenth century, American courts, following British precedent, enforced a harsh code of discipline for children. Children under the age of seven were exempt from prosecution, but children over fourteen were subject to capital punishment for crimes they committed. Children between the ages of seven and fourteen were generally judged innocent; if, however, they understood the difference between good and evil at the time of the offense, they could be convicted and receive punishment, including the death penalty.

By 1900, reformers in both Great Britain and the United States advocated keeping children out of jails and away from hardened criminals. New juvenile courts in this country adopted a humanitarian concern and sympathy for children. Judges attempted to locate the blame for the child's troubles in the home and neighborhood environment. They evaluated parental care and tried to determine if rehabilitation were possible before they diagnosed therapy for the child.

In the late 1960s, many Americans became concerned that children received the worst of both worlds in juvenile court: they received none of the protections accorded to adults in court and little of the solicitous care and rehabilitation prescribed by the court. Today juvenile courts try to practice a form of individualized justice in which the court recognizes the individuality of a child and adapts its orders accordingly. Judges try to accomplish three goals simultaneously: to protect the community, to act in the best interest and welfare of the child, and to uphold the dignity of the law and the public's faith in the judicial system.

1. Before 1900, what was the determining factor for punishing a child?

2. At what age was a juvenile punished as an adult?

3. True or false: By 1900, it was considered more important to improve a child's behavior than to punish him.

4. According to the humanitarian philosophy of the early twentieth century, what steps might be taken to change the behavior patterns of a child?

5. What are some concerns of society in dealing with today's juvenile offenders?

The Scope of Judicial Power: Juvenile Justice

Part A.

Label each statement *true* or *false*.

_____ 1. Judges hear most juvenile cases because juveniles do not have the right to a jury trial, unless they are tried as an adult.

_____ 2. Juveniles have a right to bail and to a public trial.

_____ 3. Fundamental elements of due process, such as the right to an attorney and self-incrimination, do not apply to a juvenile.

_____ 4. Under most state laws, juvenile offenders do not commit crimes; instead, they commit delinquent acts.

_____ 5. A prosecuting attorney must always try an offender between the ages of ten and eighteen as a juvenile, even if the crime is a violent, serious offense.

_____ 6. In some states, juveniles older than fourteen who are charged with murder, rape, or armed robbery are tried as adults.

_____ 7. In certain states, parents may be held legally responsible for crimes committed by their children, if they fail to supervise or control the children.

_____ 8. States vary widely on the basic steps of the juvenile justice system.

_____ 9. In a serious situation, a juvenile may be detained in a juvenile correctional facility without bail while the matter is resolved.

_____ 10. All crimes by children or teens lead to juvenile court.

Part B.

Read each of the following statements about procedures and protocols in the juvenile justice system. Then place the statements in their proper sequence, lettering them from *a* to *j*.

_____1. A second juvenile court hearing is held to determine the disposition of a matter. If the juvenile is not considered to be dangerous to others, he or she may be placed on probation and be required to follow rules established by the court, be required to perform community service, or be sentenced to a work camp.

_____2. When a child denies the allegations in a petition, a hearing like an adult criminal trial is held. An attorney represents the child, and a judge makes a ruling.

_____3. The court intake officer evaluates the case to determine whether further action is necessary and determines whether the case needs to be referred to a social service agency or to a formal juvenile court proceeding.

_____4. The court intake officer determined that a formal hearing is unnecessary and refers the child to school counselors or a mental health or youth service agency.

_____5. The judge decides that allegations have been proven and rules the child is delinquent or dismisses the case because the allegations have not been proven.

_____6. If the matter proceeds to juvenile court, and the child admits to the allegations in the petition, a treatment program may be ordered.

_____7. In cases of serious offenses, such as rape or murder, the matter could be referred for adult criminal prosecution, and the child is charged, tried, and, if convicted, sentenced as an adult.

_____8. The intake officer decides that the case should be heard in juvenile court and files a petition listing the statutes the child has been accused of violating.

_____9. It has been determined that the situation is serious, so the juvenile is detained in a correction facility pending resolution of the matter or sent to an alternative placement facility.

_____10. Matter is brought to the court's attention when the police apprehend a minor who has violated a law, or if a school official, parent, or guardian refers a problem to the court.[1]

Part C.

Read the following case studies of juvenile offenses. Indicate whether the treatment is characteristic of *a*, early American juvenile justice; *b*, early twentieth-century juvenile justice; or *c*, recent juvenile justice. Be prepared to explain your reasoning.

_____1. Ronald, age sixteen, had been in juvenile court sixty-seven times, most recently for robbing and beating a ninety-two-year-old man who later died. Ronald's case was referred to criminal court.

_____2. A ten-year-old boy was found guilty and whipped for stealing thirty yards of lemon-colored satin ribbon.

_____3. An appeals court overturned the conviction of a ten-year-old boy who had been sentenced to death for stealing a watch. The court placed him under the care of a charitable organization.

_____4. Gary, who lived in California, was arrested for shoplifting. He had already been in trouble for theft. He was freed when his mother promised to get him private psychiatric care.

_____5. A fourteen-year-old boy accused of stealing was acquitted when his attorney argued that prison would further corrupt him.

_____6. Thirteen-year-old Nancy was arrested for shoplifting. Her mother was an alcoholic, and her father had left home when she was a small child. She was placed in a foster home.

[1]Adapted from "What to Expect: Juvenile Court Chronology," *Find Law: Consumer Law Center,* <http://www.wbns.findlaw.com/criminal/life_events/le2_9.html> (4 November 2004).

In Re Gault (1967)

Read the following information about a landmark Supreme Court decision, *In Re Gault*, and write a short paragraph explaining how the Court's decision defined the rights of a juvenile in a criminal justice system.

In Arizona, a woman complained to the sheriff that she had received an obscene phone call from some neighborhood teenagers. The sheriff took two boys to the detention center. One of them, Gerald Gault, was a fifteen-year-old already on probation for another offense. Gerald's parents were not immediately informed of his detention or of the hearing scheduled for the following day.

At the hearing, Gerald admitted that he had dialed the call but claimed that he had then handed the phone to his friend. The complainant was not present at the hearing, no one was sworn in before giving evidence, and no record of the proceedings was kept.

After a second hearing, Gerald was assigned to the reformatory until he reached the age of twenty-one. If he had been over eighteen and tried in criminal court, his maximum fine would have been $5 to $50 or imprisonment for not more than two months.

While he was in the reformatory, his parents appealed his case and eventually won a hearing in the Supreme Court. Their lawyer argued that Gerald should have been informed of the exact charges against him; he should have had the right to a lawyer; he should have been told of his freedom from self-incrimination and his right to remain silent; he should have had the right to cross-examine and confront witnesses; he should have had the right to a transcript of the proceedings; and he was entitled to appellate review. The state argued that such protections would completely alter the informality of the juvenile hearing. In its landmark decision in the case, the Supreme Court upheld the rights of the defendant and asserted that similar standards apply in both juvenile proceedings and adult trials.

Part 6
Public Policy

Part 6 helps students to define and understand the concept of public policy. Lesson 34 develops an understanding of the perception held by most Americans of the efficiency of governmental bureaucracy. Lesson 35 examines the conflict between the president in his role as commander-in-chief and the U.S. military. Lesson 36 develops an understanding of the cost of securing elective office in America and the need for campaign finance reform. Lesson 37 develops an understanding of the decision-making process needed to craft the federal budget through an examination of the funding for Head Start. Lesson 38 discusses the different views of the role of the federal government in helping the nation's poor. Lesson 39 examines the need for government regulation of actions that might threaten the environment. Lesson 40 explores several major factors that have influenced recent presidents in determining American foreign policy.

Lesson 34

Bureaucracy:
The Fourth Branch of Government

Objective

- To develop an understanding of the perception held by most Americans of the efficiency of governmental bureaucracy

Notes to the Teacher

The Declaration of Independence stemmed, in part, from a rebellion against a foreign bureaucracy that imposed regulations, restrictions, and controls on the American colonies. With the establishment of the Constitution, bureaucracy was reborn. Governments make laws and oversee their administration; however, bureaucrats implement the laws. Bureaucrats do not establish policy; they merely enforce it. For this reason, bureaucrats often appear uncompromising and unconcerned about citizens and their problems.

In the nineteenth and early twentieth centuries, bureaucracy was relatively small. At the time, the American philosophy of government focused on laissez-faire and social Darwinism, which stressed the idea of rugged individualism. Most government officials believed that what was appropriate and useful would survive without any governmental assistance. However, out of the Great Depression came the New Deal, which gave new meaning to the belief that the government should promote the general welfare. Government has come to play an increasingly active role in the daily lives of its citizens. An increase in the enactment of legislation, all of which requires implementation, has resulted in the mushrooming of government agencies. Officials within these agencies, who have civil service status and expertise in their field, wield such power that they have been referred to as the "fourth branch of government." Despite the services they perform, the security of their tenure and the nature of their functions, at times, make them appear unresponsive to the president, the Congress, and the people.

In this lesson, students read selections about the development of civil service in America and complete an information organizer. Students determine the validity of statements dealing with bureaucracy and whether a series

of actions are democratic or bureaucratic. To conclude, students conduct a survey in which respondents are asked to indicate their feelings about dealing with government agencies.

Procedure

1. Ask students for examples of government agencies they may have to deal with during their lifetime (*IRS, Postal Service, Bureau of the Census, Public Health, Federal Home Loan Bank, Food and Drug Administration, and Social Security*). Explain that when the federal government was established, there were very few government agencies within the executive branch. Most of the examples listed date to post-Depression America.

2. Distribute **Handout 60**. Have students read the selections in part A and complete the information organizer in part B. Review students' responses.

Suggested Responses, Part B:

Cause—*Allowing only the aristocratic, educated elite to hold office seemed undemocratic; the spoils system permitted every man who had the support of the president to gain access to public office.*

Effect—*The merit system distributed jobs on the basis of competition on tests to demonstrate one's ability to handle the tasks of the job. There was a more democratic access to offices for white males, but the system discriminated against minorities and females.*

Cause—*This discrimination against minorities and females was the cause of affirmative action reform in the 1970s; this system used quotas and other methods to correct the underuse of women and minorities.*

Effect—*There has been a more democratic access to government offices for women and minorities but probably some discrimination against qualified applicants who were denied jobs to make room for the required number of women and minorities.*

233

Ask students whether they believe civil service hiring today discriminates against any group. Have them explain why or why not. Then ask them why government hiring practices might become discriminatory in the future. (*Legislation or court rulings could change the rules.*)

3. Distribute **Handout 61**, and have students complete part A as directed. Review students' responses.

Suggested Responses:

1.	*true*	6.	*false*
2.	*false*	7.	*true*
3.	*false*	8.	*true*
4.	*true*	9.	*false*
5.	*false*	10.	*true*

4. Have students complete part B of **Handout 61**. Review students' responses.

Suggested Responses:

All the items in the first column should be labeled D; all items in the second column, B.

5. Ask students to name some of the primary problems in making a bureaucracy more democratic (*appointive access to office; lack of responsibility to elected officials; unionization of federal employees; power of bureaucratic expertise*).

6. Distribute **Handout 62**, and have students conduct the survey as directed. Allow time to debrief students' survey results.

Enrichment/Extension

1. Have students find examples of various roles of the bureaucracy as reflected in contemporary cartoons. Display cartoons on posters labeled "Perceptions of Bureaucracy."

2. Have students collect articles from current newspapers and newsmagazines dealing with the federal bureaucracy. Ask students to summarize and evaluate the articles in light of this lesson.

Discrimination and Democracy in Bureaucracy

Part A.

Read the following selections.

The Spoils System

With the defeat of the Federalists in 1800, the Jeffersonians employed the "spoils system" to replace many Federalist officeholders, since few Federalist incumbents had resigned when the Federalists lost control of Congress and the presidency. However, affluent and educated freeholders, not laborers, gained office. It seems fair to conclude that no president before Andrew Jackson undertook to buy leadership or legislation with patronage. President Jackson, a Democrat, justified his widespread removal of incumbent Republicans and their replacement with his supporters thus: "There are, perhaps, few men who can for any great length of time enjoy office and power without being more or less under the influence of feelings unfavorable to the faithful discharge of their public duties. . . . In a country where offices are created solely for the benefit of the people no one man has any more intrinsic right to official station than another. . . . "[1]

Merit System or Civil Service

Bureaucracy under the spoils system employed from the Jackson administration to the term of President Chester A. Arthur reflected the ideals of nineteenth-century agrarian democracy. Public office became almost a requirement of citizenship and fit the individualism of the day.

Public outrage at the widespread abuse of public office in the Grant era, in particular, reflected changing values about who should hold public office. As the Senate Commission on Civil Service and Retrenchment, reporting on the Pendleton Act, put it: "The single, simple, fundamental, pivotal idea of the whole bill is, that whenever, hereafter, a new appointment or promotion shall be made in the subordinate civil service in the departments or larger offices, such appointments or promotion shall be given to the man who is best fitted to discharge the duties of the position, and that such fitness shall be ascertained by open, fair, honest, impartial, competitive examination."[2]

Civil Service and Affirmative Action

In more recent times, the federal government's Civil Service Reform Act of 1978 has mandated fairly specific regulations designed to promote equal opportunity, insure that the federal service is representative of the nation, and end the legacy of past discrimination. The 1978 act aims "to produce comprehensive efforts by Federal agencies to correct systemic problems that have resulted in the underutilization of minorities and women." The act also established the Equal Employment Opportunity Commission to create guidelines to end the long-standing underrepresentation of minorities and women in federal agencies.[3]

---

[1]Andrew Jackson, "First Annual Message to Congress," in *A Compilation of the Messages and Papers of the Presidents 1789–1897*, vol. 2, ed. James D. Richardson (Washington D.C.: Government Printing Office, 1920), 442.

[2]Senate Report 576, 47th Congress, 1st sess. (1882), 13–14.

[3]U.S. Commission on Civil Rights, *Federal Affirmative Action Efforts in Mid-America* (Washington, D.C.: Government Printing Office, 1983), 9.

Part B.

Complete the information organizer.

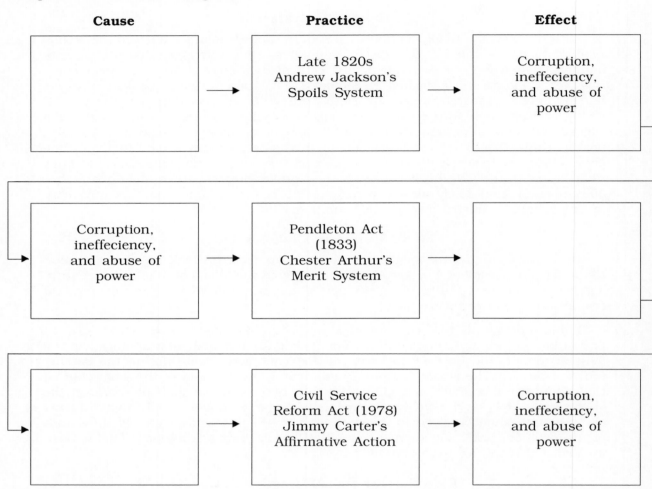

Cause	Practice	Effect
	Late 1820s Andrew Jackson's Spoils System	Corruption, ineffeciency, and abuse of power
Corruption, ineffeciency, and abuse of power	Pendleton Act (1833) Chester Arthur's Merit System	
	Civil Service Reform Act (1978) Jimmy Carter's Affirmative Action	Corruption, ineffeciency, and abuse of power

Our Nation's Bureaucracy

Part A.

Read the following short selections. Then label each numbered statement *true* or *false*, based on the point of view of the author.

The Nature of Bureaucracy

Bureaucracy implements the policy of the government as determined by elected officials. Bureaucracy cannot operate democratically, for it has the duty of carrying out federal policy efficiently and effectively with a minimum of debate.

In order to function, a bureau is organized in a pyramidal hierarchy with the flow of power directed from the top. The bureau is divided into divisions for specialization of tasks requiring a high level of expertise. Communication within and beyond the bureau is done in writing; memos are circulated and filed for permanence. Civil servants operate the bureau and are promoted on the basis of merit and seniority. This gives the bureau stability and permanence for serving the public's needs effectively and efficiently.

_____1. Bureaucracy is a necessary part of the federal government today.

_____2. Bureaucrats make laws.

_____3. Bureaucrats are promoted by the president.

_____4. Bureaucrats are knowledgeable about the workings of their divisions.

_____5. The bureau chief has limited power within his agency.

Public Perception of Bureaucracy

No American today is safe from federal bureaucrats. If you eat, drink, breathe air, dress, work, play, go to school, drive, read, watch TV, listen to radio, travel, own a house, rent an apartment, operate a farm, run a business, buy, sell, advertise, publish, spend money, save money, borrow money, invest, ship goods, import and export, use the mails, have children, get sick, or grow old, you are automatically in the grasp of at least one major federal bureau, and within reach of scores or hundreds more. If you think you can escape by dying, you haven't reckoned on the ultimate bureau, the Internal Revenue Service.[1]

_____6. The commentator shows a high regard for bureaucrats.

_____7. The federal bureaucracy is present in every facet of American life.

_____8. Bureaucrats are concerned with the public welfare.

_____9. The only time an individual is safe from the federal bureaucracy is after death.

_____10. Bureaucracy is large and complex.

[1]George Roche, *America by the Throat: The Stranglehold of Federal Bureaucracy* (Hillsdale, Mich.: Hillsdale College Press, 1985), 18.

Part B.

Using information in part A and your textbook, separate the following characteristics of democracy and bureaucracy by placing *D* in front of democratic features and *B* in front of the bureaucratic features.

_____ equality	_____ hierarchy
_____ rotation in office	_____ duration in office
_____ openness to suggestions for improving a program	_____ determination to implement a program without change
_____ equal access to participation in government	_____ differentiated access to office based on merit
_____ election to office	_____ appointment to office

Name_____

Date_____

Bureaucracy: The Fourth Branch of Government

Interview five adults about their dealings with one of the following federal agencies. Were they very pleased, pleased, displeased, or very displeased with the outcome of their encounter with the agency? Why? Record their responses in the chart.

Federal Agencies

Internal Revenue Service	Nuclear Regulatory Agency
Postal Service	Federal Communications Commission
National Park Service	Federal Reserve System
Bureau of the Census	Veterans Administration
Public Health Service	Commission on Civil Rights
U.S. Coast Guard	Environmental Protection Agency
Federal Aviation Administration	Selective Service System
National Highway Safety Administration	National Aeronautics and Space Administration
Department of Education	Equal Employment Opportunities Commission
Federal Home Loan Bank	National Labor Relations Board
Food and Drug Administration	Small Business Administration
Social Security Administration	Occupation Safety and Health Administration
Federal Deposit Insurance Corporation	

Agency	Assessment	Comments

Lesson 35
Civilian Authority v. Military Supremacy

Objective
- To examine the conflict between the president, in his role as commander in chief, and the U.S. military

Notes to the Teacher
The signing of the terms of surrender by Germany and Japan in 1945 did not end the turmoil in the world. Japan had created a satellite state in Korea, and when the war ended, the responsibility for Korean sovereignty was assumed by the fledgling United Nations. Korea was split in two politically. Northern Korea was heavily influenced by Communist China, while the south favored the establishment of a democracy similar to the structure that had been implemented in occupied Japan.

When fighting broke out between the north and the south, UN peacekeeping forces were dispatched under the command of General Douglas MacArthur. MacArthur came from a military family. His father had been awarded the Congressional Medal of Honor, and Mac-Arthur had followed in his footsteps and attended West Point. MacArthur had served with distinction and during World War II had commanded the American forces in the Pacific. He was the logical choice to serve as commander of American forces in Korea.

Initially, MacArthur had some success. This changed when Communist China threw its military might behind North Korea and thousands of troops crossed the thirty-eighth parallel and attacked UN peacekeepers. MacArthur was devastated by the losses his troops incurred, and he urged President Harry S. Truman to allow him to use allied forces to invade Communist China. Truman took a cautious approach and refused to consider MacArthur's request, fearing that an invasion of China would precipitate a third world war. MacArthur continued to press his point and made several speeches supporting a change in America's policy of containment. MacArthur challenged Truman's role as commander in chief by implying that Truman was not competent to make a military decision. Truman continued to maintain his position,

stating that he feared an invasion of China would damage the fragile peace between Communist China, under the leadership of Mao Tse-tung, and the Nationalists, under the leadership of Chiang Kai-shek, who controlled the islands of Formosa and Taiwan off the Chinese coast. This belief was further bolstered when MacArthur proposed the use of Nationalist troops to fight against the Communists.

MacArthur wrote several letters to members of Congress; in his letters, he suggested that the administration's policy was faulty. One of the letters, written to Congressman Joseph Martin, openly challenged Truman's authority, and appeared in the *Congressional Record*. Truman wasted no time and took action. He dismissed MacArthur as commander of American forces in Korea and essentially forced MacArthur to retire. Truman regarded the clash with MacArthur as a conflict between the right of the executive branch to make foreign policy and the responsibility of the military to carry out that policy. Truman referred to his action as an assertion of civil authority over the military.

In this lesson, students read a selection of primary source documents and answer questions for discussion. In addition, students write a letter of support to either President Truman or General MacArthur.

Procedure
1. Explain that one of the most important roles of the president is to act as commander in chief. During times of war and civil crisis, presidents have often clashed with military leaders. Abraham Lincoln continually clashed with General George McClellan, who trained the Army of the Potomac for months and basically refused to fight when ordered to do so by Lincoln. Military leaders, like George Washington, Andrew Jackson, Ulysses S. Grant, and Dwight D. Eisenhower, became president. Others, like William J. Clinton, have never performed military service. Stress that the president in his role as commander in chief, regardless of his military experience, has the final word.

2. Distribute **Handout 63**, and explain that the documents contained in the handout involve a clash between President Harry Truman and General Douglas MacArthur during the Korean conflict. Divide the class into small groups of three or four, and have the groups read the documents and answer the questions. Review students' responses.

Suggested Responses:

1. *MacArthur proposed to meet force with maximum force.*

2. *Europe will inevitably fall.*

3. *The military needed to do whatever it had to do to win.*

4. *MacArthur belittled the efforts of diplomats; MacArthur's victory was the wrong kind of victory; MacArthur's letter was openly insubordinate to the commander in chief.*

5. *The president was the commander in chief.*

6. *MacArthur was openly critical of Truman's policy and defied the civilian authority.*

7. *The military should be kept from taking control of the government; power resides in the people; military will never be voted out of office; military leaders never develop humility; the military is dominated by "command" and "obedience."*

8. *MacArthur challenged the civilian control of the military, and these actions endangered the fundamental principle of free government.*

9. *MacArthur said Communism was a global issue, and its success in one area would lead to success in others.*

10. *The invasion created a new war. The situation called for changes in departments and decision making.*

11. *MacArthur wanted to intensify the economic blockade against China, impose a naval blockade along the Chinese coast, remove restrictions of air reconnaissance over China and Manchuria, and use Nationalist Chinese troops against Communist troops on the mainland of China.*

12. *Appeasement leads to a sham peace; it results in successive and greater demands.*

13. *MacArthur said policy makers were afraid of all-out war with China and possible Soviet intervention.*

3. Ask students whether they feel that Truman's actions were justified. Have students explain why or why not. Then instruct students to write a letter to either Truman or MacArthur in support of his position. Allow class time for students to share their letters.

Enrichment/Extension

Have students research and report on the role of the president as commander in chief. Have them examine current attitudes toward the role of the president as a military commander.

242

Conflict between Civilian Authority and Military Supremacy

Read the documents. Then answer the questions.

MacArthur's Indiscretion

General Douglas MacArthur, commander of American forces in Korea, replied to a letter from House minority leader Joseph W. Martin in which Martin expressed his dismay at the failure to use Nationalist Chinese troops against the aggressors in Korea. Martin read MacArthur's reply on the floor of the House of Representatives, and it appeared in the *Congressional Record*. MacArthur's indiscreet reply strengthened the position of President Harry S. Truman, which was that MacArthur had overstepped the boundaries laid down in the Constitution regarding the control of the military by civil authority.

> I am most grateful for our note of the eighth forwarding me a copy of your address of February 12. The latter I have read with much interest, and find that with the passage of years you have certainly lost none of your old-time punch.
>
> My views and recommendation with respect to the situation created by Red China's entry into war against us in Korea have been submitted to Washington in most complete detail. Generally these views are well known and clearly understood, as they follow the conventional pattern of meeting force with maximum counter-force, as we have never failed to do in the past. Your view with respect to the utilization of the Chinese forces in Formosa is in conflict with neither logic nor this tradition.
>
> It seems strangely difficult for some to realize that here in Asia is where the Communist conspirators have elected to make their play for global conquest, and that we have joined the issue thus raised on the battlefield; that here we fight Europe's war with arms while the diplomats there still fight it with words; that if we lose the war to Communism in Asia the fall of Europe is inevitable; win it, and Europe most probably would avoid war and yet preserve freedom.
>
> As you point out, we must win. There is no substitute for victory.[1]

Truman v. MacArthur: No Substitute for Victory

Of course the third paragraph of MacArthur's letter was the real "clincher." I do not know through what channels of information the general learned that the Communists had chosen to concentrate their efforts on Asia—and more specifically on his command. . . . Actually, of course, my letter of January 13 [to MacArthur] had made it clear that Communism was capable of attacking not only in Asia but also in Europe and that this was one reason why we could not afford to extend the conflict in Korea. But then MacArthur added a belittling comment about our diplomatic efforts and reached his climax with the pronouncement that "there is no substitute for victory."

But there is a right kind and a wrong kind of victory, just as there are wars for the right thing and wars that are wrong from every standpoint. . . .

The kind of victory MacArthur had in mind—victory by the bombing of Chinese cities, victory by expanding the conflict to all of China—would have been the wrong kind of victory.

[1]*Congressional Record*, 82nd Congress, 1st sess. (5 April 1951), 3380.

To some professional military men, victory—success on the battlefield alone—becomes something of an end in itself. Napoleon, during his ill-fated Moscow campaign, said, "I beat them in every battle, but it does not get me anywhere."

The time had come to draw the line. MacArthur's letter to Congressman Martin showed that the general was not only in disagreement with the policy of the government but was challenging this policy in open insubordination to his Commander in Chief.[2]

Truman Asserts Civil Supremacy, 1951

A brilliant strategist whose strong opinions often made him enemies, Douglas MacArthur was responsible for most of the American success in the Pacific during World War II. He was appointed commander of American forces in Korea and had initial success. The war expanded when the Communist Chinese sent thousands of troops against a United Nations peacekeeping force. MacArthur recommended a blockade of the Chinese coast to cut supply lines, a bombing of supply bases in China, and the use of Nationalist Chinese troops as part of the peacekeeping forces. Fearing that direct intervention by the Soviet Union on behalf of the Chinese would escalate into another world war, President Truman disagreed with MacArthur's recommendations. When MacArthur issued an ultimatum to the Communists in March 1951, Truman could no longer allow MacArthur to command America's troops in Korea. Truman essentially fired MacArthur, citing the need for the military to be subordinate to civil authority.

If there is one basic element in our Constitution, it is civilian control of the military. Policies are to be made by the elected political officials, not by generals or admirals. Yet time and again General MacArthur had shown that he was unwilling to accept the policies of the administration. By his repeated public statements he was not only confusing our allies as to the true course of our policies but, in fact, was also setting his policy against the President's.

I have always had, and I have to this day, the greatest respect for General MacArthur, the soldier. Nothing I could do, I knew, could change his stature as one of the outstanding military figures of our time—and I had no desire to diminish his stature. I had hoped, and I had tried to convince him, that the policy he was asked to follow was right. He had disagreed. He had been openly critical. Now, at last, his actions [in issuing an ultimatum] had frustrated a political course decided upon, in conjunction with its allies, by the government he was sworn to serve. If I allowed him to defy the civil authorities in this manner, I myself would be violating my oath to uphold and defend the Constitution.

I have always believed that civilian control of the military is one of the strongest foundations of our system of free government. Many of our people are descended from men and women who fled their native countries to escape the oppression of militarism. We in America have sometimes failed to give the soldier and the sailor their due, and it has hurt us. But we have always jealously guarded the constitutional provision that prevents the military from taking over the government from the authorities, elected by the people, in whom the power resides. . . .

One reason that we have been so careful to keep the military within its own preserve is that the very nature of the service hierarchy gives military

[2]Harry S. Truman, *Memoirs: Years of Trial and Hope*, vol. 2 (New York: Doubleday and Company, 1956), 446–47.

commanders little if any opportunity to learn the humility that is needed for good public service. The elected official will never forget—unless he is a fool—that others as well or better qualified might have been chosen and that millions remained unconvinced that the last choice made was the best one possible. . . .

These are things a military officer is not likely to learn in the course of his profession. The words that dominate his thinking are "command" and "obedience," and the military definitions of these words are not definitions for use in a republic.

That is why our Constitution embodies the principle of civilian control of the military. This was the principle that General MacArthur threatened. I do not believe that he purposefully decided to challenge civilian control of the military, but the result of his behavior was that this fundamental principle of free government was in danger.

It was my duty to act.[3]

Douglas MacArthur Addresses Congress

. . . I do not stand here as an advocate for any partisan cause, for the issues are fundamental and reach quite beyond the realm of partisan consideration. They must be resolved on the highest plane of national interest if our course is to prove sound and our future protected. . . . I address you with neither rancor nor bitterness in the fading twilight of life with but one purpose in mind, to serve my country.

The issues are global and so interlocked that to consider the problems of one sector oblivious to those of another is but to court disaster for the whole.

While Asia is commonly referred to as the gateway to Europe, it is no less true that Europe is the gateway to Asia, and the broad influence of one cannot fail to have its impact upon the other. . . .

The Communist threat is a global one. Its successful advance in one sector threatens the destruction of every other sector. You cannot appease or otherwise surrender to communism in Asia without simultaneously undermining our efforts to halt its advance in Europe. . . .

I now turn to the Korean conflict. While I was not consulted prior to the President's decision to intervene in support of the Republic of Korea, that decision from a military standpoint proved a sound one . . . as we hurled back the invaders and decimated his forces. Our victory was complete and our objectives within reach when Red China intervened with numerically superior ground forces. This created a new war and an entirely new situation, a situation not contemplated when our forces were committed against the North Korean invaders, a situation which called for new decisions in the diplomatic sphere to permit the realistic adjustment of military strategy. Such decisions have not been forthcoming. . . .

I felt that military necessity in the conduct of the war made necessary:

First, the intensification of our economic blockade against China.

Second, the imposition of a naval blockade against the China coast.

Third, removal of restrictions on air reconnaissance of China's coastal areas and of Manchuria.

[3]Truman, *Memoirs*, vol. 2, 444–45.

Fourth, removal of restrictions on the forces of the Republic of China [Nationalist] on Formosa with logistical support to contribute to their effective operation against the Chinese mainland.

For entertaining these views . . . I have been severely criticized in lay circles, principally abroad, despite my understanding that from a military standpoint the above views have been fully shared in the past by practically every military leader concerned with the Korean campaign, including our own Joint Chiefs of Staff. . . .

But once war is forced upon us, there is no other alternative than to apply every available means to bring it to a swift end. War's very object is victory—not prolonged indecision. In war, indeed, there can be no substitute for victory.

There are some who for varying reasons would appease Red China. They are blind to history's clear lesson. For history teaches with unmistakable emphasis that appeasement but begets new and bloodier war. It points to no single instance where the end had justified the means—where appeasement has led to more than a sham peace. Like blackmail, it lays the basis for new and successively greater demands, until, as in blackmail, violence becomes the only other alternative. Why, my soldiers asked of me, surrender military advantages to an enemy in the field? I cannot now answer. Some may say to avoid the spread of the conflict into an all-out war with China; others, to avoid Soviet intervention. Neither explanation seems valid. For China is already engaging with the maximum power it can commit and the Soviet will not necessarily mesh its actions with our moves. Like a cobra, any new enemy will more likely strike whenever it feels that relativity in military or other potential is in its favor on a worldwide basis. . . .

I am closing my 52 years of military service. When I joined the Army even before the turn of the century, it was the fulfillment of all my boyish hopes and dreams. The world has turned over many times since I took the oath on the plain at West Point, and the hopes and dreams have long since vanished. But I since remember the refrain of one of the most popular barrack ballads of that day which proclaimed most proudly that—"Old soldiers never die; they just fade away." And like the old soldier of that ballad, I now close my military career and just fade away—an old soldier who tried to do his duty as God gave him the light to see that duty.

Good-by.[4]

[4]*Congressional Record*, 82nd Congress, 1st sess. (19 April 1951), 4123–25.

1. What action had MacArthur proposed when the Chinese invaded Korea?

2. What did MacArhur say would happen if Communism was allowed to take hold in Asia?

3. What did MacArthur mean by "no substitute for victory"?

4. Why was Truman angry with MacArthur?

5. To whom did Truman say the power to set policy had been given?

6. Why did Truman feel he had to dismiss MacArthur?

7. Why did Truman say the military needed to be controlled?

8. Why did Truman act against MacArthur?

9. What did MacArthur say about the threat of Communism?

10. How did the invasion of North Korea by Communist China change the Korean conflict?

11. How did MacArthur propose winning the war?

12. What did MacArthur say would happen if America tried to appease China instead of trying for victory?

13. Of what did MacArthur say policy makers were afraid?

Lesson 36
Campaign Finance Reform

Objectives
- To develop an understanding of the cost of securing elective office in America

- To examine the need for campaign finance reform

Notes to the Teacher
Over the past fifty years, conducting a campaign for elected office in the United States has become more and more expensive. At one time, a few fundraisers and contributions from the party faithful were all that were needed for a successful political campaign. Today billions of dollars are spent on television and radio commercials, print advertisements, and, in the case of national candidates, appearances at meetings and rallies across the country. Today much of the money supporting campaigns comes from companies, organizations, and individuals who support a particular position or cause. Of course, these contributors will expect the candidate to espouse their causes or beliefs openly. Lobbyists for large organizations and corporations constantly bombard congressional representatives and senators for support.

In the past, money from these donors has been loosely controlled. Today as war chests grow and the political leadership in America argues about soft money and hard money, the cry has risen for change in campaign financing.

In this lesson, students read a selection on campaign finance reform and answer questions for discussion. Students interpret a series of tables that document campaign expenditures for the House of Representatives and the Senate. To conclude, students, working in small groups, create a proposal for a campaign finance reform bill, present it to the class for consideration, and attempt to reach consensus on the content of a passable bill.

Procedure
1. Ask students to describe the ideal candidate for public office. (*Someone who is educated, well-spoken, honest, owes nothing to special interest groups, and supports the views of the issues held by his or her constituency would be a good candidate.*) Ask why it is necessary for a candidate to be a good fundraiser. (*Campaigns are very expensive, and in today's media-dominated world, television and radio time are necessary to make voters aware of the candidate.*)

2. Ask students to define the following terms:

    political action committees (PACs)—*organizations established by corporations, labor unions, and special interest groups to provide contributions to a specific candidate's political campaign*

    hard money—*political contributions restricted by election law*

    soft money—*political contributions that are made to political parties, are unregulated, and may be spent on such things as "party-building" and "get out the vote" campaigns*

    issue ads—*advertisements aimed at informing voters about a candidate's or party's stand on a particular issue*

    public financing of presidential campaigns—*government funds available for candidates who accept certain limits on spending and stop fundraising*

3. Explain that some attempts at campaign finance reform have been attempted in the past. In March 2002, President George W. Bush signed into law the Bipartisan Campaign Reform Act. Distribute **Handout 64**, and have students read the selection on the McCain-Feingold Bill and answer the questions for discussion. Review students' responses.

Suggested Responses:
1. Soft money *refers to political contributions that are made to political parties, are unregulated, and may be spent on such things as "party-building" and "get out the vote" campaigns. Hard money refers to political contributions restricted by election law.*

2. *running issue ads mentioning a candidate prior to an election*

3. *will affect the way soft money will be raised*

249

4. *declared soft money ban unconstitutional; restricted how soft money could be spent; prohibited issue ads; adopted stricter rules about laws aired anytime during a campaign*

5. *The Supreme Court upheld the soft money and issue ads portion of the bill and declared unconstitutional the restriction placed on contributions by minors to political campaigns.*

4. Consider preparing an overhead transparency of the charts in **Handout 65** for use in class. Distribute **Handout 65**, and have students interpret the charts and answer the discussion questions. Review students' responses.

Suggested Responses:

1. *Republican candidates traditionally raise more money than Democratic candidates.*

2. *Candidates for Senate have to run a statewide campaign, which is more expensive than a local district campaign.*

3. *Campaigns between two incumbents for a newly created district after reapportionment were the most expensive.*

4. *An incumbent has the advantage of name recognition.*

5. *none*

6. *Florida*

7. *James F. Humphreys (D-W.Va.); Wayne Hogan (D-Fla.); Frances Folk Marcum (D-Tenn.)*

8. *Democrats—unions; human rights, women, and pro-choice issues; entertainment industry; more liberal; professional groups, such as lawyers, publishing*

   Republicans—gun rights, mining, oil and gas, building materials, chemicals; businesses large and small; ranchers and agribusiness; conservative

9. *No, the political issues that each group supports are very different.*

10. *Microsoft's headquarters are located in Inslee's district.*

11. *banks and financial institutions, law firms, big business*

5. Divide students into groups of four or five. Have students prepare a campaign finance reform bill. Allow time for groups to present their bill for consideration. Have students attempt to reach consensus on the content of a passable bill.

Enrichment/Extension

1. Have students research and report on the cost of a campaign in their area. They might choose a local campaign for mayor or city council, or a statewide campaign for office, such as governor.

2. Have students contact candidates after an election and interview them about running a political campaign.

Bipartisan Campaign Reform Act

Read the selection, and answer the questions.

Elections: Campaign Finance Reform

The campaign finance reform bill signed into law [in 2002] would ban soft money (unlimited campaign contributions to political parties) and prevent special interest groups from running so-called "issue" ads that mention a candidate just prior to an election. The law also doubles the hard money limits for individuals. The law's soft money restrictions would greatly impact the way campaign funds are raised: Political parties collected more than $400 million in soft money contributions during the 2002 elections. Shortly after the bill was signed by President Bush, several groups filed lawsuits, challenging the law's constitutionality. The AFL-CIO, American Civil Liberties Union, and the National Rifle Association say the legislation's curbs on issue ads are an unconstitutional limit on free speech. Sen. Mitch McConnell (R-Ky.), an outspoken critic of the new law, and the Republican National Committee also filed lawsuits, asking for the law's ban on soft money contributions to be struck down. In May [2002], a federal court ruled that the new law's ban on soft money contributions was unconstitutional, allowing the political parties to resume raising the unlimited campaign contributions. The court restricted how soft money can be spent, however, prohibiting political parties from using it to run issue ads. The court also rejected the law's ban on issue ads by special interest groups in the weeks leading up to an election, instead adopting a stricter standard that applies to ads aired at any time.

The decision was automatically appealed to the U.S. Supreme Court, and the justices heard the case on September 8 [2002]. Three months later, in a 5–4 decision, the Court upheld McCain-Feingold's soft money and issue ad restrictions. The Court did declare unconstitutional the law's prohibition on minors making contributions to candidates and political parties.[1]

1. Define *soft money* and *hard money*.

2. What did the law prevent special interest groups from doing?

3. What would be the effect of the limitations on soft money?

4. What was the decision of the federal district court in the case?

5. What was the ruling of the Supreme Court in the appeal?

[1]"Elections: Campaign Finance Reform," *Open Secrets.org*, 9 January 2003, <http://www.opensecrets.org/payback/issue.asp?issueid=CFR&CongNo=107> (25 May 2004).

Raising Money Is Easy; Winning an Election Is Hard

Interpret the charts, and answer the questions.

The Price of Admission

Running for Congress has never been an easy proposition, or an inexpensive one. But even in these years of low inflation, the cost of winning a seat in the U.S. Senate or House of Representatives keeps climbing upwards, with no guarantee of success when all the votes are counted. Here's how the numbers broke down in the last election.

House

Party	Number of Candidates	Average Raised	Average Spent	Average Cash on Hand	Average from PACs	Average from Individuals
All	435	$966,670	$898,184	$307,187	$413,140	$498,044
Democrats	205	$920,567	$854,497	$315,581	$403,649	$463,534
Republicans	229	$1,009,294	$938,497	$298,269	$423,063	$528,807

Senate

Party	Number of Candidates	Average Raised	Average Spent	Average Cash on Hand	Average from PACs	Average from Individuals
All	34	$5,029,904	$4,812,159	$512,999	$1,230,238	$3,363,413
Democrats	12	$4,992,408	$4,742,986	$785,410	$1,166,425	$3,423,442
Republicans	22	$5,050,356	$4,849,891	$364,412	$1,265,044	$3,330,669

1. Why do you think the amount of money raised by the Republicans was greater than that raised by the Democrats?

2. Why do you think candidates for Senate had to raise more money?

Different Races, Different Costs

Getting reelected is a lot cheaper than winning a seat in Congress in the first place. That fact is evident in these charts, which show averages for winners and losers in different types of races.

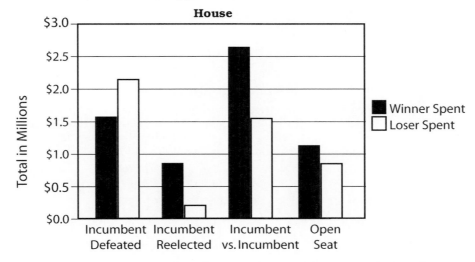

Type of Race	Spent by Winner	Spent by Loser	Number of Races
Incumbent Defeated	$1,595,805	$2,141,671	4
Incumbent Reelected	$826,942	$179,000	378
Incumbent vs. Incumbent	$2,670,768	$1,552,073	4
Open Seat	$1,246,114	$838,242	49

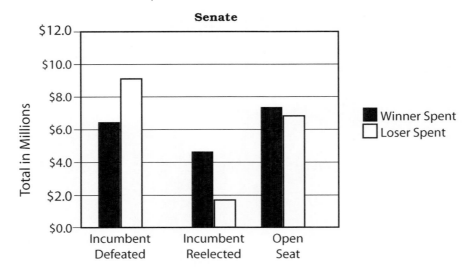

Type of Race	Spent by Winner	Spent by Loser	Number of Races
Incumbent Defeated	$6,826,395	$9,315,654	3
Incumbent Reelected	$4,681,870	$1,644,130	24
Open Seat	$7,123,787	$6,767,665	7

3. Which campaigns were the most expensive?

4. Why do you think the cost of running for a open seat is almost 50 percent higher than a race run by an incumbent?

Millionaire Candidates

As the costs of running for office have escalated, more and more candidates are jumping into politics using their personal fortune, rather than trying to raise all those funds from other people. The following chart shows the top ten millionaire candidates in the 2002 election cycle.

Chamber	Candidate	Self-Funding	Raised from Others	Percentage Self-Funded	Result
House	James F. Humphreys (D-W.Va.)	$7,794,500	$369,340	95.5%	Lost
Senate	Douglas R. Forrester (R-N.J.)	$7,485,000	$2,580,199	74.4%	Lost
Senate	Erskine B. Bowles (D-N.C.)	$6,791,550	$6,485,229	51.2%	Lost
House	Wayne Hogan (D-Fla.)	$4,482,475	$184,736	96.1%	Lost
House	Harry Jacobs (D-Fla.)	$3,270,000	$753,632	81.3%	Lost
House	Roger Kahn (D-Ga.)	$2,802,394	$841,861	76.9%	Lost
House	Tom Reiser (R-Tex.)	$1,759,619	$385,515	82.0%	Lost
House	Janet Robert (D-Minn.)	$1,707,587	$472,970	78.3%	Lost
House	Frances Folk Marcum (D-Tenn.)	$1,700,000	$158,872	91.5%	Lost Primary
House	Martha Fuller Clark (D-N.H.)	$1,580,000	$1,957,316	44.7%	Lost

5. Of the top ten candidates, how many were elected?

6. Which state had two self-funded candidates?

7. Which three candidates self-funded more than 90 percent of their election campaign?

Most Heavily Partisan industries

The list below shows the industries and interest groups that gave the highest proportion of their dollars to one party or the other.

Rank	Industry/ Interest Group	Donations to Democrats	Percentage to Democrats
1	Democratic/Liberal	$11,051,234	99.8%
2	Industrial Unions	$19,068,114	98.7%
3	Misc. Unions	$13,172,231	95.9%
4	Women's Issues	$7,248,482	93.4%
5	Public Sector Unions	$25,386,834	93.1%
6	Bldg. Trade Unions	$19,785,359	92.6%
7	Environment	$1,856,480	87.0%
8	Human Rights	$3,592,725	84.9%
9	Transport Unions	$12,518,237	84.1%
10	Non-Profits	$6,110,641	82.7%
11	Pro-Choice	$1,646,820	79.8%
12	TV/Movies/Music	$31,094,270	77.9%
13	Pro-Israel	$6,319,011	75.1%
14	Lawyers/Law Firms	$70,701,488	74.1%
15	Publishing	$11,201,876	72.0%

Rank	Industry/ Interest Group	Donations to Republicans	Percentage to Republicans
1	Republican/Conservative	$13,392,562	99.7%
2	Gun Rights	$2,613,497	93.7%
3	Business Associations	$2,468,224	84.4%
4	Poultry & Eggs	$1,578,106	82.7%
5	Mining	$4,652,168	82.3%
6	Trucking	$3,708,932	80.5%
7	Building Materials	$5,629,707	80.0%
8	Oil & Gas	$19,901,981	79.8%
9	Chemicals	$5,704,797	78.7%
10	Tobacco	$7,191,015	78.7%
11	Railroads	$5,246,963	76.8%
12	Forest Products	$3,616,921	76.3%
13	Automotive	$11,451,129	76.1%
14	Misc. Mfg./Distrib.	$14,576,203	75.5%
15	Livestock	$2,702,773	75.5%

8. How would you characterize the contributors to the Democratic and Republican parties?

9. Are there any groups that appear on both lists? Why or why not?

Bundles of Money: Biggest Contributions in the 2002 Elections

While federal contribution limits ensure that no single individual can give enormous sums of money to any candidate, there's no limit to what groups of individuals from the same organization can give. Indeed, many groups bundle large numbers of checks and deliver them en masse to candidates they strongly support. This list shows the biggest bundles delivered to candidates in the 2002 election cycle. Totals include money from individuals connected with the organization, their immediate family members, and contributions, if any, from the organization's political action committee.

Contributor	Total	Recipient—Senate
Goldman Sachs	$585,870	Jon S. Corzine (D-N.J.)
Emily's List	$500,389	Deborah Ann Stabenow (D-Mich.)
Emily's List	$494,211	Jean Carnahan (D-Mo.)
Emily's List	$426,645	Jeanne Shaheen (D-N.H.)
Goldman Sachs	$331,600	Charles E. Schumer (D-N.Y.)
Emily's List	$297,753	Barbara Boxer (D-Calif.)
Citigroup Inc.	$261,416	Charles E. Schumer (D-N.Y.)
MBNA Corp.	$253,250	William V. Roth Jr. (R-Del.)
MBNA Corp.	$171,000	Olympia J. Snowe (R-Maine)
Robins, Kaplan et al.	$159,516	Michael V. Ciresi (D-Minn.)

Contributor	Total	Recipient—House
Emily's List	$236,816	Lynn N. Rivers (D-Mich.)
Emily's List	$115,537	Stephanie Herseth (D-S.D.)
Club for Growth	$102,930	Tom Feeney (R-Fla.)
Emily's List	$93,925	Julie Thomas (D-Iowa)
Emily's List	$90,000	Martha Fuller Clark (D-N.H.)
Anheuser-Busch	$84,450	Richard A. Gephardt (D-Mo.)
Club for Growth	$80,350	John Swallow (R-Utah)
Emily's List	$77,650	Carol A. Roberts (D-Fla.)
Microsoft Corp.	$75,100	Jay Inslee (D-Wash.)
Dresdner, Kleinwort & Wasserstein	$71,250	Rahm Emanuel (D-Ill.)

10. Why do you think Microsoft made a large contribution to Inslee?

11. How would you characterize the contributors?

Source: Center for Responsive Politics, "The Big Picture: 2002 Cycle," *Open Secrets.org,* <http://www.opensecrets.org/bigpicture/index.asp?cycle+2002> (20 May 2004).

Lesson 37
The Federal Budget:
Head Start, a Case Study

Objectives

- To develop an understanding of the decision-making process needed to craft the U.S. Budget

- To examine the funding for Head Start

Notes to the Teacher

The federal budget is spent on activities ranging from the maintenance of lodges in Yellowstone National Park to the purchase of fighter planes for the military. The federal budget is a plan for how the government spends taxpayers' money. It depends on the revenue gained from different kinds of taxes, such as income tax, excise tax, and social security insurance tax. It is a plan for the borrowing of money or the repayment of loans and debts. When revenues exceed spending, the government has a surplus. Some of this money is applied to the national debt. The spending by the government, including money for improvements in education and support for science and technology, can raise income, produce jobs, and increase future productivity. Taxes, on the other hand, reduce income and leave people with less money to spend. When the economy is good, people are paid higher wages, and unemployment is low. The nation's revenue increases, and the deficit shrinks.

A budget reflects the president's requests for money sent to Congress. These requests include the administration's priorities for the coming fiscal year, which begins on October 1. This budget affects both the American people and the economy. State and local budgets affect the economy as well. They are independent of the federal budget, and the states and cities have their own sources of revenue. But the federal government supplements state and local revenues. About 20 percent of the money spent by state and local governments comes from the federal budget. The Gross Domestic Product (GDP) measures the size of the economy. The federal budget allocates a small percentage of the GDP to government spending.

In general, both Congress and the president determine how much money the government is expected to receive in each of the next several years, where it will come from, and how much will be available to spend in order to help the administration reach its goals. Wartime has affected the proposed budgets of Abraham Lincoln, Woodrow Wilson, Franklin D. Roosevelt, Harry Truman, and George W. Bush. Presidents John F. Kennedy and Ronald Reagan supported a commitment to space exploration.

Both Congress and the president decide how much they will spend through taxes and how much through borrowing. They must reach an agreement on how to use the budget to help the economy grow.

The federal government pays most of its bills by using revenues from taxes, such as corporate income taxes, excise taxes on tobacco, alcohol, gasoline, and telephone services, estate and gift taxes, and custom duties. Budgets have reflected the need to finance defense spending, the war on terrorism, and social programs, such as Head Start and Medicare. The agencies that receive discretionary spending may see their share of the pie change each budget cycle. Nondiscretionary spending, which is mandated by laws that create special programs, changes very little. These programs are usually referred to as entitlement programs. Some of these entitlements are means-tested, which means that a set of criteria determines who is eligible for a specific program. Some spending limits, such as Social Security, Medicare, and Medicaid, are set by law.

The president must submit a budget to Congress by the first Monday in February. The White House Office of Management and Budget (OMB) helps to prepare the budget after consulting with the president and his advisors. Then Congress and the president decide how much to spend on each program.

The government measures spending in two ways: budget authority and outlays. Budget authority is the amount the law authorizes the federal government to spend on certain programs, projects, or activities. What the government actually spends in a given year is called the outlay. For example, the president and Congress may agree to spend $1 billion on a space station. Congress appropriates $1 billion in budget authority. But the system takes ten years to build, and the government might spend $100 million in outlays the first year, and $900 million over the next nine years as construction continues. To monitor spending, the government uses an Inspector General; the General Accountability Office (GAO), an auditing arm of Congress; congressional committees; and the OMB.

In this lesson, students complete a short activity on the process of producing a budget. They then examine the Head Start program and the budgetary allocations for the program. To conclude, students write a letter to their congressional representative requesting continued support for the Head Start program.

Procedure
1. Ask students to explain what a budget is (*a plan for proposed spending*). Distribute **Handout 66**, and have students complete part A as directed. Discuss students' responses, which will vary.

2. Have students complete parts B and C of **Handout 66**. Review students' responses.

   Suggested Responses:
   Part B.

a.	5	e.	4
b.	3	f.	7
c.	1	g.	6
d.	2		

   Part C.
   - *individual income tax*
   - *corporate income tax*
   - *excise tax*
   - *estate and gift taxes*
   - *Federal Reserve earnings*
   - *social insurance payroll taxes*

3. Distribute **Handout 67**, and have students read part A and answer the questions. Review students' responses.

   Suggested Responses:
   1. *to provide extra help to get disadvantaged children ready for school*

   2. *provide better teachers, stress academics, protect Head Start programs against budget cuts, and encourage states to fund early childhood education*

4. Have students complete **Handout 67**, part B, as directed. Review students' responses. Students might use the Internet to obtain more recent statistics regarding Head Start allocations.

   Suggested Responses:
   Top ten states—*large populations, large populations of non-English-speaking children; industrial rust belt and rural south, where there are large numbers of disadvantaged children*

   Bottom ten states—*small populations, small numbers of children who do not speak English*

5. Have students write their congressional representative a letter in which they request continued support for the Head Start program. Allow time for students to share their letters.

Enrichment/Extension
1. Have students research and report on the budgets of other entitlement programs.

2. Have students interview a Head Start teacher or program participant about the Head Start program.

Making Choices

Part A.

Determine which of these items are most important to you personally. Rank them in order from 1, most important, to 14, least important.

_____	personal safety	_____	paying off bills and debts
_____	shelter	_____	faith
_____	financial security	_____	emotional happiness
_____	health	_____	books
_____	clothes	_____	educational opportunity
_____	entertainment	_____	transportation
_____	furniture	_____	retirement

Part B.

Congress and the president determine the federal budget in a way similar to how you might determine your personal budget. Use the information in your textbook and other sources to place the following steps in the budgetary process in the proper sequence from 1 to 7.

_____a. The heads of agencies execute the budget and spend money provided by law.

_____b. Congress reviews the president's budget proposal, develops its own budget, and approves spending and revenue bills.

_____c. The agencies of the executive branch develop requests for funding and submit them to the Office of Management and Budget. The president reviews requests and makes final decisions of what will appear in the budget.

_____d. The executive branch prepares and transmits the budget documents to Congress.

_____e. The fiscal year begins.

_____f. The government makes available data on actual spending and receipts, by agency, for the completed fiscal year.

_____g. Once the president and Congress approve spending, the government monitors the budget through agency program monitors, including Inspector General, the OMB, and the General Accounting Office.

Part C.

Determine which of the following are sources of income for the federal government.

_____	individual income tax	_____	Stealth bomber construction
_____	road construction	_____	corporate income tax
_____	excise taxes	_____	import taxes paid to other countries
_____	estate taxes	_____	Federal Reserve earnings
_____	social insurance payroll taxes		

Head Start: A Case Study

Part A.

Read the following bill summary, and be prepared for class discussion.

The School Readiness Act of 2003
House Education and the Workforce Committee

Head Start is a great program that is capable of achieving even greater results. Studies show that while children in Head Start show improvement, they still leave the program with knowledge levels far below national averages for U.S. children. The U.S. Department of Health and Human Services (HHS) has released a report . . . showing that Head Start children lag behind their more affluent peers in the crucial early learning knowledge areas that have been shown to be an excellent predictor of later school success. As a result of this "readiness gap," Head Start children are not being adequately prepared for school in key areas of cognitive development that have been shown to be critical for later school success.

To close the readiness gap and strengthen Head Start, the School Readiness Act, authored by Rep. Mike Castle (R-Del.), would

- Emphasize "what works" in preparing disadvantaged children for school through the strengthening of the academic components of the program.
- Allow faith-based centers to hire individuals of the same religion.
- Improve teacher quality by requiring teachers be trained in early childhood development on the college or university level.
- Provide incentives for states to maintain and expand funding for early childhood education.
- Shield Head Start and other early childhood education programs against state budget cuts.
- Increase Head Start funding.
- Require no new testing.
- Ensure that local Head Start centers are fairly evaluated on their performance.
- Continue to provide extra help for Head Start centers identified as underachieving.
- Grant additional funds for migrant and seasonal Head Start and quality improvement.
- Provide all current health and nutrition services for Head Start children.
- Keep Head Start at the U.S. Department of Health and Human Services.[1]

1. What is the purpose of Head Start?

2. What suggestions were made for improving the program?

[1]Adapted from "Summary: The School Readiness Act of 2003," *Committee on Education and the Workforce,* <http://ed-workforce.house.gov/issues/108th/education/earlychildhood/billsummary.htm> (21 May 2004).

Part B.

Review the following data about allocations, enrollment, and expenditures for Head Start in fiscal year 2003. How would you characterize the top ten states? the bottom ten?

Top Ten States

	State	Dollars	Enrollment	Expenditure per Child
1.	California	$811,486,631	98,767	$8,216.17
2.	Texas	$465,421,856	67,764	$6,868.27
3.	New York	$422,349,645	49,473	$8,536.97
4.	Illinois	$263,046,115	39,640	$6,635.90
5.	Florida	$255,501,245	35,350	$7,227.75
6.	Ohio	$239,770,120	38,017	$6,309.92
7.	Michigan	$228,044,810	35,099	$6,497.19
8.	Pennsylvania	$222,603,242	30,908	$7,202.12
9.	Georgia	$163,757,113	23,400	$6,998.17
10.	Mississippi	$157,164,747	26,762	$5,872.68

Bottom Ten States

	State	Dollars	Enrollment	Expenditure per Child
1.	Wyoming	$12,027,897	1,803	$6,671.05
2.	Alaska	$12,126,424	1,817	$6,673.87
3.	Delaware	$12,536,909	2,214	$5,662.56
4.	New Hampshire	$13,018,299	1,632	$7,976.90
5.	Vermont	$13,182,631	1,573	$8,380.56
6.	North Dakota	$16,696,830	2,357	$7,083.93
7.	Montana	$20,365,406	2,952	$6,898.85
8.	Rhode Island	$21,445,541	3,150	$6,808.11
9.	Idaho	$22,248,160	2,939	$7,424.20
10.	Hawaii	$21,819,720	3,063	$7,263.52

Source: U.S. Department of Health and Human Services, "Head Start Program Fact Sheet," *Adminstration for Children and Families*, <http://www.acf.hhs.gov/programs/hsb/research/2004.htm> (28 June 2004).

Lesson 38
Poverty in America

Objective
- To understand different views of the role of the federal government in helping the nation's poor

Notes to the Teacher

Historically, one of the most contentious issues between America's political parties has been the extent of the government's responsibility in helping the poor. In colonial America, churches assumed the responsibility for the poor in their community, following biblical exhortations to contribute alms to the poor. By the beginning of the twentieth century, the growth of cities and a corresponding growth in the number of urban poor led to a change in the practices that had been effective in a rural community. Poor children were sent to work for wealthy families. At times, entire families were sent to the workhouse or farm, where they were expected to earn their keep. The elderly went to an almshouse. In the 1930s, when the Great Depression struck, local resources were strained, and President Franklin D. Roosevelt's administration created a plan to provide relief for the poor. Roosevelt's New Deal was a radical expansion of the government's role in all areas, from its use of local labor in road and park building (Civilian Conservation Corps) to projects that documented the lives of former slaves and chronicled the history and culture of America's states (Public Works Administration). Food distribution and rural electrification projects were created at government expense. New Deal programs to clear slums and aid tenant farmers established a federal responsibility for victims of society.

In the years since the Great Depression, some aspects of the welfare state have become an established, but politically controversial, fact in American politics. Conservatives see the expanded programs of the federal government as a violation of the spirit of the Founding Fathers, who were strict constructionists and desired that the federal government act only on those ideals that were spelled out in the Constitution. Conversely, more liberal interpreters of the Constitution cite the Preamble as a basis for providing social and economic aid to the unfortunate and promoting the general welfare.

In this lesson, students read a selection and answer questions for discussion about the responsibility of American society to the poor. To conclude, students interpret data and draw conclusions about the changing role of government in a welfare state.

Procedure

1. Discuss our nation's attitude toward the poor. Stress the idea of being responsible for the well-being of those less fortunate. Explain that the way in which American society has approached the problem of poverty has changed over time.

2. Divide the class into small groups of three or four. Distribute **Handout 68**, and have each group complete the activity as directed. Review students' responses.

   Suggested Responses:
   1. *Ronald Reagan*
   2. *Thomas Jefferson*
   3. *Calvin Coolidge*
   4. *New Deal Era*
   5. *Leviticus*
   6. *George W. Bush*
   7. *William J. Clinton*

3. Distribute **Handout 69**. Have students read and interpret the chart in part A and then answer the questions. Review students' responses.

   Suggested Responses:
   1. *1970*
   2. *1970*
   3. *1970s*
   4. *the disabled, the elderly, and retired people*

4. Explain that for many years, reformers have called for changes in our welfare system. These efforts at reform may be on the local, state, or national level. Have students complete part B of **Handout 69**. Review students' responses.

263

Suggested Responses:

1. *Answers might include new state work requirements and status of benefits for noncitizens.*

2. *healthy marriages and provision for the involvement of the father in the life of children born out of wedlock; an increase in childcare benefits*

3. *States may claim specific waivers and exemptions; funds from Temporary Assistance for Needy Families (TANF) stay at current levels.*

4. *a dramatic drop of over 50 percent*

5. Have each group prepare a list of five reforms it would propose if it were responsible for welfare reform. Have each group make a brief presentation and explain its reasoning. Have students attempt to reach consensus on a class list of five proposed reforms.

Enrichment/Extension

Have students collect examples from current newspapers and magazines about efforts to reform welfare programs across the country. Instruct students to prepare a bulletin board display of the articles.

Care of the Poor: A Historical Perspective

Read each of the following statements on the care of the poor at different times in history. Then answer the questions.

> When you harvest your fields, do not cut the grain at the edges of the fields, and do not go back to cut the heads of grain that were left. Do not go back through your vineyard to gather the grapes that were missed or to pick up the grapes that have fallen; leave them for poor people and foreigners. I am the LORD your God.
>
> —*Leviticus 19:9* (TEV)

> The poor, unable to support themselves, are maintained by an assessment on the [tithable] persons in their parish. This assessment is levied and administered by twelve persons in each parish, called vestrymen . . . chosen by the housekeepers of the parish . . . afterwards . . . by their own choice. . . . The poor who have neither property, friends, nor strength to labor are boarded in the houses of good farmers, to whom a stipulated sum is annually paid. To those who are able to help themselves a little, or have friends from whom they derive some succor, inadequate however to their full maintenance, supplementary aids are given, which enable them to live comfortably in their own houses or in the houses of their friends. Vagabonds, without visible property or vocation, are placed in workhouses, where they are well [clothed], fed, lodged, and made to labour. Nearly the same method of providing for the poor prevails through all our states; and from Savannah to Portsmouth you will seldom meet a beggar. In the large towns . . . sometimes . . . foreigners . . . never obtained a settlement in . . . [the] parish. I never yet saw [an] American begging in the streets or highways. A subsistence is easily gained here: and if, by misfortunes, they are thrown on the charities of the world, those provided by their own country are so comfortable and so certain, that they never think of relinquishing them to become strolling beggars.
>
> —Thomas Jefferson

> We cannot finance the country, we cannot improve social conditions, through any system of injustice, even if we attempt to inflict it upon the rich. Those who suffer the most harm will be the poor. This country believes in prosperity. It is absurd to suppose that it is envious of those who are already prosperous. The wise and correct course to follow in taxation and all other economic legislation is not to destroy those who have already secured success but to create conditions under which every one will have a better chance to be successful. . . . All owners of property are charged with a service. These rights and duties have been revealed through the conscience of society, to have a divine sanction. The very stability of our society rests upon production and conservation.
>
> —Calvin Coolidge

> From the beginning we strove to make methods of emergency relief differ deeply from practices of local poor relief, which still held a heavy hand over many local agencies. Under the philosophy of this ancient practice, the applicant was in some way morally deficient. He must be made to feel his pauperism. Every help which was given to him was to be given in a way to intensify his sense of shame. Usually he was forced to plead his destitution in an offensively dreary room. We asked for the establishment of respectable light quarters continently placed in the neighborhoods of those who had to use them. We tried to have the applicant received by an

intelligent, sympathetic human being who did not, in his own mind, put a stigma upon the unfortunate person before him. We tried to see that relief officials were people who understood that the predicament of the worker without a job is in an economic predicament not of his own making; that his religion, race, or party is irrelevant. His need was the only thing that had to be established.

—Harry Hopkins, advisor to Franklin D. Roosevelt

Very simply, it has concerned me that many programs that Washington administers aren't efficient and don't really help the people they were designed to help. I suggested that we consider them prime candidates for an orderly, phased transfer to state and local governments. This was not a budgetary proposal but one for transfer of control—authority and responsibility—from the federal government to those closer to the people. The people, through their state and local governments, would and should decide if they wanted to expand, modify, change, or replace these programs and how best to do so.

—Ronald Reagan

So we did what your president said with the unfunded mandates. But we also worked out the partnership in welfare reform, which many people said would never work and result in terrible injustice to children. And fewer people on welfare and two million fewer children in poverty, the lowest poverty rate among children in more than twenty years. The only thing I would say is, I hope all of you will fully spend all those . . . funds to make sure that we are actually doing right by the kids as we move their parents from welfare to work. But it has been . . . a successful partnership between the National Government and the States and our private sector friends who've been hiring people from welfare to work. . . . [As] a result of everybody doing their jobs, . . . twenty million more Americans have jobs. . . . [W]e have the lowest unemployment rates in thirty years, the lowest welfare rolls in thirty years, the lowest crime rates in twenty-five years. And that is a good thing.

—William Jefferson Clinton

We will not leave people in need to their own struggle, and we will not leave them to their own fate. . . . Across America, no doubt about it, single mothers do heroic work. They have the toughest job in our country. In many cases, their lives and their children's lives would be better if their fathers lived up to their responsibilities. . . . Abstinence is the surest way and the only completely effective way to prevent unwanted pregnancies and sexually transmitted diseases. When our children face a choice between self-restraint and self-destruction, government should not be neutral.

—George W. Bush

1. Whose philosophy of government returns responsibility for care of the poor to the local level and sounds similar to Calvin Coolidge's attitude toward problems during the Great Depression?

2. Who places the responsibility for taking care of the poor primarily on religious groups?

3. Who suggests that the individual is expected to "make it on his own"?

4. At what point in American history did the national government first assume responsibility for the welfare of the poor?

5. Which selection placed the responsibility of the poor on neighbors and friends?

6. Whose philosophy encompasses the idea of individual responsibility and the role of the national government in helping the poor reform welfare?

7. Whose philosophy most resembles the New Deal philosophy of active government participation in helping the poor but also stresses, like Coolidge, the role of the private sector?

The Steady Growth of the Welfare State

Part A.

Use the data in the chart to answer the questions.

Recipients of Government Benefits
(in millions of individuals)

	1945	1950	1960	1970	1980	1990	2000
Medicare (includes disabled)	—	—	—	20,491	28,478	34,203	36,620
Medicaid	—	—	—	14,507	23,311	25,255	42,763
Aid to Families with Dependent Children	1,450	3,099	4,317	9,659	11,101	11,439	N/A
Food Stamps	—	—	—	4,340	2,332*	21,500*	18,200*
School Lunches	—	8,600	14,100	23,100	3,235*	11,600*	27,600*
Subsidized Housing	—	—	.426	.932	1,093*	4,339*	4,689
Unemployment Insurance	—	1,600	2,100	2,100	25,823*	N/A	N/A

*indicates households served rather than individuals

1. In what year did Medicare and Medicaid first appear in the table as funded by the federal government?

2. In which year did food stamps appear?

3. In which decade did a dramatic increase occur in health and welfare benefits?

4. Which three groups benefited from welfare expenditures: the disabled, the elderly, retired people, or teachers?

Part B.

Study the examples of welfare reform proposed by George W. Bush. Then answer the questions.

- **Welfare Block Grants**—Spending on the main welfare program, Temporary Assistance for Needy Families, would continue at current levels. States would get $16.5 billion a year from 2002 to 2007.

- **Work Requirements**—By 2007, at least 70 percent of a state's adult welfare recipients must be engaged in work or job-preparation activities. . . . Welfare recipients must engage in supervised activity for forty hours a week, including a minimum of twenty-four hours of actual work.

- **Marriage and Fatherhood**—[The federal] government would provide up to $300 million per year to promote "healthy marriage" and $20 million a year for projects encouraging fathers to be more involved in children's lives.

- **Child Care**—States could get $26 billion over five years for child care. . . . In addition, a state could use as much as 50 percent of its federal welfare grant for child care.

- **Waivers**—States could seek exemptions from many federal laws and rules governing welfare, food stamps, public housing, job training, child care, aid to the homeless, and other programs for poor people.

- **Immigrants**—Most legal immigrants who have not become citizens would be ineligible for federal welfare benefits, as under current law.[1]

1. What are two of the most extreme elements of the welfare reform bill?

2. What elements encourage support to members of the family?

3. Is there any flexibility built into the program for the states?

4. What has happened to the welfare rolls in America since President William Jefferson Clinton signed a reform bill in 1996?

[1]Robert Pear, "House Passes a Welfare Bill with Stricter Rules on Work," *The New York Times* (17 May 2002): A20.

Lesson 39
Government Regulation and the Environment

Objective

- To examine the need for government regulation of actions that might threaten the environment

Notes to the Teacher

Since 1900, federal legislation has protected Americans against unsafe, unfair, or wasteful practices by corporations and industries. This legislation includes the Pure Food and Drug Act (1906), which prohibited processing violations in food and patent medicines; the Wagner Act (1935), which established the right of workers to organize unions and to bargain collectively with employers; and the Surplus Property Act (1944), which mandated that surplus government property must be disposed of in a manner that encourages competition between buyers and sellers. Regulatory legislation dealing with environmental issues has sought to ensure that all citizens would be able to live in conditions that were as environmentally safe and healthy as possible.

America is a land of many wildernesses. Foreign visitors often marvel at the diversity of the geography of the United States. One of the problems confronting today's leaders is how to use the rich resources of our environment while still preserving the environment of wilderness lands. Strip-mining, particularly in the Southwest, and oil drilling, both offshore and in wilderness areas, have become important issues to both environmentalists and legislators.

In this lesson, students examine the possible impact of oil drilling in the Arctic National Wildlife Refuge (ANWR). They conclude by deciding whether drilling for oil in the ANWR is necessary to offset American dependence on foreign oil and writing an editorial supporting their position.

Procedure

1. Ask the following questions:

    - What are nonrenewable resources? (*resources that cannot be replaced once they are used*)

    - What are some examples of nonrenewable resources? (*fossil fuels such as oil and coal*)

    - What are the two largest consumers of fossil fuels in the world? (*cars and home heating*)

    - Where is most of the fossil fuel used in the world found? (*Middle East, North Sea, Indonesia, Gulf of Mexico, Caribbean, Africa*)

    - Where is oil found in the United States? (*Gulf of Mexico, offshore along the West Coast, Texas, Oklahoma, Alaska*)

2. Distribute **Handout 70**, and have students locate and label areas where oil is found.

3. Explain that one of the most controversial environmental issues in the United States today involves fossil fuels. Explain that newly discovered oil fields sometimes raise environmental questions and that fields in the Arctic National Wildlife Refuge in Alaska have caused much controversy over whether drilling should be permitted in a protected area. Distribute **Handout 71**, and have students read the selection and answer the questions. Review students' responses.

Suggested Responses:

1. *If Congress had adopted his administration's energy plan, there would not be high gasoline prices.*

2. *The Energy Information Administration said that drilling would not decrease prices enough to justify drilling, since the ANWR accounts for less than 2 percent of the world's oil production.*

3. *Real savings would be in money (wages, taxes, etc.) that would be retained in the United States and not sent overseas.*

4. Ask students whether drilling in the ANWR would violate the principles upon which it was established. Encourage students to justify their responses.

5. Have students write an editorial supporting or opposing drilling in the ANWR. Have students share their editorials with the class.

Enrichment/Extension

1. Have students create posters illustrating support or opposition of drilling in the ANWR. Display finished posters in the classroom.

2. Have students use the Internet and other sources to monitor the status of drilling in the ANWR. Allow class time for students to report their findings.

Name_____

Date_____

Where Is Oil Found?

Locate and label areas where oil is found.

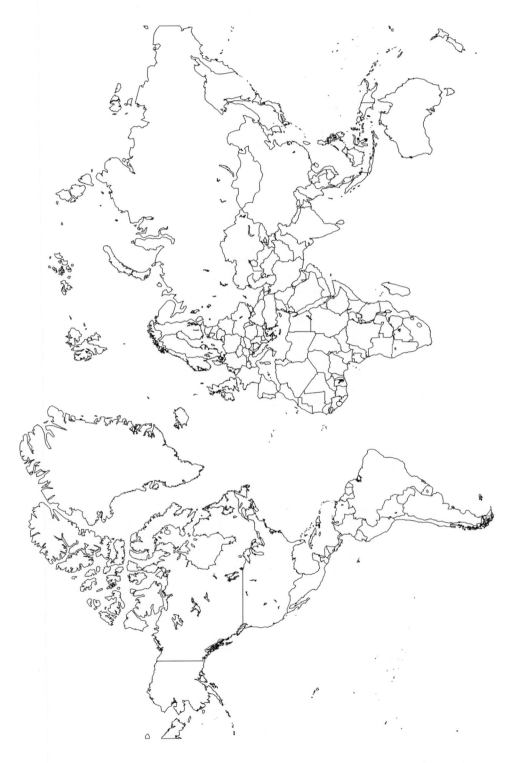

Drilling for Oil in the Arctic National Wildlife Refuge

Read the following selections, and answer the questions.

History of the Arctic National Wildlife Refuge

Created by President Dwight Eisenhower in 1960 and expanded when President Jimmy Carter signed the 1980 Alaska National Interest Lands Conservation Act (ANILCA), America's Arctic Refuge has been one of the greatest conservation legacies of both Republican and Democratic administrations.

The Arctic Refuge was established to conserve fish and wildlife populations and habitats in their natural diversity; fulfill the international treaty obligations of the United States with respect to fish and wildlife and their habitats, such as migratory waterfowl agreements and the Canada-U.S. Porcupine River caribou herd agreement; provide the opportunity for local residents to continue their subsistence way of life; and to protect water quality and quantity.

The U.S. Fish and Wildlife Service, which manages the Arctic National Wildlife Refuge, . . . calls it "the only conservation system unit that protects, in an undisturbed condition, a complete spectrum of the arctic ecosystems in North America."[1]

Bush Links ANWR Drilling to Gas Prices

WASHINGTON—Advocates of drilling for oil in the Arctic National Wildlife Refuge say record oil prices could help their case. But environmental groups and other organizations say that the refuge's oil would do little to lower prices and that the public opposes drilling there.

Gasoline prices are averaging more than $2 per gallon, and some oil prices have topped $40 per barrel.

President Bush said this week that drilling in ANWR could have made a difference.

"Had ANWR been passed—had it not been vetoed in the past—we anticipate additional barrels of oil would have been coming out of that part of the world, which would obviously have a positive impact for today's consumers," Bush said.

The president made the comments while speaking to the news media about a Wednesday Cabinet meeting, according to a White House transcript of the comments obtained by the Fairbanks *Daily News-Miner.*

Bush has previously said that if Congress had adopted the energy plan the administration developed three years ago—which included ANWR drilling—that would have kept oil prices lower.

Sen. Ted Stevens, R-Alaska, also made the ANWR-gas price link this week.

"That is part of the problem we have. Our supply is dwindling. Our demand is increasing as the rest of the world is increasing their demand," he said.

However, a number of organizations, among them advocates on both sides of the issue and government agencies, have said ANWR oil would have little effect on oil prices.

The U.S. Energy Information Administration in March said if ANWR were developed by 2013, that would probably cut world oil prices by 30 to 50 cents per barrel, not per gallon.

[1]"History of the Arctic National Wildlife Refuge," *Alaska Wilderness League,* <http://www.alaskawild.org/campaigns_arctic_history.html> (30 July 2004).

"The impact on world oil prices is not expected to be significant," the EIA said. That's in part because ANWR would make up only 0.5 percent to 1.3 percent of world oil production, the agency estimated.

Pro-drilling economists say the real benefit of drilling is not its price effect but the money generated for the United States in taxes, wages, and dollars retained in the country instead of being sent overseas.

Environmental groups say they have surveys showing the public is not buying the pro-drilling arguments.

The Republican-led House has approved ANWR drilling twice in the last two years, but the idea runs into trouble in the Senate. Republicans also hold a majority there, but not by enough to overcome procedural blocks by drilling opponents.

Stevens told Alaska reporters . . . that if the procedural hurdles were overcome, drilling supporters would have fifty-one votes "under some circumstances."

Rep. Don Young, R-Alaska, said he thinks the high prices will push Congress into action. He didn't specifically address ANWR but said energy prices could at least help a proposed Alaska natural gas pipeline.

In 1995, both the House and Senate passed legislation to drill in the refuge, but President Clinton vetoed it.[2]

1. According to President Bush, what action could have stopped an increase in gasoline prices?

2. What is the argument against drilling?

3. What do pro-drilling economists argue?

[2]Associated Press, "Bush Links ANWR Drilling to Gas Prices," *Anchorage Daily News*, 24 May 2004, <http://www.adn.com/alaska/story/5107775p-5034634c.html> (30 July 2004).

Lesson 40
Viewpoints on Foreign Affairs

Objective

- To understand several major factors that have influenced recent presidents in determining American foreign policy

Notes to the Teacher

From its economic ties to the Dutch, French, and British during the sixteenth and seventeenth centuries to the whale oil, shipbuilding, timber, cotton, tobacco, porcelain, and silk trade relationships with Europe and Asia during the era of the clipper ships, the United States has developed intricate political and economic relationships with nation-states around the world. America has relied, sometimes reluctantly, on productive political, economic, and social ties with foreign countries.

In his farewell address, George Washington urged members of Congress not to form entangling alliances with foreign states. He warned against treaties and pacts that obligated the United States to provide assistance to other countries, even as our nation was increasing international trade. His warning defined the early years of American foreign policy as anti-revolutionary and isolationist, two principles which were easily defended across the deep water that divided America from other nations.

Recent, complicated historical events—the horrific terrorism spawned among militant Islamic extremists; violent clashes between India and Pakistan, two growing nuclear powers; continuing conflict between Israelis and Palestinians—have refocused America's foreign policy agenda.

Each presidential decision represents a fraction of the wide spectrum of American foreign policy, such as military intervention, peace and trade talks, international reforestation, environmental and economic summits, vaccination and drug interdiction programs. Under the Articles of Confederation, the federal government had no power to compel the states to comply with trade or military treaties negotiated by Congress. This posed a potential threat to the stability of the country, because there was no judiciary to handle trespasses against those treaties. The new Constitution placed these powers directly within the executive branch. Formal treaties and trade agreements were to be ratified by the Senate.

The president, as chief diplomat and commander in chief, takes the lead in determining U.S. foreign policy. Because of the globalization of markets and growing economic ties around the world, America's role in foreign affairs has become more complex and requires a president to use patience and thought in assuring that America's security remains the primary goal of American foreign policy. In addition, our desire for peace and human rights also has helped shape our relations with the rest of the world.

In this lesson, students read seven excerpts, mostly from presidential addresses since World War II, and analyze the changing emphasis in American foreign policy. Students evaluate statements about the excerpts and arrange the statements in the correct sequence to illustrate the changing attitudes toward American foreign policy.

Procedure

1. Distribute **Handout 72**, and have students read the documents in part A either aloud or silently. Explain the context of each speech, using the information that follows:

   a. Four days after he gave his "Four Freedoms" speech in 1941, Franklin D. Roosevelt appealed to Congress to respond to an urgent request from Great Britain for war materials needed to continue the fight against Nazi Germany. A month earlier, Winston Churchill had announced that Britain's inability to continue purchases of U.S. military equipment left them in mortal danger. Despite considerable opposition to the idea, Congress enacted the Lend–Lease Act, which, in effect, offered all aid, short of war, to any country whose defense the president considered vital to the defense of the United States.

   b. By 1947, Russia, not Nazi Germany, posed the major threat to American security. Russia had expanded into

277

Eastern Europe and threatened to take control of Greece and Turkey. Britain, the traditional defender of these nations, appealed to the United States to help preserve the independence of these countries which provided vital access to the oil-rich Middle East. In a historic shift in foreign policy, Harry S. Truman persuaded Congress to appropriate $400 million in peacetime aid to these troubled countries.

c. By the 1960s, John F. Kennedy had become convinced that Communist opposition to American ideals would not soon end. Therefore, the United States should strive "to make the world safe for diversity." Shortly thereafter, Kennedy revived test-ban talks with the Soviet Union and, in September 1963, concluded a partial test-ban treaty with the USSR and Britain that outlawed nuclear tests in outer space, the atmosphere, and underwater.

d. Richard M. Nixon, who had a long record of strong opposition to Communism, visited Communist China, reversing U.S. opposition to China's entrance into the United Nations. Then, in 1972, he renewed diplomatic relations with China.

e. Steadily rising Soviet defense expenditures, coupled with a declining emphasis on U.S. defense spending, prompted Ronald Reagan to propose massive increases in defense spending as the best way to insure American security.

f. During William Jefferson Clinton's two terms in office, the international world was torn apart by wars that were fueled by ethnic and racial hatred. Civil war erupted in Bosnia among Orthodox Christian, Catholic, and Muslim factions. American Marines were killed while on peacekeeping duty in Somalia's capital, Mogadishu. Ethnic hatred between the Tutsi and Hutu tribes in central Africa resulted in alternating sprees of revenge killings. Ongoing peace talks between Palestinians and Israelis did little to stop the violence, which has raged for decades.

g. George W. Bush's refusal to comply with international treaties, such as the Kyoto agreement and some aspects of NAFTA, have raised angry, bitter protests from our friends and allies. After the terrorist bombings of September 11, 2001, Bush has been faced with the issues of international terrorism and homeland security. The complicated relationship between India and Pakistan, countries with nuclear capabilities; the actions of Al-Qaeda and other terrorist groups in Afghanistan, Indonesia, and the Philippines; and the continued problems with Israel and the Palestinians have forced Bush to recognize America's complex role on the international stage. These factors, coupled with the desire of NATO states to assert their independence from U.S. influence and the growing power of the European Union in the world economy, have resulted in changes in American foreign policy.

2. Have students complete **Handout 72**, part B. Instruct them to identify to which paragraph each statement applies. Review students' responses.

Suggested Responses:

1. *true; paragraph 4*

2. *true; paragraph 5*

3. *false; paragraph 3*

4. *true; see all documents*

5. *false; paragraph 6 of Roosevelt and paragraph 1 of Kennedy*

6. *true; see all documents*

7. *true; paragraph 1 or 3*

8. *true; paragraph 1*

9. *false; no evidence in any paragraph*

10. *true; see all paragraphs of Roosevelt*

11. *true; paragraph 1*

12. *false; paragraph 1*

13. *false, paragraphs 3 and 5*

14. *true; see all paragraphs of Roosevelt*

15. *true, paragraph 4*

3. Have students write a structured paragraph as directed in part C of **Handout 72**. Have selected students share their paragraphs.

Suggested Responses:

Topic sentence—*statement 4*

Evidence—*statements 10, 14, 2, 1, 8, 7, 15, 11*

Conclusion—*statement 6*

Enrichment/Extension

Have students bring in current newspapers and newsmagazines and locate articles that illustrate the development of current American foreign policy. Have them develop a bulletin board display, with a world map and current articles, to show this ongoing development.

Viewpoints on American Foreign Policy

Part A.

Read the following passages from speeches given by American presidents and a secretary of state since World War II.

President Franklin D. Roosevelt, 1941

In the future days, which we seek to make secure, we look forward to a world founded upon four essential human freedoms.

The first is freedom of speech and expression—everywhere in the world.

The second is freedom of every person to worship God in his own way—everywhere in the world.

The third is freedom from want—which, translated into world terms, means economic understandings which will secure to every nation a healthy peacetime life for its inhabitants—everywhere in the world.

The fourth is freedom from fear—which, translated into world terms, means a worldwide reduction of armaments to such a point and in such a thorough fashion that no nation will be in a position to commit an act of physical aggression against any neighbor—anywhere in the world.

That is no vision of a distant millennium. It is a definite basis for a kind of world attainable in our own time and generation.

President Harry S. Truman, 1947

I believe that it must be the policy of the United States to support free peoples who are resisting attempted subjugation by armed minorities or by outside pressures.

I believe that we must assist free peoples to work out their own destinies in their own way.

I believe that our help should be primarily through economic and financial aid which is essential to economic stability and orderly political processes.

The world is not static, and the status quo is not sacred. But we cannot allow changes in the status quo in violation of the Charter of the United Nations by such methods as coercion, or by such subterfuges as political infiltration. In helping free and independent nations to maintain their freedom, the United States will be giving effect to the principles of the Charter of the United Nations.

It is necessary only to glance at a map to realize that the survival and integrity of the Greek nation are of grave importance in a much wider situation. If Greece should fall under the control of an armed minority, the effect upon its neighbor, Turkey, would be immediate and serious. Confusion and disorder might well spread throughout the entire Middle East.

President John F. Kennedy, 1963

First: Examine our attitude towards peace itself. Too many of us think it is impossible. Too many think it is unreal. But that is a dangerous defeatist belief. It leads to the conclusion that war is inevitable—that mankind is doomed—that we are gripped by forces we cannot control.

We need not accept that view. Our problems are manmade. Therefore, they can be solved by man. And man can be as big as he wants. No problem of human destiny is beyond human beings. Man's reason and spirit have often solved the seemingly unsolvable—and we believe they can do it again. . . .

In short, both the United States and its allies, and the Soviet Union and its allies, have a mutually deep interest in a just and genuine peace and in halting the arms race. Agreements to this end are in the interests of the Soviet Union as well as ours—and even the most hostile nations can be relied upon to accept and keep those treaty obligations and only those treaty obligations, which are in their own interest.

So, let us not be blind to our differences—but let us also direct attention to our common interests and the means by which those differences can be resolved. And if we cannot end now our differences, at least we can help make the world safe for diversity. For, in the final analysis, our most basic common link is that we all inhabit this small planet. We all breathe the same air. We all cherish our children's future. And we are all mortal.

President Richard Nixon, 1968

. . . [W]e simply cannot afford to leave China forever outside the family of nations, there to nurture its fantasies, cherish its hates, and threaten its neighbors. There is no place on this small planet for a billion of its potentially most able people to live in angry isolation. . . .

Only as the nations of non-Communist Asia become so strong—economically, politically and militarily—that they no longer furnish tempting targets for Chinese aggression, will the leaders in Peking be persuaded to turn their energies inward rather than outward. And that will be the time when the dialogue with mainland China will begin. For the short run, then, this means a policy of firm restraint, of no reward, of a creative counter-pressure designed to persuade Peking that its interests can be served only by accepting the basic rules of international civility. For the long run, it means pulling China back into the world community—but as a great and progressing nation, not as the epicenter of world revolution.

President Ronald Reagan, 1982

I have discussed on other occasions, including my address on May 9, the elements of Western policies toward the Soviet Union to safeguard our interests and protect the peace. What I am describing now is a plan and a hope for the long term—the march of freedom and democracy which will leave Marxism–Leninism on the ash heap of history as it has left other tyrannies which stifle the freedom and muzzle the self-expression of the people.

That is why we must continue our efforts to strengthen NATO even as we move forward with our zero-option initiative in the negotiations on intermediate range forces and our proposal for a one-third reduction in strategic ballistic missile warheads.

Our military strength is a prerequisite to peace, but let it be clear we maintain this strength in the hope it will never be used. For the ultimate determinant in the struggle now going on for the world will not be bombs and rockets but a test of wills and ideas—a trial of spiritual resolve: the values we hold, the beliefs we cherish, the ideals to which we are dedicated.

Secretary of State Madeleine K. Albright, 2000

Mr. Chairman, over the past decade, we have had to reevaluate our entire approach to international affairs in light of the geopolitical and technological changes transforming our world. . . . [We] have had to adapt our institutions, adjust our thinking, and steer a course between isolation, which is not possible, and overreaching, which is not sustainable.

Our goal has been to keep America secure, prosperous, and free. And our means have included everything from military force to quiet diplomacy. . . .

. . . Twenty years ago when American diplomats sat down with their counterparts overseas, the agenda was dominated by cold war concerns, and America's interests were measured primarily by the single yardstick of superpower rivalry. . . .

. . . American diplomacy in the twenty-first century ranges across almost the full spectrum of human activity. In the past four years, I spent most of my time on big-ticket issues of security, war, and peace but I spent some of my time on everything, from the war against AIDS, to explaining our position on biotechnology, to trying to crack down on the trafficking in human beings. The reaon is that our nation's interests and responsibilities and reach are truly global and that problems abroad, if left unaddressed, will all too often come home to America.

President George W. Bush, 2002

. . . Our generation faces new and grave threats to liberty, to the safety of our people, and to civilization itself. We face an aggressive force that glorifies death, that targets the innocent, and seeks the means to matter—murder on a massive scale.

We face the global tragedy of disease and poverty that take uncounted lives and leave whole nations vulnerable to oppression and terror. We'll face these challenges together. We must face them together. Those who despise human freedom will attack it on every continent. Those who seek missiles and terrible weapons are also familiar with the map of Europe. Like the threats of another era, this threat cannot be appeased or cannot be ignored. By being patient, relentless, and resolute, we will defeat the enemies of freedom. . . .

By remaining united we are meeting modern threats with the greatest resources of wealth and will ever assembled by free nations. Together, Europe and the United States have the creative genius, the economic power, the moral heritage, and the democratic vision to protect our liberty and to advance our cause of peace. . . .

Our response will be reasoned, and focused, and deliberate. We will use more than our military might. We will cut off terrorist finances, apply diplomatic pressure, and continue to share intelligence. . . .

We must recognize that violence and resentment are defeated by the advance of health, and learning, and prosperity. Poverty doesn't create terror—yet, terror takes root in failing nations that cannot police themselves or provide for their people. Our conscience and our interests speak as one . . . we must create a better world.

Part B.

Label each statement *true* or *false*. Cite evidence from the documents in part A to support your choice.

_____ 1. Kennedy, recognizing the improbability of ever achieving a world of uniform beliefs, stressed the need to emphasize the common links among nations "to make the world safe for diversity."

Evidence:

_____ 2. Harry Truman believed in the domino effect of Communism and felt that if Greece fell, Turkey would follow.

Evidence:

_____ 3. According to Reagan, diplomacy should replace a nuclear buildup as the best way to promote world peace and resolve differences among nations.

Evidence:

_____ 4. American foreign policy, over the past half-century, has reflected both a concern for American security and a sense of mission to create a better world.

Evidence:

_____ 5. Both Roosevelt and Kennedy viewed world peace as an unrealistic dream.

Evidence:

_____ 6. Even though the United States accepts diversity today, American foreign policy strives to prevent change unfavorable to the democratic way of life.

Evidence:

_____ 7. Reagan's concern that Communist tyranny again threatens American security prompted him to urge vast increases in spending for military preparedness.

Evidence:

_____8. In reestablishing relations with the Red Chinese, Nixon accepted the diversity of people in the world.

Evidence:

_____9. Kennedy specifically advocated that the United States and USSR should cooperate in combating ignorance, poverty, and disease in the world under United Nations auspices.

Evidence:

_____10. The freedoms for other countries emphasized by Roosevelt are similar to those espoused in the Preamble to the Constitution and the Bill of Rights.

Evidence:

_____11. Bush stated that the greatest threat to liberty is terrorism, which glorifies death, targets the innocent, and seeks murder on a massive scale.

Evidence:

_____12. Nixon did not fear the effects of isolation on the people of China.

Evidence:

_____13. Bush did not think the European Union and the United States could fight disease and poverty with health, education, and prosperity and that poverty does not create terror.

Evidence:

_____14. Roosevelt vigorously pursued the agenda of freedom for all countries of the world.

Evidence:

_____15. Albright stated that America's foreign policy involves more than military intervention and diplomacy.

Evidence:

Part C.

Cross out the statements you have marked false. Then rearrange the remaining sentences into a paragraph on the changing attitudes toward American foreign policy. Your topic sentence should explain the main idea of the paragraph, the body should include several sentences of evidence in appropriate order, and the conclusion should focus on American foreign policy today.

Acknowledgments

For permission to reprint all works in this volume, grateful acknowledgment is made to the following holders of copyright, publishers, or representatives.

Every effort has been made to trace the owners of copyrighted material. The publisher apologizes for any omissions, and would be grateful to know of them so that acknowledgment may be made in future editions.

Lesson 5, Handout 8

Lesson 7, Procedure 6

For use of excerpts from *The American Political Tradition and the Men Who Made It* by Richard Hofstadter, copyright © 1948. Reprinted by permission of Alfred A. Knopf, Inc.

Lesson 6, Notes to the Teacher and Handout 10

For use of an excerpt from *Amending America* by Richard B. Bernstein and Jerome Agel, copyright © 1993 by Richard B. Bernstein and Jerome Agel. Used by permission of Times Books, a division of Random House, Inc.

Lesson 12, Handout 24

For use of an excerpt from *ASCD Update*, September 1988, John O'Neill, editor. Reprinted with the permission of the Association for Supervision and Curriculum Development. Copyright © 1988 by the Association for Supervision and Curriculum Development. All rights reserved.

Lesson 27, Handout 49

For use of an 1828 lithograph cartoon, President Jackson destroying the Bank of the United States. The Granger Collection, New York.

For use of a 1972 political cartoon by Hugh Haynie. Reprinted with permission of Hugh Haynie and The Courier-Journal and Times, Louisville, Kentucky. Courtesy of Manuscripts and Rare Books Department, Earl Gregg Swem Library, College of William and Mary.

Lesson 29, Handout 52
Documents A, C, D, E

For use of excerpts from *The Modern American Vice Presidency: The Transformation of a Political Institution* by Joel K. Goldstein. Copyright © 1982 by Princeton University Press. Excerpts reprinted with permission of Princeton University Press.

Lesson 36, Handout 64

For use of an excerpt from "Elections: Campaign Finance Reform" as it appeared on the *Open Secrets.org* Web site. Reprinted with permission from The Center for Responsive Politics.

Lesson 38, Handout 68

For use of Scripture taken from the Today's English Version—Second Edition Copyright © 1992 by American Bible Society. Used by Permission.

Lesson 39, Handout 71

For use of the Associated Press article "Bush Links ANWR Drilling to Gas Prices" as it appeared on the *Anchorage Daily News* Web site 24 May 2004. Reprinted with the permission of The Associated Press.

The Publisher

All instructional materials identified by the TAP® (Teachers/Authors/Publishers) trademark are developed by a national network of teachers whose collective educational experience distinguishes the publishing objective of The Center for Learning, a nonprofit educational corporation founded in 1970.

Concentrating on values-related disciplines, the Center publishes humanities and religion curriculum units for use in public and private schools and other educational settings. Approximately 500 language arts, social studies, novel/drama, life issues, and faith publications are available.

While acutely aware of the challenges and uncertain solutions to growing educational problems, the Center is committed to quality curriculum development and to the expansion of learning opportunities for all students. Publications are regularly evaluated and updated to meet the changing and diverse needs of teachers and students. Teachers may offer suggestions for development of new publications or revisions of existing titles by contacting

The Center for Learning

10200 Jefferson Blvd.
P.O. Box 802
Culver City, CA 90232-0802
(800) 421-4246 • Fax (800) 944-5432
E-mail: access@centerforlearning.org
Web: www.centerforlearning.org